Post Card

FOREIGN LANGUAGES PRESS · 外文出版社

33

Gilded Changxin Palace Lamp, Han Dynasty. Unearthed from the tomb of Dou Wan, wife of Liu Sheng, prince of the State of Zhongshan, in Mancheng, Hebei Province, in 1968.

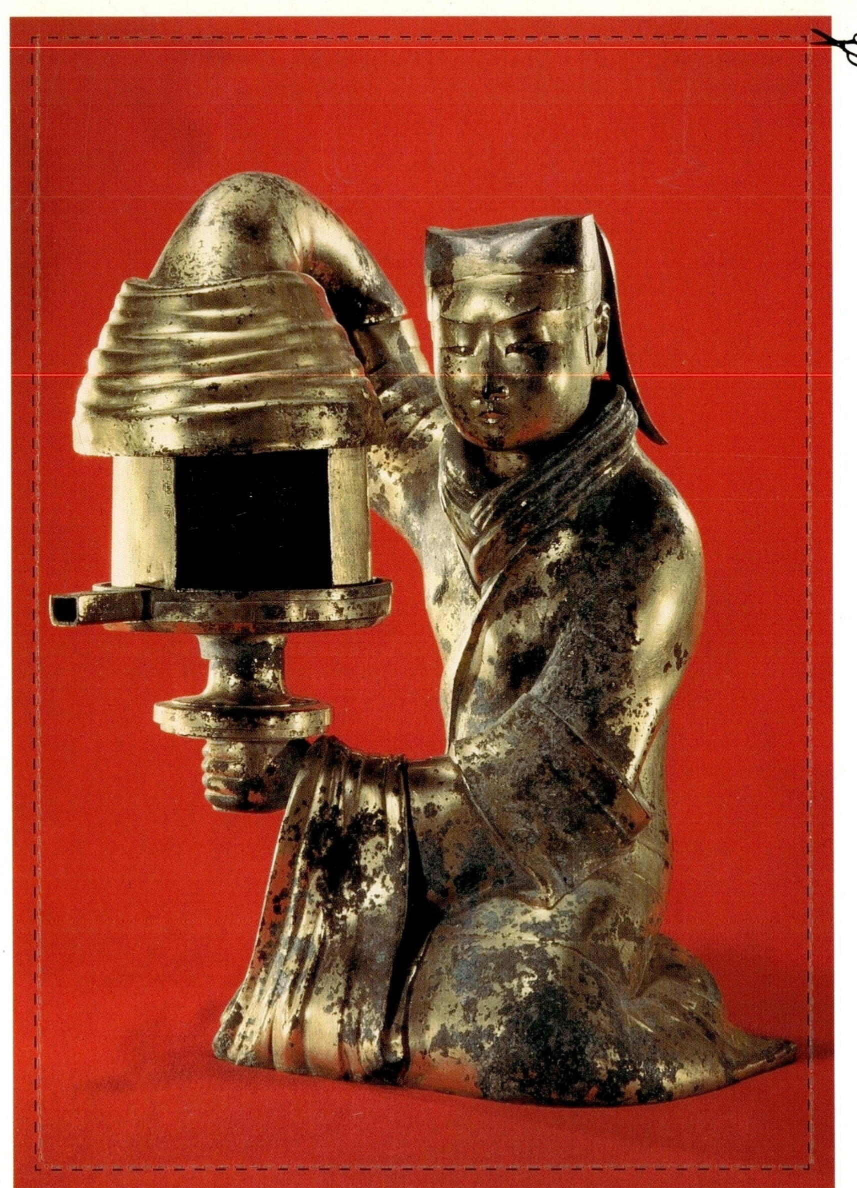

Ancient Sculpture

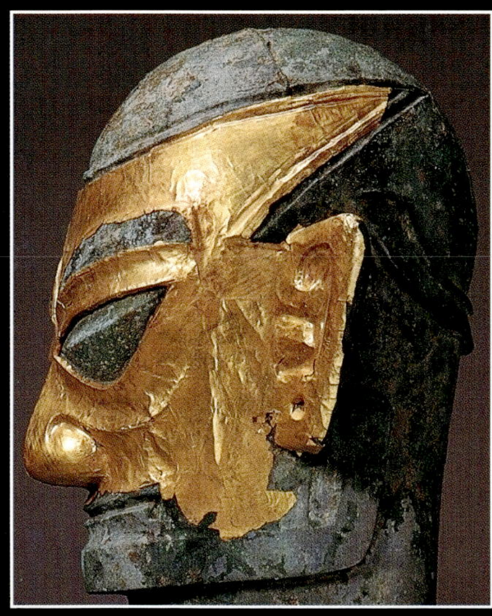

Foreign Languages Press Beijing

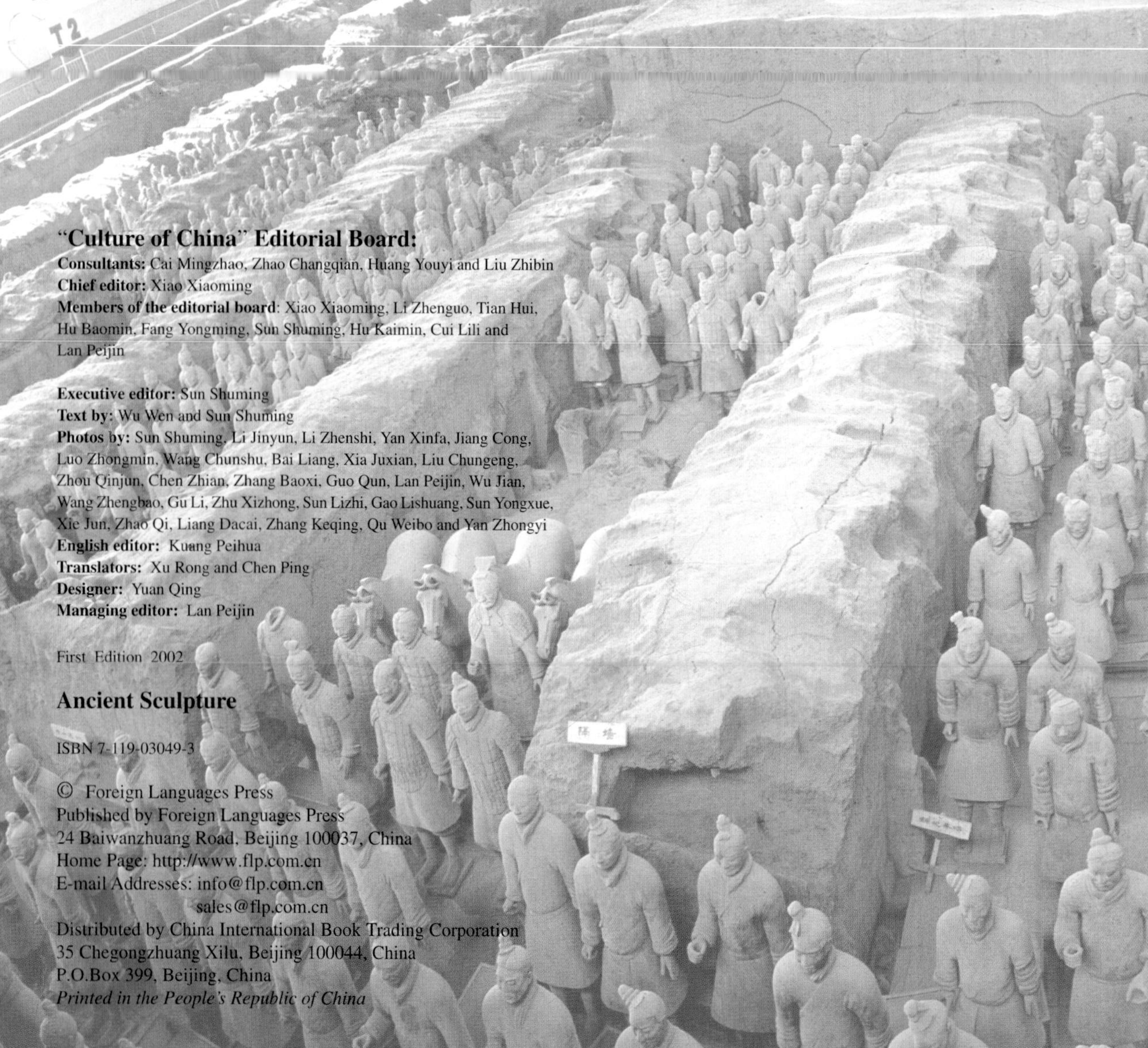

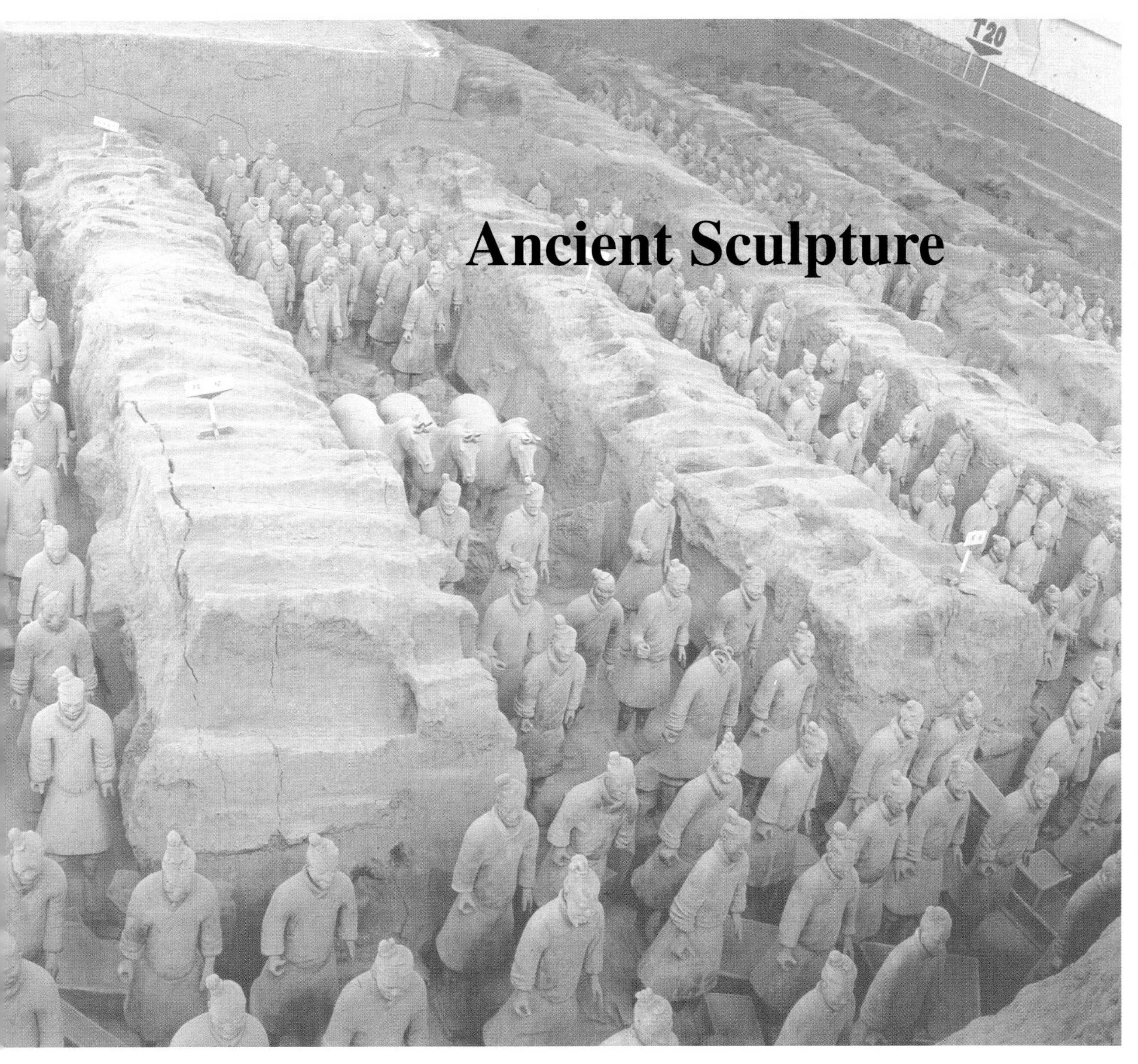

Ancient Sculpture

Foreword

Sculpture refers to the making of three-dimensional works of art in stone, clay, metal, wood, etc. The art of sculpture emerged in China along with the first glimmerings of civilization. Over the millennia of Chinese cultural development, sculptural works with distinct national characteristics have been created, and famous sculptors have added luster to the Chinese people's artistic achievements from epoch to epoch.

Sculpture in the Period of Primitive Society, and the Xia, Shang and Zhou Dynasties

The late leading architect Liang Sicheng once stated, "Sculpture is the starting point of art. When our forefathers lived in caves in the wilderness, they had to carve stones into various items for daily use. Then, when building houses, they carved patterns as decorations. Thus, we can say the art of sculpture started in the Stone Age, and is the oldest artistic form."

In remote antiquity, with the appearance of primitive agriculture and an embryonic handicrafts industry, earthenware became important in people's life and work. Human aesthetic creation began to manifest itself in a basic way in the shaping and decorating of earthenware items.

Exquisite pottery products have been excavated belonging to the Yangshao, Maojiayao, Dawenkou and Hongshan cultures of the Neolithic Age, between 10,000 and 4,000 years ago. Great achievements were also made in jade carving at that time. Unearthed jade artifacts include jade axes, *bi* (ornamental flat pieces of jade with holes in the center), *cong* (jade ornaments in square shape with a hole in the middle), and jade battle-axes. Noteworthy is *zhulong* or *yulong* (jade ornaments with a bearing pattern resembling the dragon with a beast head).

During the Xia (2070-1600 B.C.), Shang (1600-1046 B.C.) and Western Zhou (1046-771 B.C.) dynasties, China was in the period of slave society. In the course of the Eastern Zhou Dynasty, which was conventionally divided into the Spring and Autumn (770-476 B.C.) and Warring States (476-221 B.C.) periods, a feudal society gradually emerged in China. During these dynasties, with the further division of social labor, the handicrafts industry became quite developed, and was divided into many categories. The sculpture category included bronze smelting and founding, pottery making, and jade, stone, bone and ivory carving. As the artistic achievements in bronze ware manufacture were the most significant, this period was also called the Bronze Age. Bronze ware production, mixing the characteristics of pottery making and jade carving, evolved into a new artistic tradition. Not only tools and weapons, but also large numbers of sacrificial vessels and musical instruments were made of bronze. Sacrificial vessels included *ding* (three-legged tripod or four-legged cauldron for meat and cereals), *li* (cauldron for meat and cereals), *yan* (steamer for vegetables and cereals), *gui* (deep circular vessel with two or four handles, used as a container for grain), *gong* (lidded drinking vessel with spout at the front, handle at the back and a square stand or four legs), *jue* (tripod vessel with handle and open spout), *zun* (cup, used for drinking or warming wine), *you* (jar, round or oval in horizontal section, with cover and swing handle), and *hu* (jar, round, rectangular or compressed in shape). Sacrificial musical instruments included large and small bells, *nao* (in the shape of a big bell, with hollow handle, to be struck by wooden mallet), *bo* (bell with plane opening and circular knob on top) and drums. Bronze wares from the Shang Dynasty were noted for their distinctive carved patterns, such as *taotie* and *kui* (mystical beasts), clouds and lightning, dragons, tigers, elephants, deer, oxen, phoenixes and human faces. The patterns were stylized and delicately structured.

Sculpture in the Qin and Han Dynasties

The Qin (221-207 B.C.) and Han (206 B.C.-A.D.220) dynasties saw China become a unified feudal monarchy. In the newly powerful empire a vast range of prospects for the development of sculpture opened up. The rulers of the Qin and Han dynasties had many fine works of sculpture made to advertise their successes in enlarging their territory, demonstrate their personal power and cite courtiers and generals for distinguished services. During this period, striking achievements were also made in pottery, stone carving, bronze casting, and the shaping and designing of artifacts. Thus was formed the first golden age in the history of Chinese sculpture.

In 221 B.C., Qin Shi Huang (First Emperor of the Qin Dynasty) unified China, putting an end to the endemic warfare between the feudal states of the previous few centuries. In Lintong, Shaanxi, near the Qin Shi Huang Mausoleum, over 6,000 life-size terracotta figurines of warriors and horses have been discovered. Facing the east and standing in military formations, the terracotta warriors and horses were originally painted in bright colors, which prove that great progress was made in sculpture in the Qin Dynasty. There are thought to be many thousands more waiting to be excavated.

In the Han Dynasty, the royal palaces and gardens of Chang'an and Luoyang, the capitals of Western and Eastern Han dynasties, respectively, housed colossal sculptures, and the mausoleums and ancestral halls of the aristocrats were guarded by stone beasts as well. In recognition of the military achievements of Huo Qubing (140-117 B.C.), Emperor Wu designed his mausoleum in the shape of Mount Qilian. In the mausoleum were placed granite sculptures of horses, tigers, oxen, pigs and mythical beasts. Especially interesting is one representing Xiongnu invaders being trampled under a warhorse's hooves. This series is rated as outstanding examples of Han stone sculpture.

Stone and brick relief carving was a characteristic new variety of sculpture which appeared in the Qin and Han dynasties. Such carvings are generally found on the walls of tomb chambers, memorial shrines in front of tombs and watchtowers. The brick relief works of the late Han Dynasty excavated around Chengdu, Sichuan Province, are of a quite high artistic level. The themes are mostly taken from daily life, featuring horse-drawn carriages, feasts and celebrations, and farming and handicraft work.

In the Qin and Han dynasties, bronze was no longer used exclusively for ritual vessels and weapons, but also for ordinary utensils, especially mirrors and lanterns. An exquisite example of the latter is the gilded "Changxin Palace Lantern" found in Dou Wan's tomb in Mancheng, Hebei Province. There are masterpieces in bronze statues as well. Near the Qin Shi Huang Mausoleum, two half-size bronze chariots and horses weighing over 1,200 kg each were discovered. They are elaborately shaped, and probably represent Qin Shi Huang's own imperial chariots and horses. A more famous example is a bronze statue of a galloping horse with the foot mounted on a flying swallow, excavated from an Eastern Han tomb in Wuwei, Gansu Province.

Sculpture in the Wei, Jin and Northern and Southern Dynasties

Throughout the period of the Wei, Jin and Northern and Southern dynasties (220-581), China was divided and war-torn. Social upheavals gave rise to the spread of Buddhism, along with which Buddhist art was introduced from India by way of the "Silk Road," and influenced the art of the Central Plains. During this period, sculpture with Buddhist themes became dominant and made the most prominent achievements. This is reflected in the grotto sculptures which were begun at that time. The earliest of these are in No.16 Grotto of the Mogao Grottoes in Dunhuang, Gansu Province, and those in No.169 Grotto of the Binglingsi Grottoes in Yongjing County, Gansu Province, dating from the first year of the Jianhong reign period (420) of the Western Qin Dynasty. The images and techniques of expression here fully reflect the influence from the Western Regions. After the Northern Wei Dynasty (386-534) united the northern part of China, the dissemination of Buddhism was accelerated, and grottoes containing Buddhist statues were carved at Datong, Luoyang and other places. Large numbers of magnificent stone sculptures dating from the Northern Dynasties period still remain, representative ones being the statues in the Five Grottoes by Monk Tanyao in Yungang, and Guyang Grotto and Binyang Grotto in Longmen. From the images and attire of the Buddha and niches, we can see the blending of the characteristics of the art of the Central Plains and that of the Western Regions.

The area to the south of the Yangtze River developed under the rule of the Southern Dynasties. In today's Nanjing and the surrounding regions are scattered 30-odd tombs of emperors and aristocrats of the Song, Qi, Liang and Chen dynasties (420-589), in which large-scale memorial sculptures such as stone columns, stone tables and stone beasts occupy an important position, in addition to pottery figurines buried with emperors and high-ranking officials.

Sculpture in the Sui and Tang Dynasties

The Sui (581-618) Dynasty put an end to the state of separation and anarchy which had lasted for more than 300 years, uniting China once more. During this dynasty and the following Tang Dynasty (618-907), with the vigorous development of the handicrafts industry and commerce, closer contacts between the various ethnic groups of China, and more frequent economic and cultural exchanges between China and its neighbors, a splendid era of cultural and artistic attainments came into being. Chinese sculpture, naturally, shared in this prosperity.

Buddhist statues made at this time display richer contents, wider scopes of expression and more mature workmanship, along with a flurry of activity in the sphere of excavating grottoes and constructing temples. The Dunhuang Grottoes are a treasure house of clay sculptures and murals. Of the 476 grottoes here, 95 date from the Sui Dynasty, and 213 from the Tang Dynasty. Of the grottoes and niches in Longmen, over 60 percent were chiseled during the Tang Dynasty. The statues in the grotto of Fengxian Temple were made during the reign of Emperor Gaozong. Their gigantic scale and superb craftsmanship are outstanding in the history of grotto art.

The mausoleums of the Tang emperors were often built at the foot of a mountain, with stone figures of humans, lions and horses guarding them. The stone sculptures of the No. 18 Tang Mausoleum near Xi'an are among the great treasures of ancient Chinese sculpture. The six stone horses in front of the Mausoleum of Li Shimin, the second Tang emperor, and the groups of stone statues in the passageway of the Mausoleum of Emperor Gaozong and Empress Wu are representative of Tang sculpture.

The Tang Dynasty was famous for its characteristic tricolored glazed pottery. Funerary figurines of humans and models of animals, such as camels and horses, are among the best examples of this genre. The well-proportioned pottery horses, especially, are shown in frozen motion, emitting a lifelike spirit.

Sculpture in the Five Dynasties, Song, Liao, Kin and Yuan Dynasties Periods

With the division of the country once more during the Five Dynasties (907-960), the respective confrontations between the Northern Song Dynasty (960-1127) and the Liao Dynasty (907-1125) and the Southern Song Dynasty (1127-1279) and the Kin Dynasty (1115-1234), and the short period of unification under the Yuan Dynasty (1271-1368), this era was rather chaotic and changeable. The political situations and economic trends at different times had various influences on the art of sculpture.

The sculpture of this period lost the grandeur and forthrightness it had displayed in the Sui and Tang dynasties, but made progress in realistic techniques and precision. Religious sculpture still held an important position, and the sculptures in temples and monasteries were of quite grand scale. The 22-m-high bronze Bodhisattva of Great Sorrow (made in the Northern Song Dynasty) in Great Sorrow Pavilion in Longxing Temple, Zhengding, and the 16-m-high clay figure of Goddess of Mercy (made in the Liao Dynasty) in Dule Temple, Jixian County, Hebei Province, are outstanding examples of the large statues made in the medieval period. The 29 statues of Buddha, Bodhisattvas and arhats in the Xiahuayan Temple of the Pujia sect, and the statues of the "24 Heavenly Gods" in the Great Hall of Shanhua Temple — both in Datong, Shanxi Province, are the most magnificent such statues made in the Liao and Kin dynasties. As for the characteristic temple and monastery statues of the Song Dynasty, the best known are those in Baosheng Temple in Suzhou, the arhats in Lingyan Temple in Changqing, Shandong Province, and the colored statues of maids in the Jin Memorial Shrine in Taiyuan, Shanxi Province.

The construction of grottoes declined gradually in central China, the focus shifting to the areas of Shaanxi and Sichuan, which were relatively free from the upheavals which racked the northern parts of China following the fall of the Tang Dynasty. There are a dozen sites with stone statues in Dazu County in Sichuan Province, of which the largest are on North Mountain and Mount Baoding. The Southern Song Dynasty retained sovereignty south of the Yangtze River, and its capital, Lin'an (today's Hangzhou), was prosperous both economically and culturally. Lin'an was also a center of Buddhist worship. Near the West Lake there are several grottoes with statues, the most famous ones being Yanxia Grotto and the 380-odd statues on the Peak That Flew Here at Lingyin Temple.

Among the stone statues located at mausoleums dating from this period, the statue of Wan Jian at Wan Jian's tomb of the Former Shu Dynasty (one of the Five Dynasties) is a rare portrait-statue. The stone figures of men and animals at the imperial mausoleum of the Northern Song Dynasty in Gongxian County, Henan, are notable for their realistic features.

Sculpture in the Ming and Qing Dynasties

The Ming (1368-1644) and Qing (1644-1911) dynasties were the last two feudal regimes in China. During this time, feudal politics, economy, ideology and culture reached their zenith and began to disintegrate. This directly or indirectly influenced the progress of all artistic activities, including sculpture.

The religious sculpture in the Ming and Qing dynasties generally showed a decline, but a few fresh works did appear, such as the colored sculptures in Shuanglin Temple in Pingyao, Shanxi Province, the statue of Goddess of Mercy with 1,000 hands and 1,000 eyes in Chongshan Temple in Taiyuan, the sculptured walls of Shuilu Convent in Lantian, Shaanxi, and the 500 arhats in Biyun Temple in Beijing.

An outstanding feature of this period was the flourishing of Tibetan Buddhism (also called Lamaism). A large number of wooden and bronze statues connected with Tibetan Buddhism were erected. Especially in the Kangxi and Qianlong reigns of the Qing Dynasty, in order to unite the Mongolian and Tibetan people, these rulers energetically supported Lamaism and sponsored the building of many Lamaist temples and monasteries. From the 52nd year of the reign of Emperor Kangxi (1713) to the 45th year of the reign of Emperor Qianlong (1780), 12 magnificent Buddhist temples were built in accordance with the architectural patterns of Mongolian and Tibetan religious constructions at the summer resort of the Qing emperors at Chengde. The "Eight Outside Temples," with 55,161 statues, are still preserved there. The Yonghe Palace in Beijing was turned into a lamasery in the ninth year of the reign of Emperor Qianlong (1744). In the Forbidden City there are 35 Tibetan Buddhist halls.

Apart from the Xiaoling Mausoleum of Zhu Yuanzhang, the first emperor of the Ming Dynasty, which is situated in Nanjing, all the mausoleums of the Ming emperors are located on the southern side of Mount Tianshou in Changping County, Beijing, reaching 13 in total. As for the imperial mausoleums of the Qing Dynasty, a few are in the northeast of China, and the Eastern Tombs of the Qing Dynasty are scattered in Zunhua City, and the Western Tombs, Yi County, in Hebei Province. Large stone animals and figures line the approaches to the tombs.

In the meantime, practical and visual technological and artistic sculpture for the decoration of houses flourished in the Ming and Qing dynasties. This included the carving of jade, stone, ivory, bone, bamboo and wood, and sculptures in porcelain and clay, some of which attracted great attention from connoisseurs.

CONTENTTS

CHRONOLOGY

1,000,000-10,000 B.C.   PALEOLITHIC PERIOD

10,000-ca.2100 B.C   .NEOLITHIC PERIOD
     Xia Dynasty ca. 2100-ca. 1600 B.C.

ca.1600-ca.1100 B.C.   SHANG DYNASTY

ca.1100-256 B.C.   ZHOU DYNASTY
     Western Zhou ca. 1100-771 B.C.
     Eastern Zhou ca. 770-256 B.C.
       Spring and Autumn Period 770-476 B.C.
       Warring States Period 476-221 B.C.

221-206 B.C.   QIN DYNASTY

206 B.C.-A.D.220   HAN DYNASTY
     Western (Former) Han Dynasty 206 B.C.-A.D.9
     Xin Dynasty (Wang Mang Interregnum) 9-23
     Eastern (Later) Han Dynasty 25-220

220-280   THREE KINGDOMS
     Wei 220-265
     Shu 221-263
     Wu 222-280

265-420   JIN DYNASTY*
     Western Jin 265-317
     Eastern Jin 317-420

317-589   SOUTHERN DYNASTIES*
     Liu Song 420-479
     Southern Qi 479-502
     Liang 502-557
     Chen 557-589

386-581   NORTHERN DYNASTIES
     Northern Wei 386-534
     Eastern Wei 534-550
     Western Wei 535-556
     Northern Qi 550-577
     Northern Zhou 557-581

581-618   SUI DYNASTY

618 907   TANG DYNASTY
     Great Zhou Dynasty (Wu Zetian Interregnum) 684-705

907-960   FIVE DYNASTIES (in the north)
     Later Liang 907-923
     Later Tang 923-936
     Later Jin 936-946
     Later Han 947-950
     Later Zhou 951-960

902-979   TEN KINGDOMS (in the south)
     Former Shu 907-925
     Later Shu 934-965
     Nanping or Jingnan 924-963
     Chu 927-951
     Wu 902-937
     Southern Tang 937-975
     Wuyue 907-978
     Min 909-945
     Southern Han 917-971
     Northern Han 951-979

916-1125   LIAO DYNASTY

960-1279   SONG DYNASTY
     Northern Song 960-1127
     Southern Song 1127-1279

1115-1234   JIN DYNASTY

1038-1227   WESTERN XIA DYNASTY

1271-1368   YUAN DYNASTY

1368-1644   MING DYNASTY

1644-1911   QING DYNASTY

1912-1949   REPUBLIC OF CHINA

1949-   PEOPLE'S REPUBLIC OF CHINA

*The Western and Eastern Jin dynasties together with the Southern Dynasties are frequently referred to as the Six Dynasties.

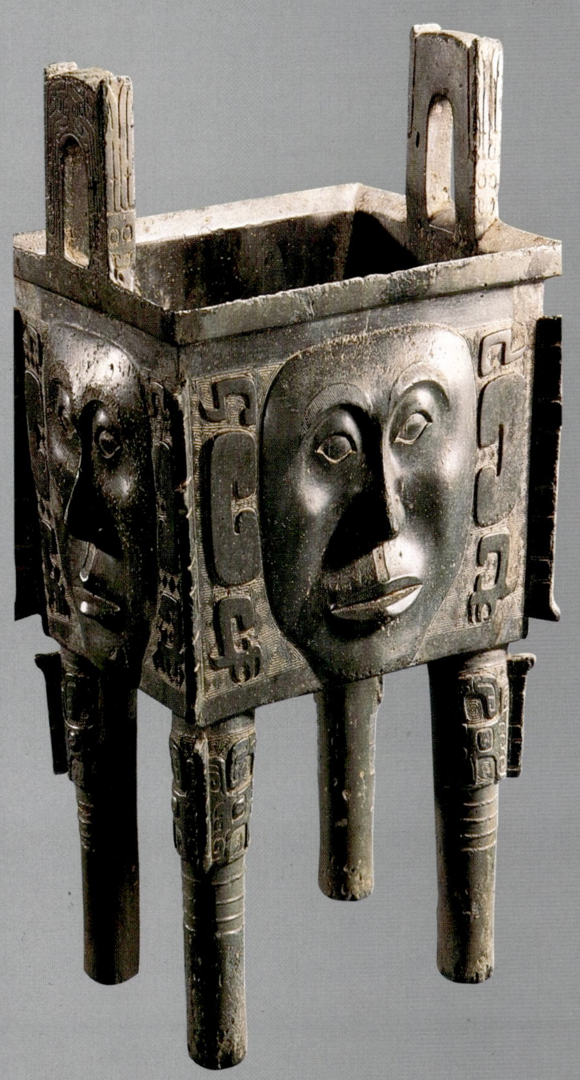

Pottery Sculpture · Bronze Ware

The appearance of pottery in primitive society not only promoted and enriched the economic life of the people of remote antiquity, but also gave free rein to man's natural aesthetic impulse. The pottery and porcelain products of this period are the best manifestation of this. The statues of goddesses and pottery sculptures of fertility symbols discovered in Lingyuan County, Liaoning Province, show that primitive sculpture had reached a quite high level.

The Xia, Shang and Zhou dynasties are known as the era of bronze, when bronze was an alloy of copper and tin. The bronze wares of the Shang and Zhou dynasties display standard molding techniques and a high degree of artistic development. The great Si Mu Wu rectangular *ding* (cooking vessel) excavated at Wuguan Village in Anyang, Henan, is 110 cm long, 77 cm wide and 137 cm high and weighs 875 kg. This cooking vessel is a majestic piece of work, with dragon patterns on the edges of its four sides, projecting images of two standing tigers and one human head on its handles and solid ornaments of beast heads on its feet. A similar rectangular *ding* (cooking vessel) with human-mask motif was excavated in Ningxiang, Hunan Province, with four large and striking half-reliefs of human masks on its four sides, respectively. The features of these human faces are complete and clear-cut, and look pretty much the same as those of modern people, except for the ears, which are big and stretch back at the two sides of the faces with cloud patterns above the ears and crooked hand-shaped patterns below them. To cast such a big pot, a large-scale foundry, sophisticated division of labor and special techniques were obviously necessary. The bronze artifacts of the Shang Dynasty have a solemn and mysterious air about them, and they are exquisitely wrought. Bronze wares were made in great quantities in this period, mostly sacrificial vessels and musical instruments, and some tools of production, weapons and daily utensils. They show that artistic endeavors were gradually maturing.

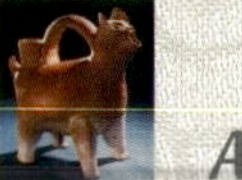

Pottery Bust, late Yangshao culture. Excavated from a site in Lixian County, Gansu Province, 1964. It is the remnant of a pottery figure. The plump face wears a simple and honest expression.

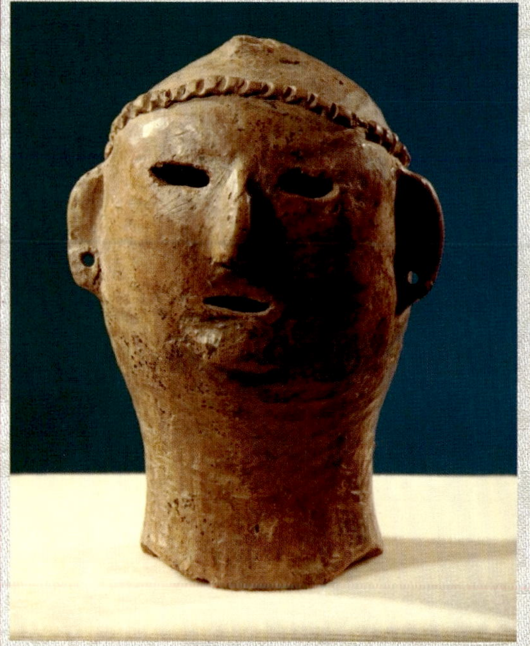

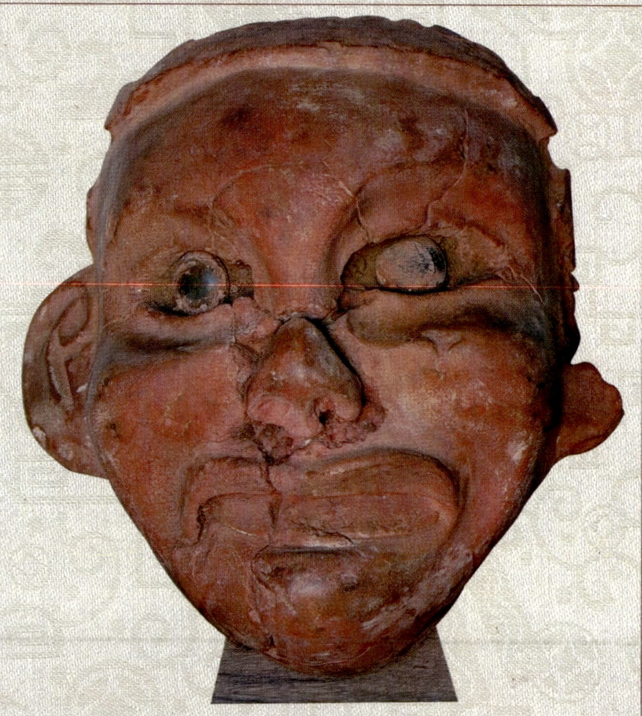

Colored Pottery Bust, Hongshan culture. Unearthed in Niuheliang, Liaoning Province. With green jade eyeballs, a broad forehead, raised eyebrows, and full lips, this life-sized sculpted head was executed in a realistic style. The five sense organs are located accurately and are well proportioned.

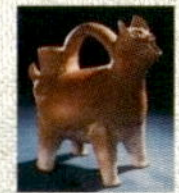

Pottery Figurines of Naked Women, Hongshan culture. Unearthed in Dongshanzui, Mongolian Autonomous County of Harqin Left Wing, Liaoning Province. These two small, incomplete naked figurines have swelling abdomens and protruding buttocks. They are thought to be fertility symbols.

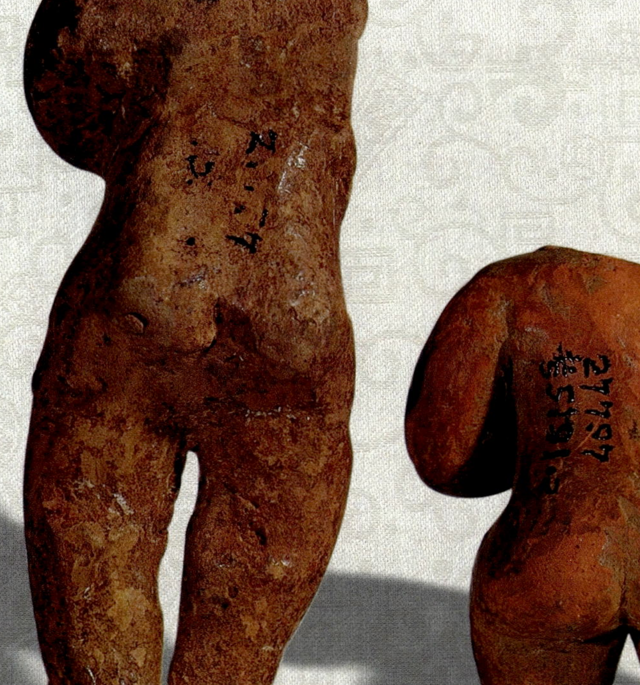

Animal-shaped Pottery Vessel, Dawenkou culture. Excavated from a site in Dawenkou, Tai'an City, Shandong Province, in 1925. This water container looks like a pig; however, its wide-open mouth looks exactly like that of a barking dog.

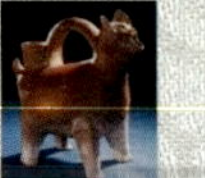

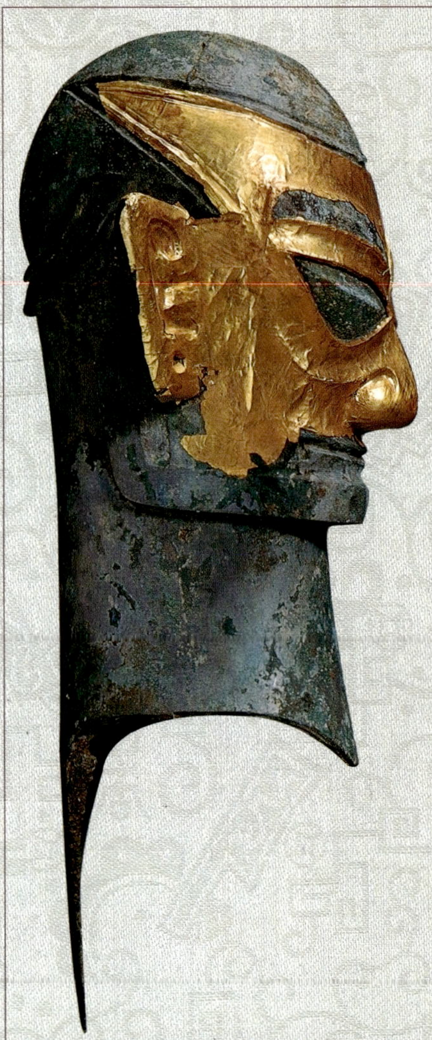

Bronze Bust with Gold Mask, Shang Dynasty. Excavated from the Sanxingdui tombs site, Guanghan City, Sichuan Province, in 1986.

Featuring an exaggerated nose, mouth and ears, the bronze human figures unearthed from the Sanxingdui tombs all look like extraterrestrial beings.

Jade Figurine of a Kneeling Man, Shang Dynasty. Unearthed from the Tomb of Fu Hao in Anyang County, Henan Province, in 1976.

This exquisite yellowish-brown jade sculpture is only seven cm high. This kneeling man, absorbed in thought and a fierce facial expression, may be a slave owner. The tube-shaped head ornament, gorgeous dress and the pendant worn at the waist are characteristics of the attire of the highest rank in ancient China.

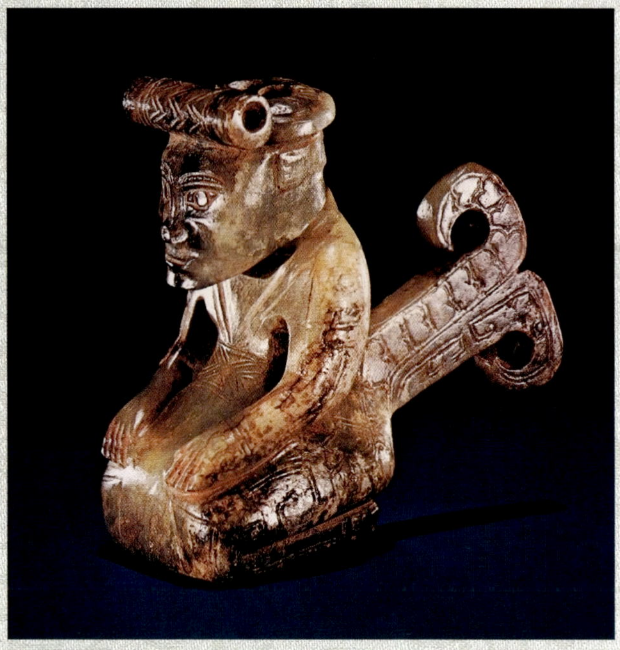

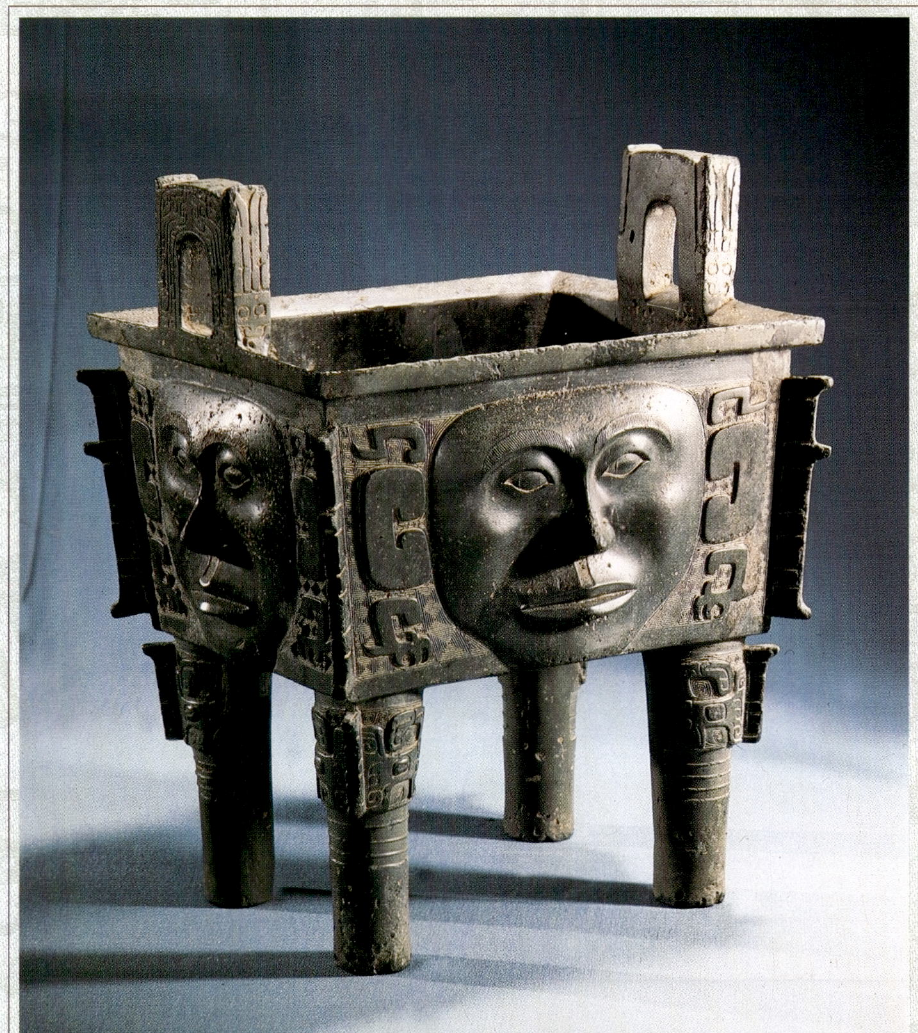

Rectangular Ding with Human-mask Motif, late Shang Dynasty. Excavated from a site in Ningxiang County, Hunan Province, in 1959. The four human faces on the four sides, respectively, of the *ding* are nearly square. The five sense organs are accurately located, the nose is sharp and pointed, and the cheekbones are high. Some people believe these details relate to the legend that Huangdi (the Yellow Emperor, legendary ruler and ancestor of the Chinese nation) had four faces; others believe it is a *taotie*, a mythical carnivorous beast.

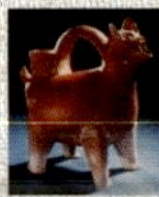

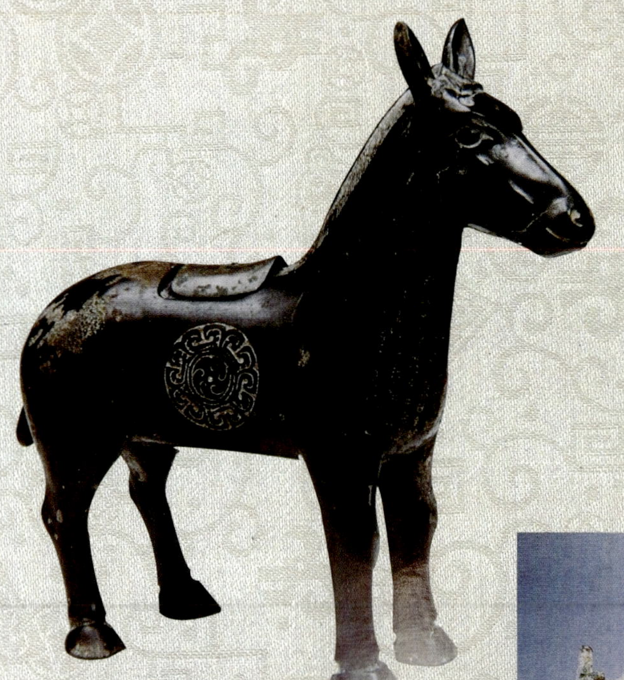

Horse-shaped Zun, Western Zhou Dynasty (ca.11th century-770 BC). Unearthed from a site in Meixian County, Shaanxi Province, in 1955.
The inscription on the breast of the animal reads that after presiding at the stabling ceremony for new horses, the emperor of the Zhou Dynasty bestowed two of them on Minister Li as gifts. Minister Li then had this *zun* made to express his thanks to the emperor.

Bronze Carriage with a Limbless Doorkeeper, early Eastern Zhou Dynasty (770-221 BC). Unearthed from a site in Wenxi County, Shanxi Province, in 1989. Figures of birds and animals are arranged around and above the carriage, dragon and tiger designs are engraved on the walls. Worthy of notice is the limbless man by the door, possibly indicating the punishment of amputation carried out during the Zhou Dynasty.

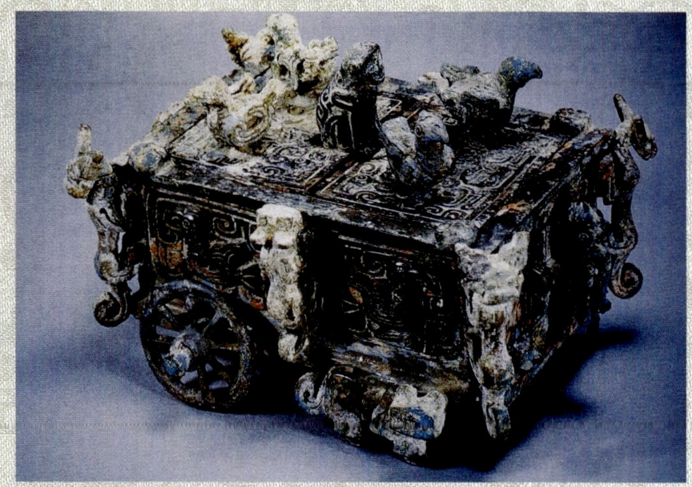

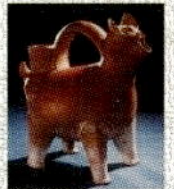

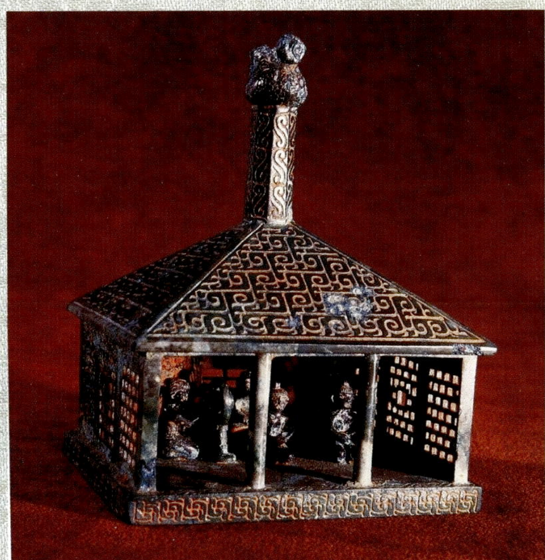

Bronze House with Cloud Design, Eastern Zhou Dynasty. Unearthed in Shaoxing City, Zhejiang Province, in 1981.
Six naked musicians are playing different types of instruments inside a temple. This sculpture probably demonstrates a performance of ritual music.

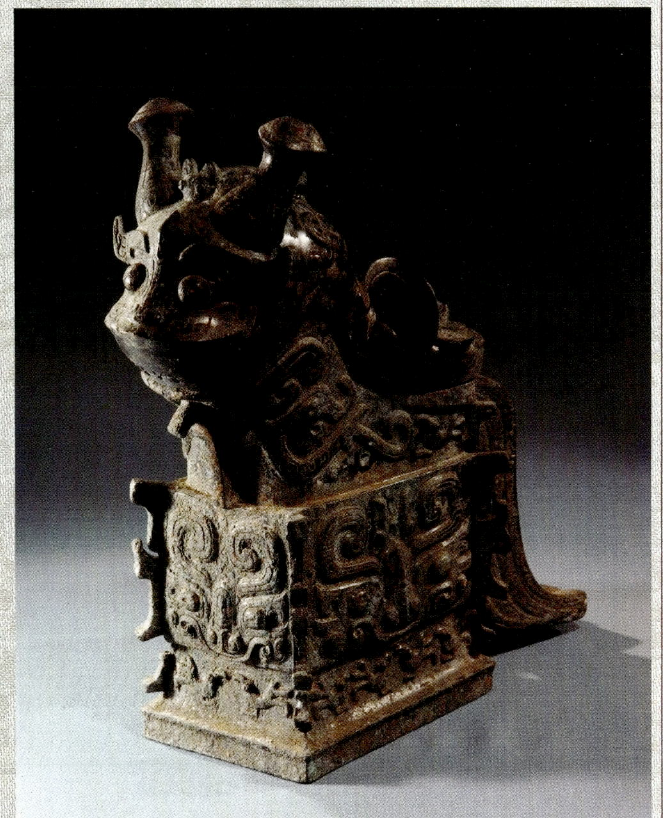

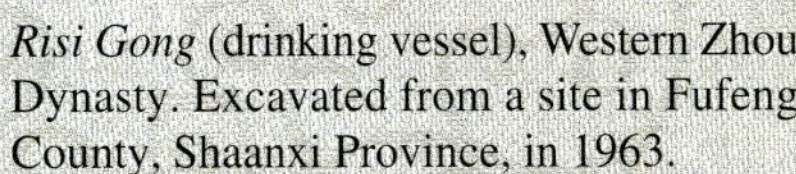

Risi Gong (drinking vessel), Western Zhou Dynasty. Excavated from a site in Fufeng County, Shaanxi Province, in 1963.

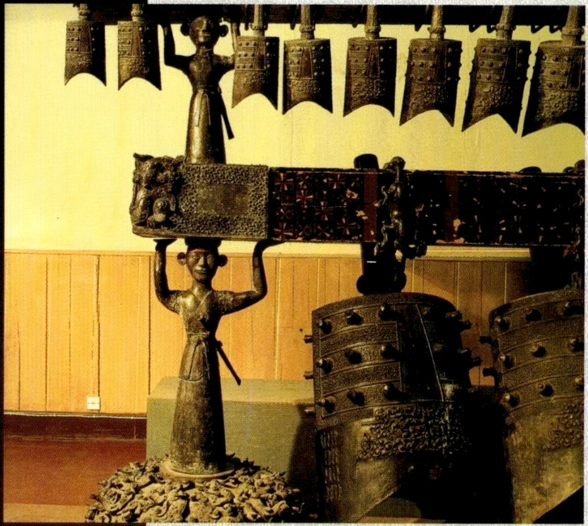

Bronze Human Figurine Chime Supports, Warring States Period. Excavated from No.1 Tomb in Leigudun, Suixian County, Hebei Province, in 1978.
Part of the rack on which chimes are hung, found in the tomb of Marquis Yi of the State of Zeng, Warring States Period.

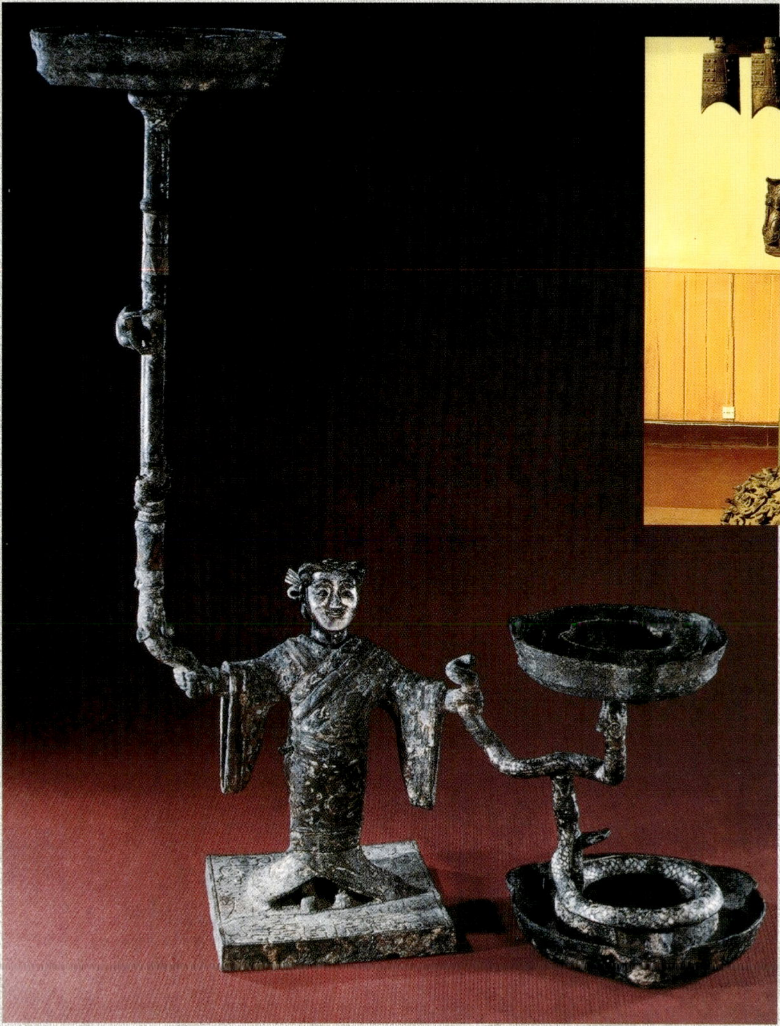

Lamp with a Silver-headed Human Figure, Warring States Period.
Unearthed from the tomb of the ruler of the State of Zhongshan, Pingshan County, Hebei Province, in 1976.

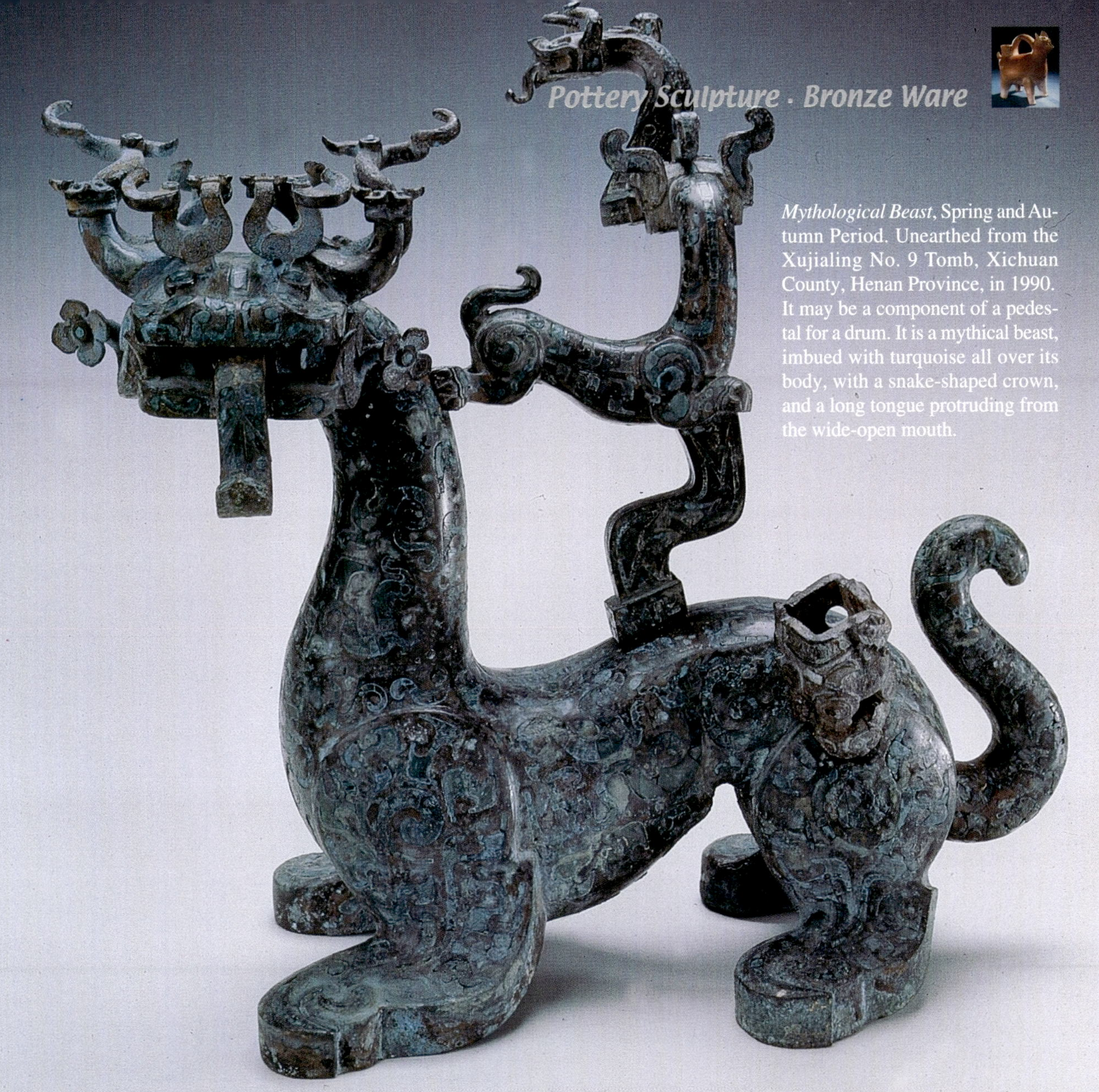

Mythological Beast, Spring and Autumn Period. Unearthed from the Xujialing No. 9 Tomb, Xichuan County, Henan Province, in 1990. It may be a component of a pedestal for a drum. It is a mythical beast, imbued with turquoise all over its body, with a snake-shaped crown, and a long tongue protruding from the wide-open mouth.

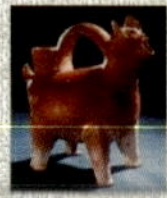

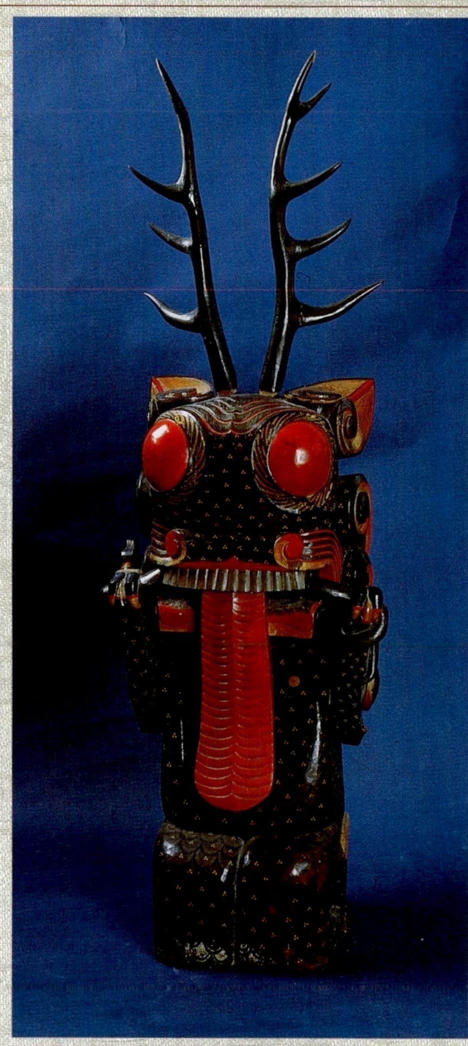

Tomb-protecting Mythical Beast, Warring States Period. Excavated from the Changtaiguan No. 1 Tomb in Xinyang, Henan Province, in 1957. The beast has a pair of antlers, big round eyes and a very long tongue. Kneeling on the floor, it is swallowing a snake. Such sculptures are found only in tombs of high-ranking officials and noblemen, which also tend to contain multiple coffins and ritual vessels.

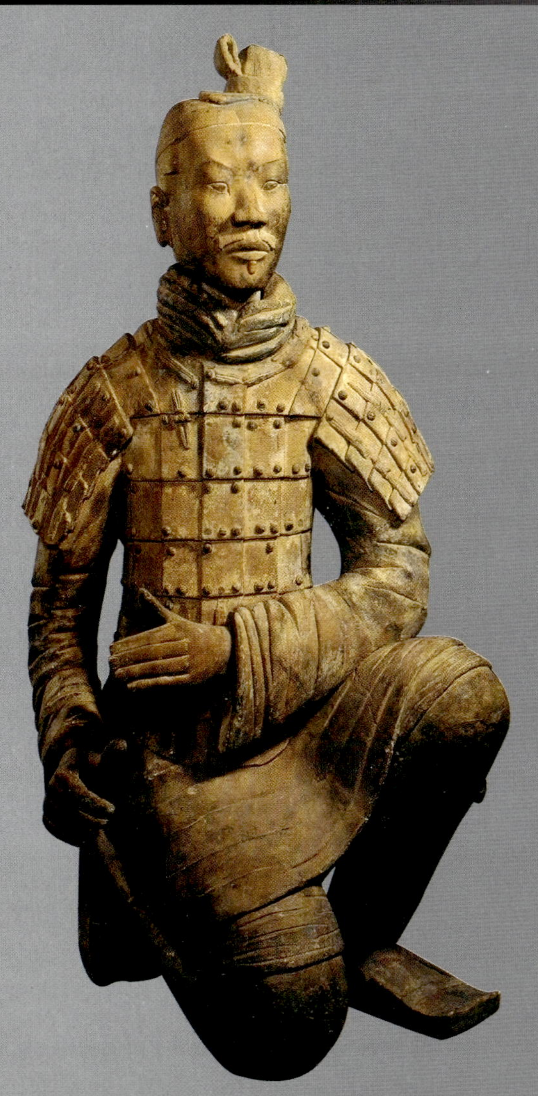

Terracotta Warriors and Horses
Groups of Stone Carvings
Bronze Galloping Horse

After Emperor Qin Shi Huang unified China, he established the first feudal regime over the huge territory. During the following Han Dynasty, the Xiongnu tribes in north China were tamed, and the boundaries of China extended and secured. The military formations of the terracotta figurines of warriors and horses guarding the Qin Shi Huang Mausoleum and the groups of stone sculptures before the grave of General Huo Qubing, conqueror of the Xiongnu, are testimony to the power and grandeur of China in this period.

The main artistic features of the Qin terracotta figurines are realism and precision in molding technique. In the general layout, the repetition of numerous motionless upright articles produces the force of a landslide and the power of a tidal wave, giving an awe-inspiring and unforgettable impression. As for the groups of stone sculptures before the tomb of General Huo Qubing, by using the artistic technique of making shapes according to the outlines of the stones, the artisans ingeniously combined the skills of solid sculpture, relief and shallow carving, and depicted the images just to the point of expression, without any unnecessary polishing. The bronze galloping horse with one foot mounted on a flying swallow, excavated at Wuwei, is 34.5 cm tall and 45 cm long. It has been the centerpiece of the exhibitions of excavated relics held by China in more than 10 countries since 1973, including Japan, the United States, Britain, France, Italy and Sweden, and is the symbol of the National Tourism Administration.

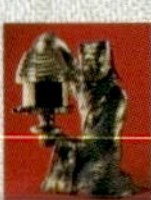

The No. 1 Pit of Terracotta Warriors and Horses of the Mausoleum of Qin Shi Huang, Qin Dynasty. Discovered in Lintong County, Shaanxi Province, in 1974.
Over 6,000 life-size terracotta warriors and horses were magnificently arranged in battle array in the No. 1 Pit, which is 210 m wide from east to west, and 62 m long from north to south.

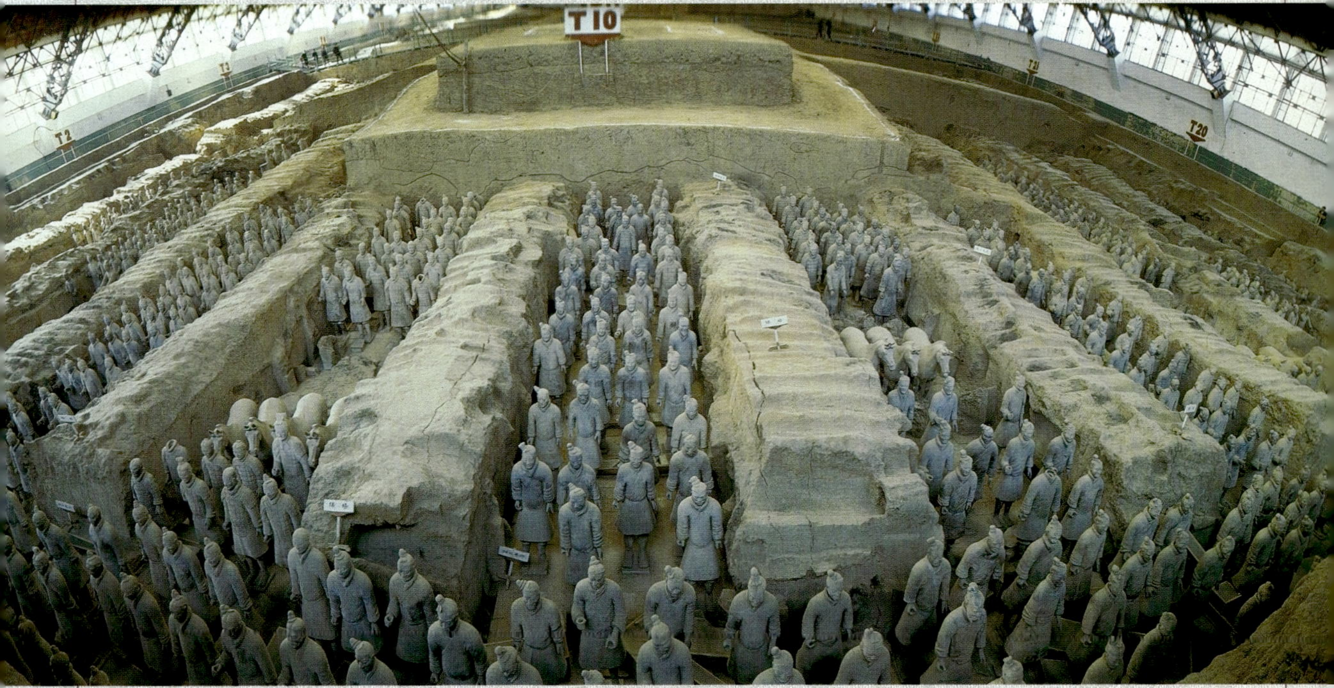

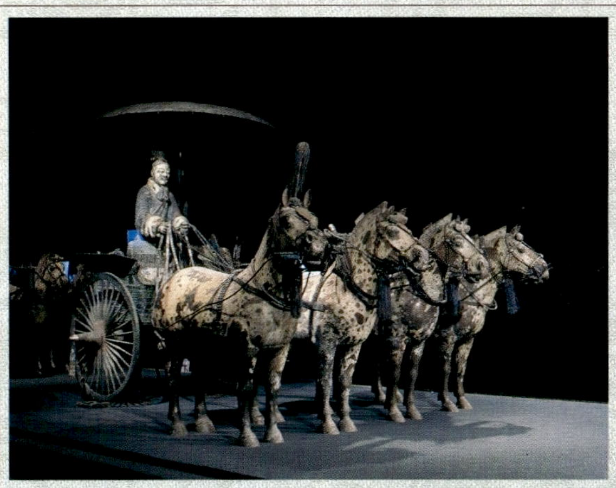

Painted Bronze Carriage and Horses, Qin Dynasty. Unearthed on the west side of the Mausoleum of Emperor Qin Shi Huang, in 1980.
This item is 317 cm long and 106.2 cm high, and weighs 1,241 kg. Most of the accessories are decorated with gold and silver, and some are cast in gold or silver. Due to its unusual structure and splendid decorations, it is thought by many to be a copy of Emperor Qin Shi Huang's own carriage.

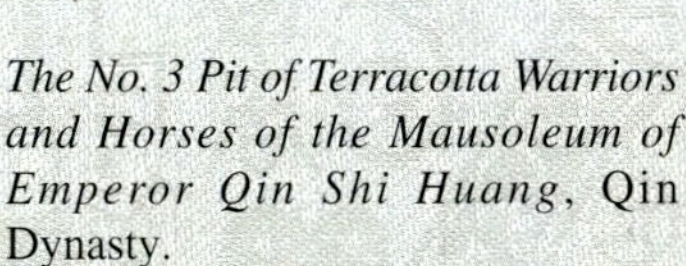

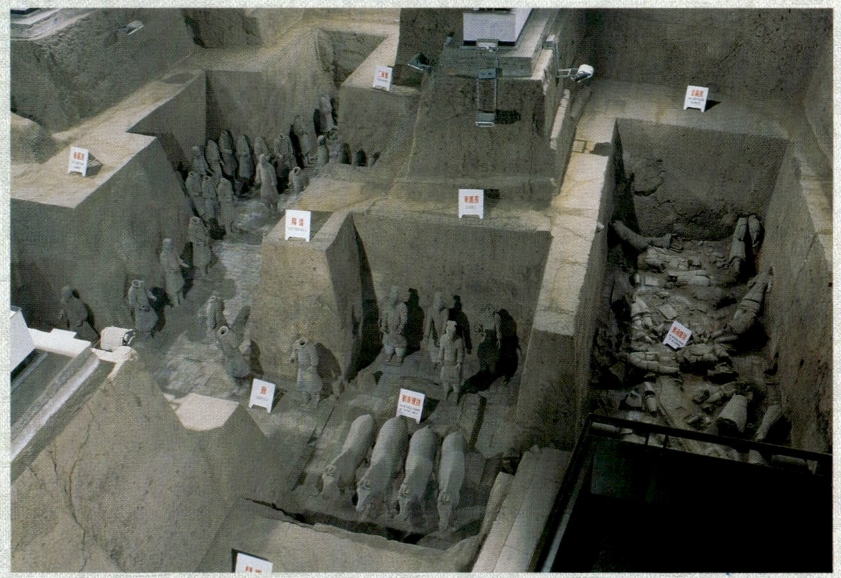

The No. 3 Pit of Terracotta Warriors and Horses of the Mausoleum of Emperor Qin Shi Huang, Qin Dynasty.
This pit is relatively small, and probably represents the command center of the army. The chariot of the commander-in-chief drawn by four horses occupies the central position in this pit.

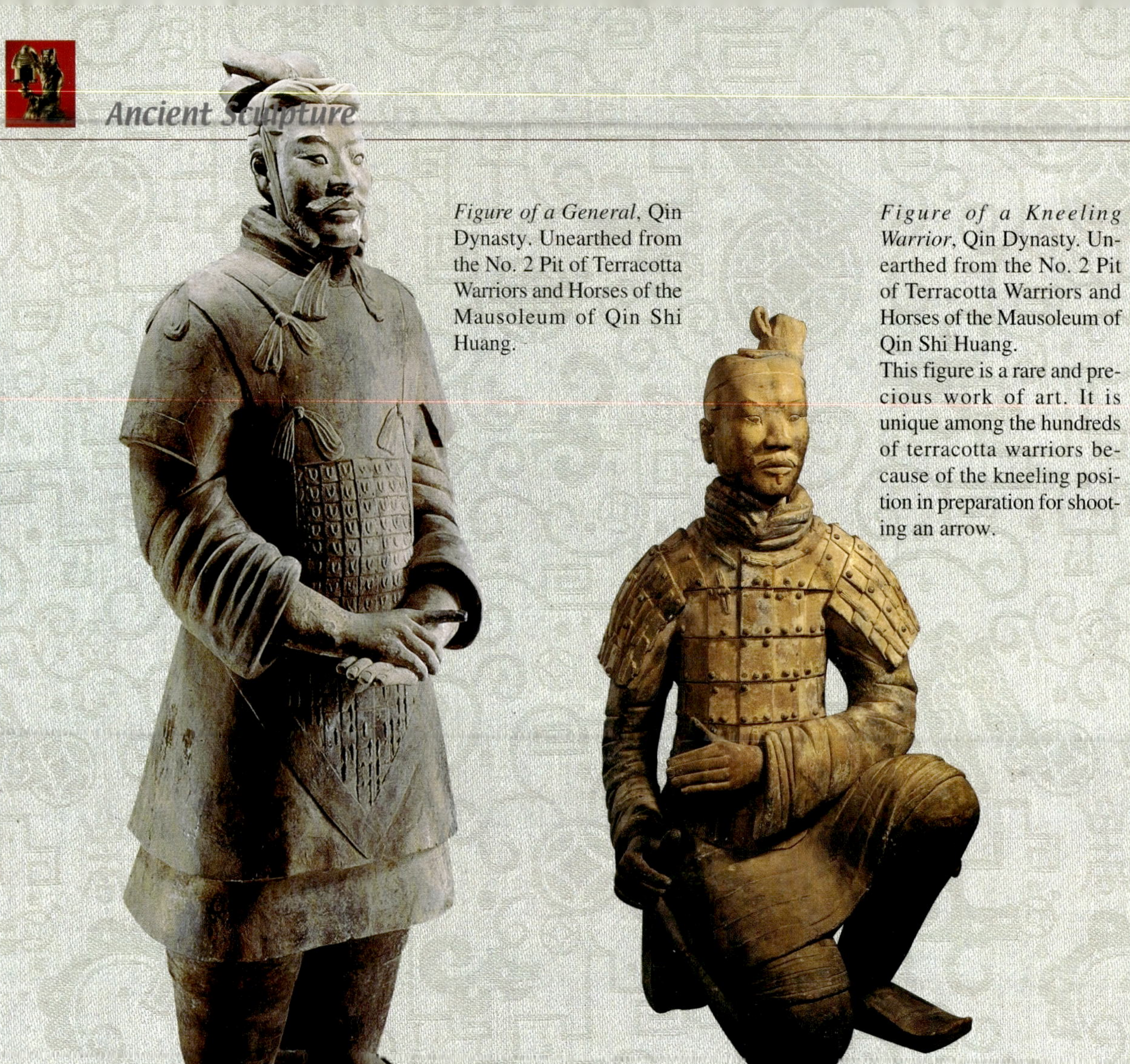

Figure of a General, Qin Dynasty. Unearthed from the No. 2 Pit of Terracotta Warriors and Horses of the Mausoleum of Qin Shi Huang.

Figure of a Kneeling Warrior, Qin Dynasty. Unearthed from the No. 2 Pit of Terracotta Warriors and Horses of the Mausoleum of Qin Shi Huang.
This figure is a rare and precious work of art. It is unique among the hundreds of terracotta warriors because of the kneeling position in preparation for shooting an arrow.

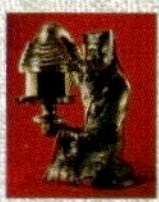

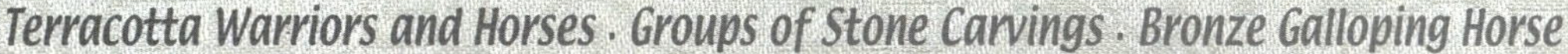

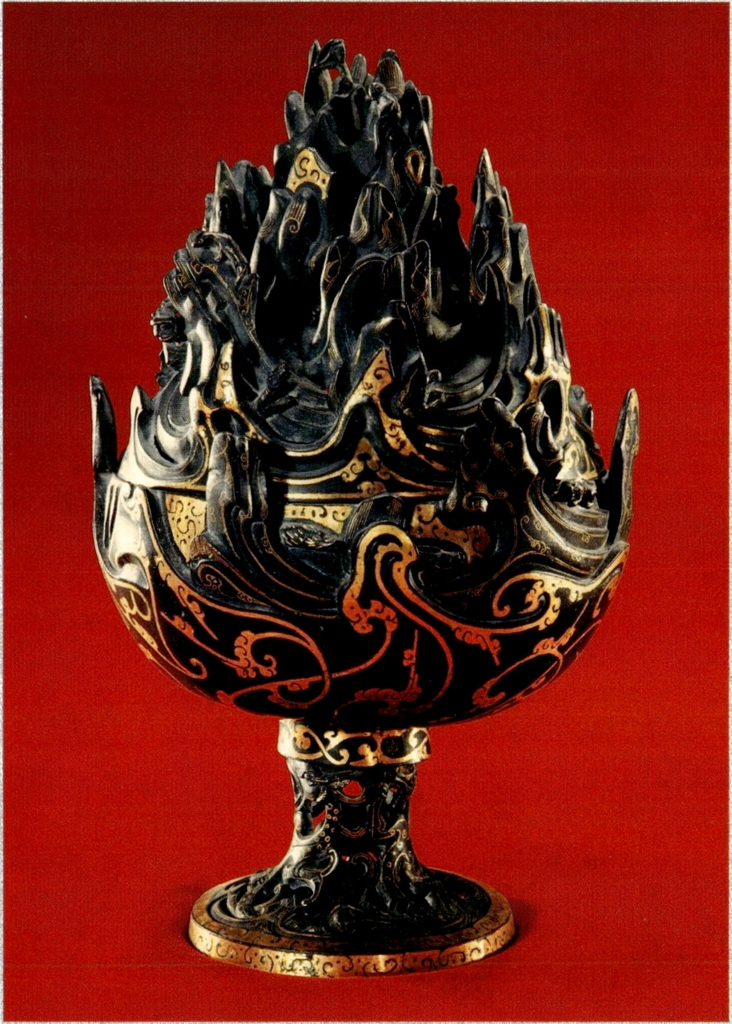

Boshan Bronze Incense Burner with Gold Inlay, Han Dynasty. Excavated from the tomb of Liu Sheng, prince of the State of Zhongshan, in Mancheng, Hebei Province. The Boshan incense burner is connected with Penglai Island in the East China Sea, legendary abode of the immortals, thus making it a suitable funerary article.

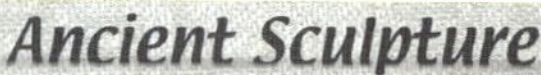

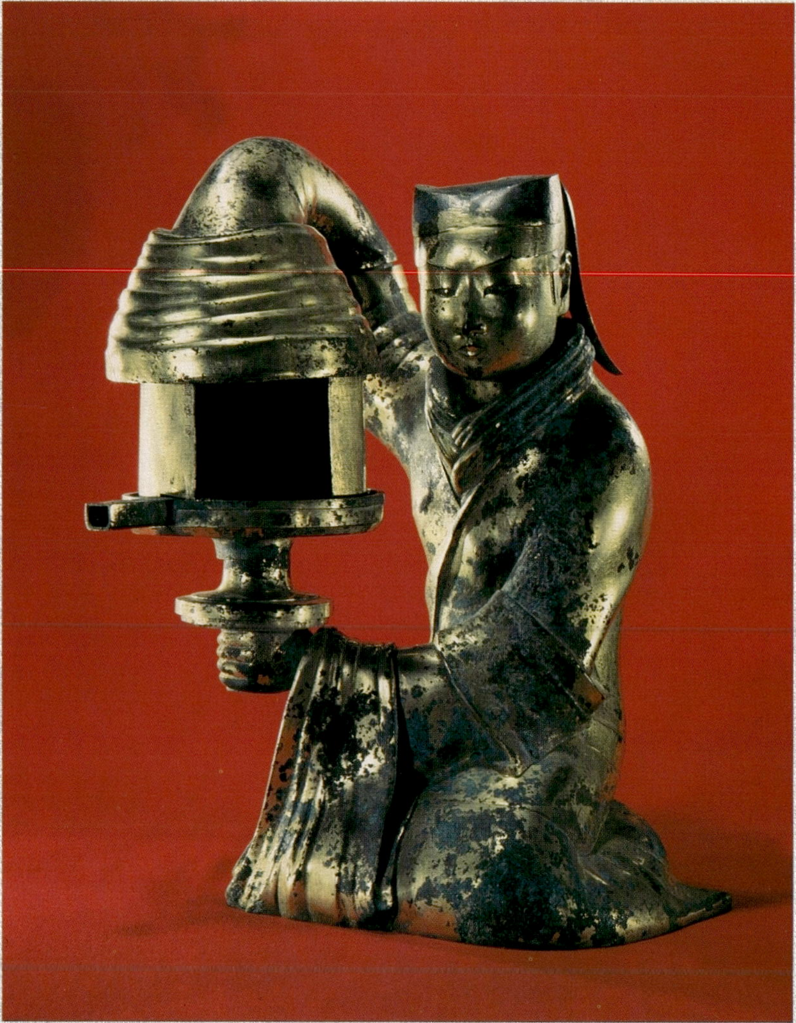

Gilded Changxin Palace Lamp, Han Dynasty. Unearthed from the tomb of Dou Wan, wife of Liu Sheng, prince of the State of Zhongshan, in Mancheng, Hebei Province, in 1968.

This beautiful lamp was probably a wedding present from Liu Sheng's grandmother. On the top of the lamp, there is a plate which can be turned to adjust the brightness and lighting direction. The smoke from the lamp travels up the right arm of the maid figure into her hollow body.

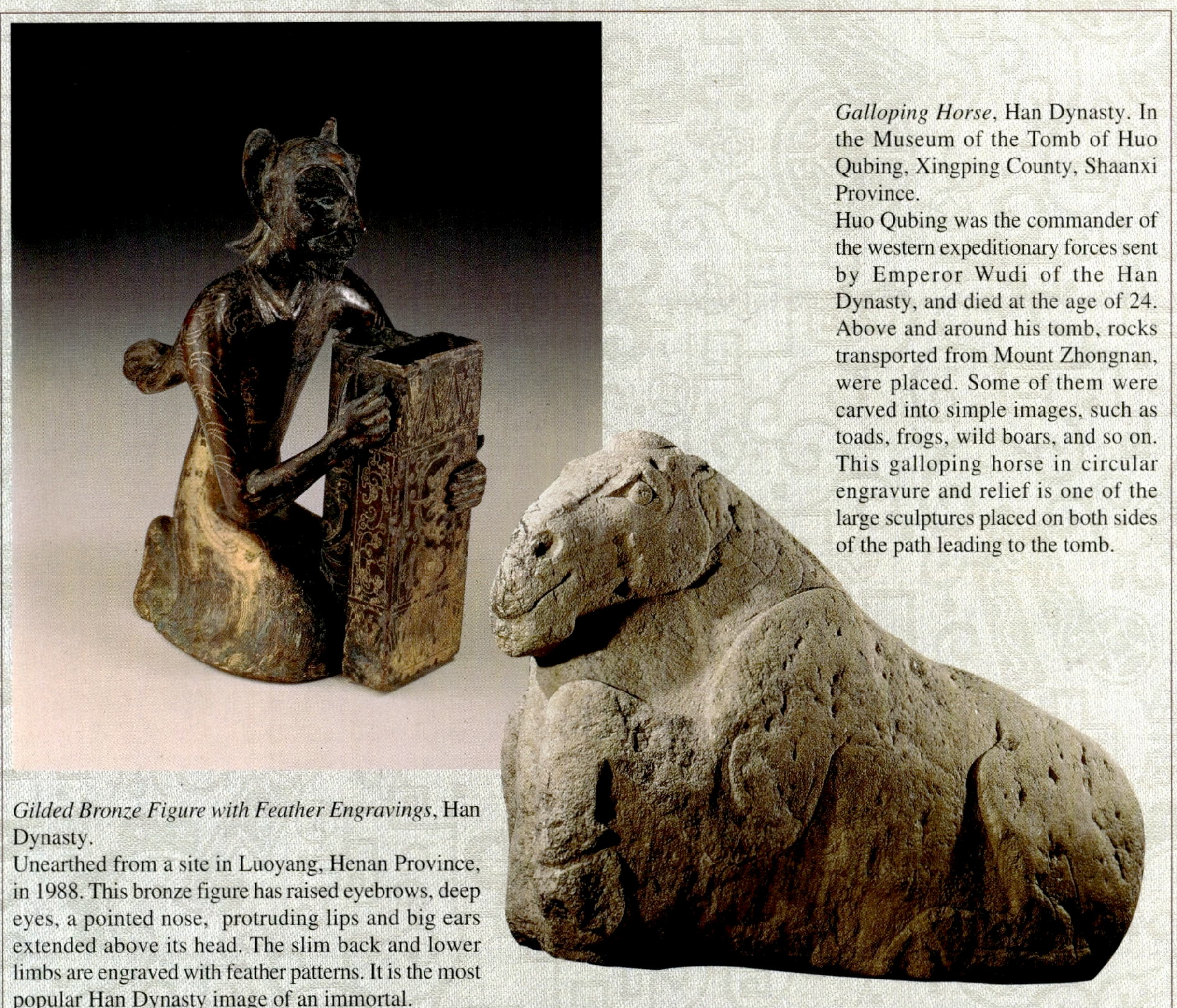

Galloping Horse, Han Dynasty. In the Museum of the Tomb of Huo Qubing, Xingping County, Shaanxi Province.

Huo Qubing was the commander of the western expeditionary forces sent by Emperor Wudi of the Han Dynasty, and died at the age of 24. Above and around his tomb, rocks transported from Mount Zhongnan, were placed. Some of them were carved into simple images, such as toads, frogs, wild boars, and so on. This galloping horse in circular engravure and relief is one of the large sculptures placed on both sides of the path leading to the tomb.

Gilded Bronze Figure with Feather Engravings, Han Dynasty.

Unearthed from a site in Luoyang, Henan Province, in 1988. This bronze figure has raised eyebrows, deep eyes, a pointed nose, protruding lips and big ears extended above its head. The slim back and lower limbs are engraved with feather patterns. It is the most popular Han Dynasty image of an immortal.

Figurine of a Comedian Beating a Drum, Han Dynasty. Excavated from a site in Pengshan County, Sichuan Province.

With amusing expression and exaggerated attitude, this figurine was probably a comedian who amused the audience with songs, jokes and humorous dances.

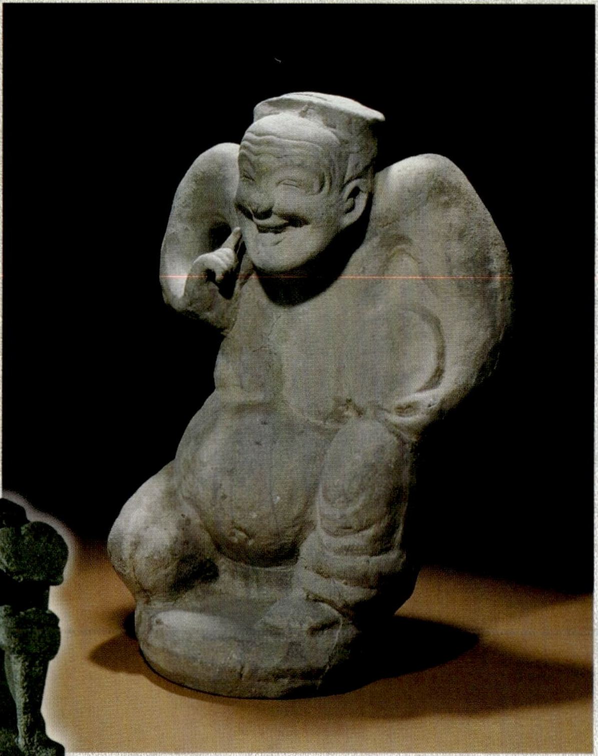

Stone Winged Beast for Warding Off Evil Spirits, Han Dynasty.

Unearthed in Yichuan County, Henan Province, in 1963. It was thought that this huge mythical winged beast had the power to protect the deceased.

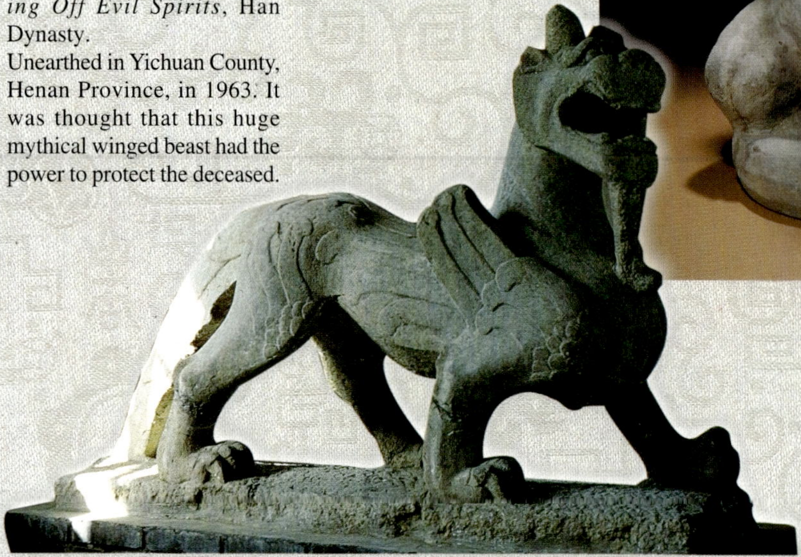

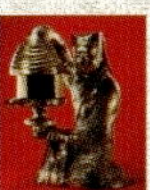

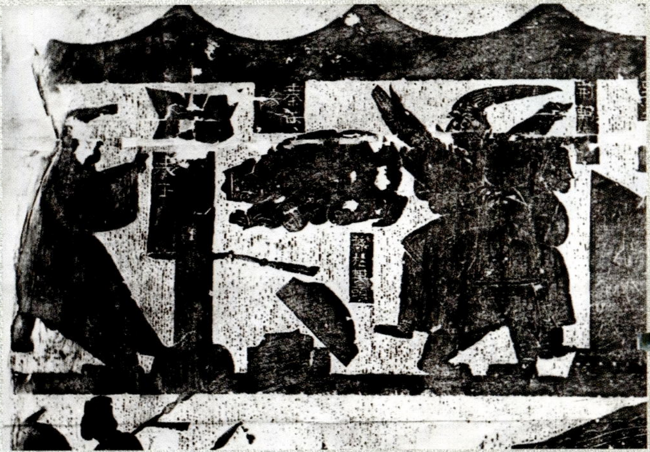

Carved Stone with Scenes from the Story of Jing Ke's Attempt on the Life of the First Emperor of the Qin Dynasty, Han Dynasty. Preserved in Wuliang Shrine, Shandong Province.

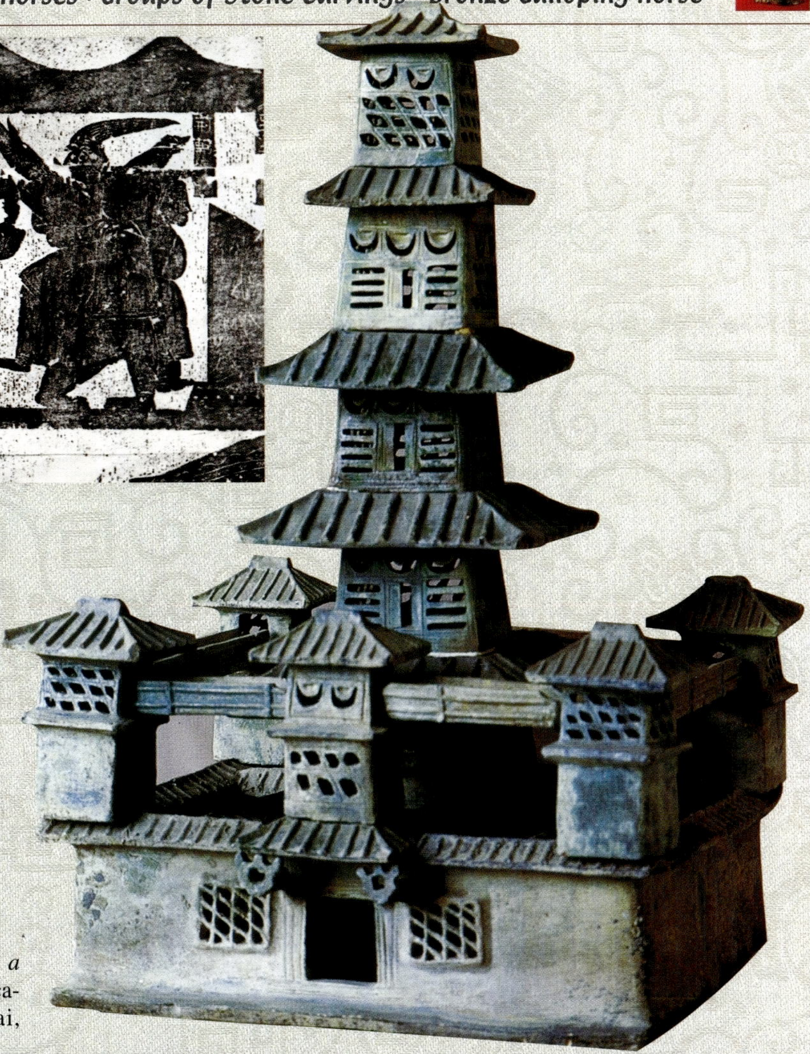

Pottery Building with a Courtyard, Han Dynasty. Excavated from a site in Leitai, Wuwei, Gansu Province.

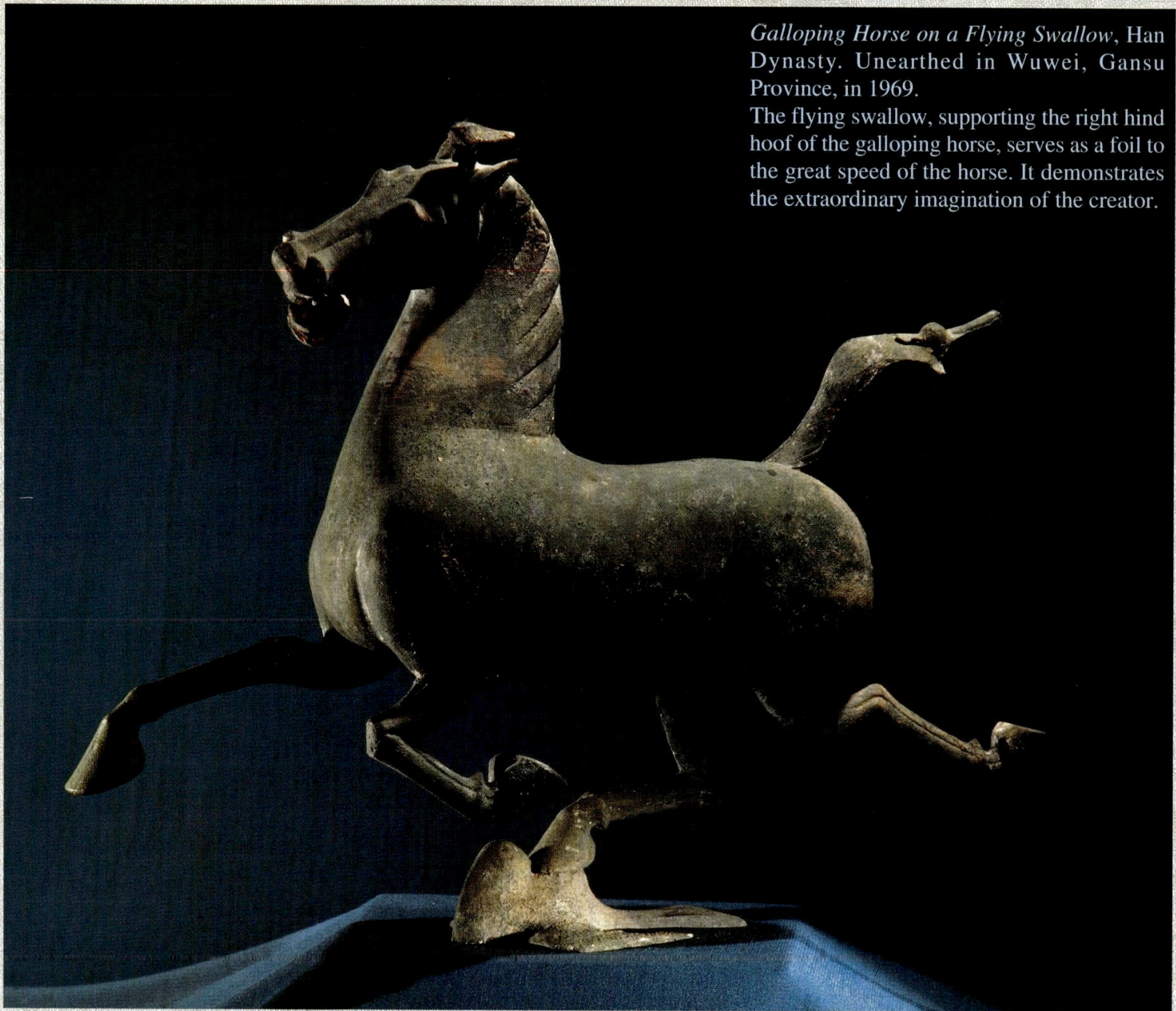

Galloping Horse on a Flying Swallow, Han Dynasty. Unearthed in Wuwei, Gansu Province, in 1969.
The flying swallow, supporting the right hind hoof of the galloping horse, serves as a foil to the great speed of the horse. It demonstrates the extraordinary imagination of the creator.

The Impact of Buddhism

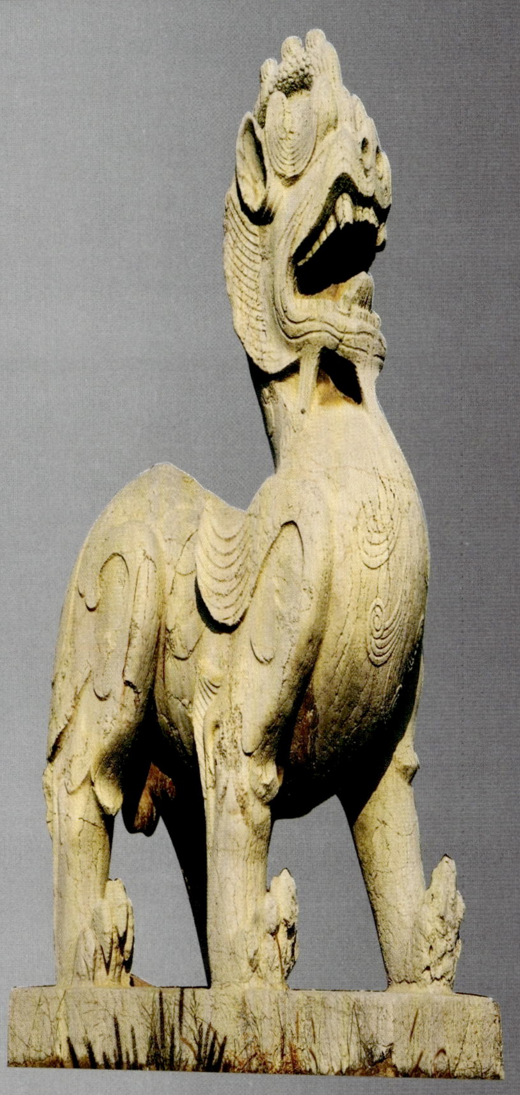

Buddhism spread rapidly during the war-ravaged period of the Wei, Jin and Northern and Southern dynasties. The common people sought relief from their sufferings by praying for Buddha's help, while their rulers used Buddhism to benumb the minds of the people and avert revolt. During this period, the chiseling of stone grottoes and building of Buddhist temples became prevalent all over China. Du Mu (803-852), a leading poet of the Tang Dynasty, described the temples of the Southern Dynasties in a poem, as follows: "Of four hundred and eighty temples of the Southern Dynasties,/ How many towers and terraces loom in the misty rain?" Since grottoes are less vulnerable than temples and palaces in times of war and natural disasters, grotto sculptures are our major source of information about the art and religion of that epoch. The famous grottoes of Datong in Shanxi Province and Luoyang in Henan Province, along with many lesser ones, were constructed in the Northern Wei Dynasty, bequeathing large numbers of stone statues of Buddha to posterity.

Of the Yungang Grottoes at Datong, five major grottoes (the 16th to the 20th) were constructed by Monk Tanyao at the order of Emperor Wencheng of the Wei Dynasty in 450. These "five grottoes by Monk Tanyao" display the rigid forms of foreign influences on Chinese sculpture, but in the grottoes constructed later, artisans seemed to be trying to abandon these forms and return to the traditional artistic forms of the Han people. The image of Buddha is usually represented with a plump forehead, long eyes, straight nose, thick lips and broad shoulders. After the Northern Wei Dynasty moved its capital to Luoyang, Monk Huicheng, a member of the Wei imperial clan, began the construction of a big grotto known as the Guyang Cave on Mount Longmen in 495. From 500 to 523, Emperor Xuanwu and Emperor Xiaoming had the north, central and south grottoes — called the Binyang Caves — carved out. Constructed over a period of more than 50 years, the Guyang Cave is full of stone statues of Buddha in various sizes. And in the Binyang Caves, a carving representing emperors and empresses praying before Buddha is the most exquisite piece of work. The sculptures of the Longmen Grottoes manifest more Chinese artistic forms than those of the Yungang Grottoes, and the postures of Buddha have changed from vigorous and awe-inspiring at Yungang to gentle and amiable at Longmen. The image of Buddha represented by the main Buddha in the Central Binyang Cave is a kindly one, shown by the benevolent smile on the face of the statue. All these show the evolution of the combination of traditional Chinese art with foreign art.

Figurines of Scribes, Western Jin Dynasty. Excavated from a site in Changsha, Hunan Province.
Two clerks sit face-to-face, writing on bamboo slips.

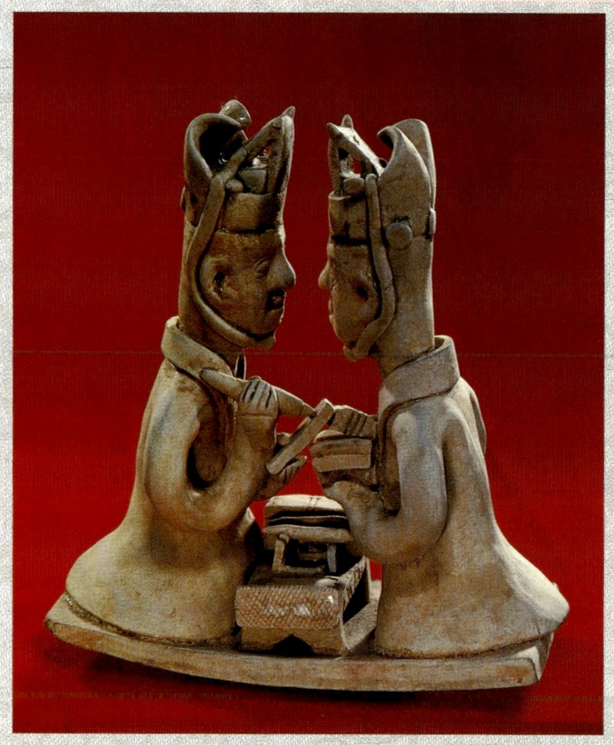

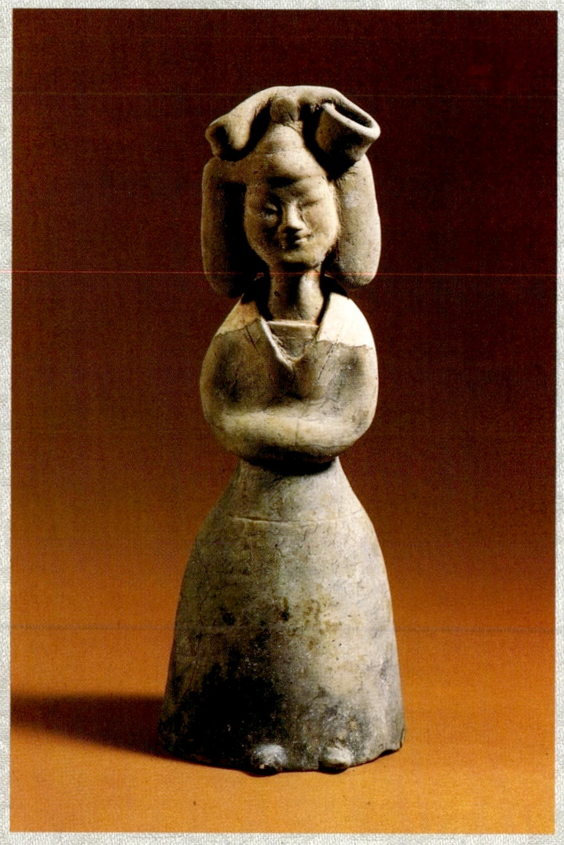

Pottery Figure of a Woman, Eastern Jin Dynasty. Unearthed on Mount Mufu, Nanjing, Jiangsu Province, in 1955.
Looking happy and relaxed, this woman wears her hair in a bun, a style which was popular in the Jin Dynasty and Southern and Northern Dynasties periods.

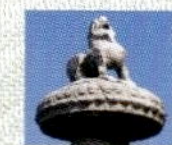

Kylin (unicorn), Southern Dynasties. Unearthed from the Chuning Mausoleum of Emperor Liu Yu of the Song Dynasty (420-479), Jiangning District, Nanjing, Jiangsu Province.

Stone mythical beasts account for the largest number among the relics that have been preserved at the tombs of the Southern Dynasties. Their body is usually three m long, and has wings. Those with horns in front of the tomb of an empress are called *tianlu* or *kylin*, and those without horns in front of the tomb of an emperor are called *pixie*.

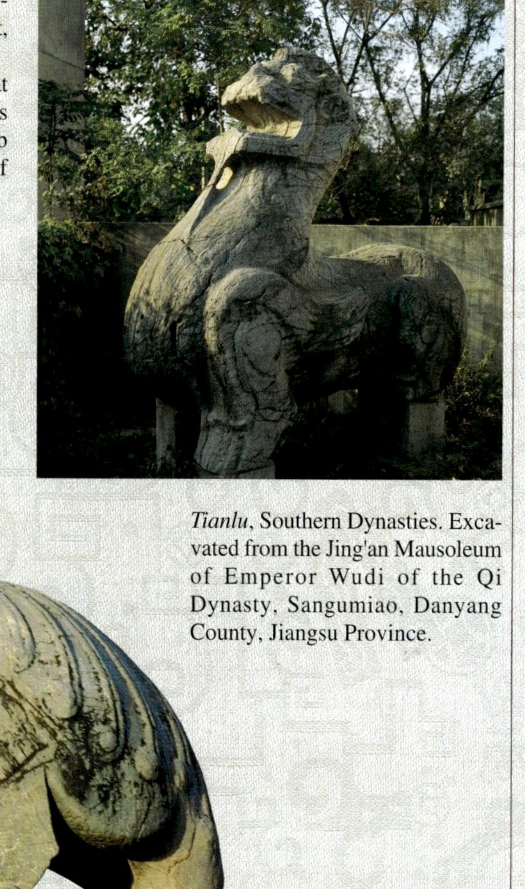

Tianlu, Southern Dynasties. Excavated from the Jing'an Mausoleum of Emperor Wudi of the Qi Dynasty, Sangumiao, Danyang County, Jiangsu Province.

31

Stone Pillar Guarding a Tomb Passage, Southern Dynasties. Unearthed from the Tomb of Marquis Xiao Jing of the Liang Dynasty, Ganjia Lane, Nanjing, Jiangsu Province.

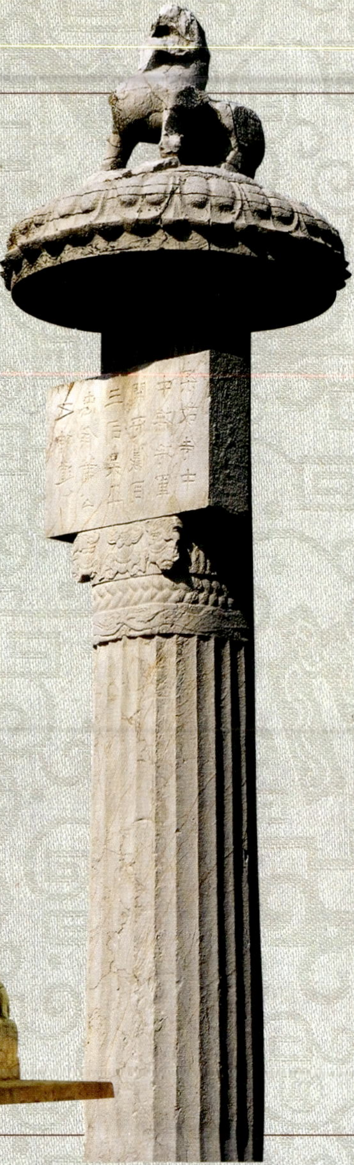

Pixie, Southern Dynasties. Excavated from the Tomb of Marquis Xiao Jing of the Liang Dynasty, Ganjia Lane, Nanjing, Jiangsu Province.

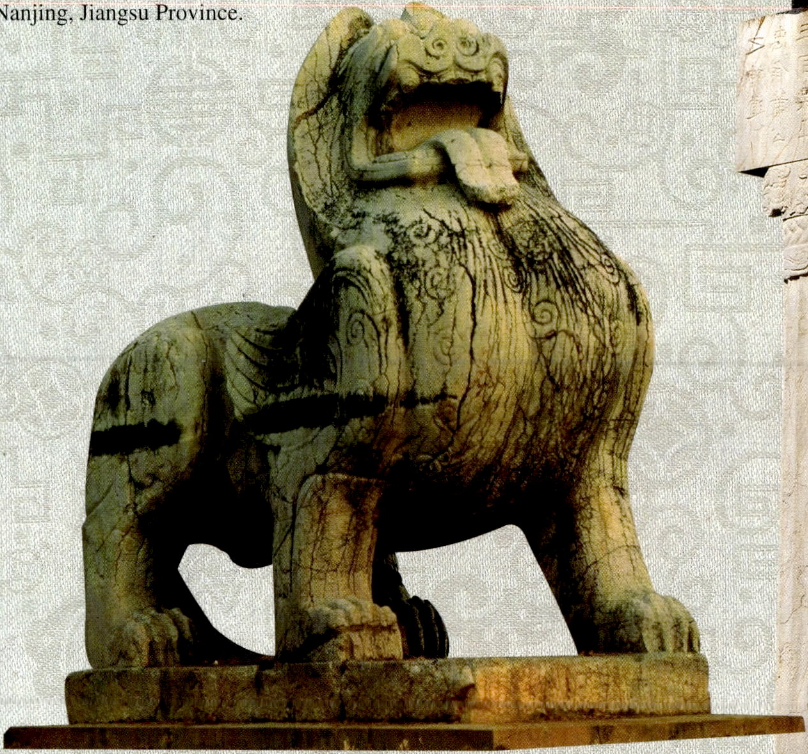

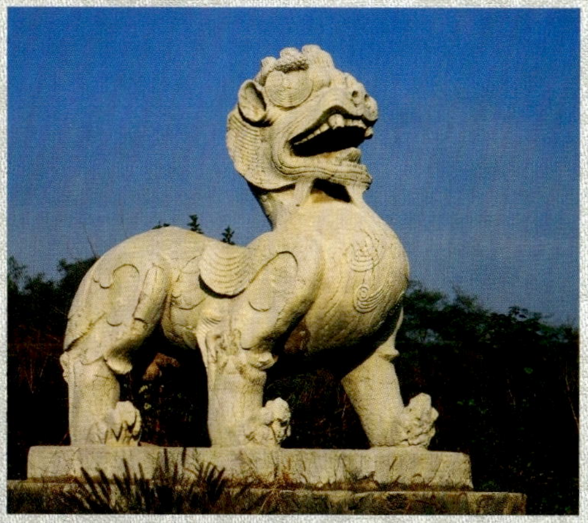

One-horned Kylin, Southern Dynasties. Unearthed from the Yongning Mausoleum of Emperor Wendi of the Chen Dynasty in Ganjia Lane, Jiangning District, Nanjing, Jiangsu Province.

Stone Steles and Pillar on the Sacred Way, Southern Dynasties.
Excavated from the Tomb of Prince Xiao Hong of the Liang Dynasty, Jiangning District, Nanjing, Jiangsu Province.

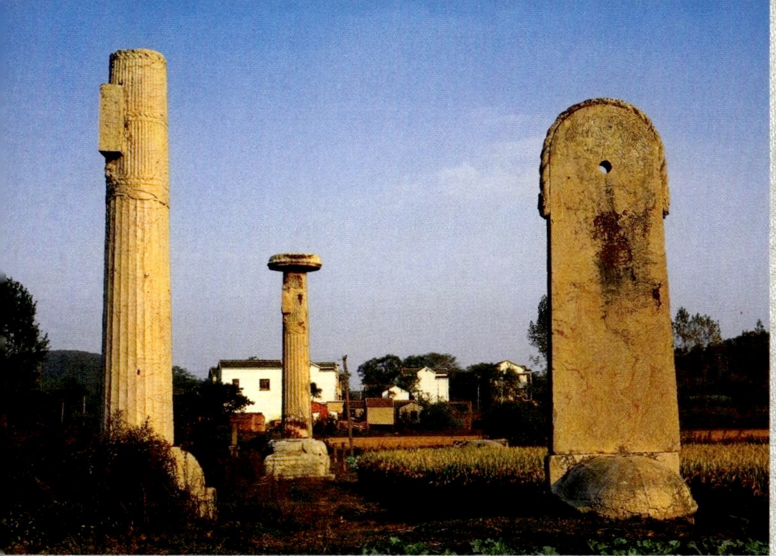

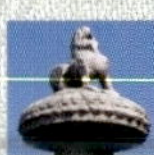

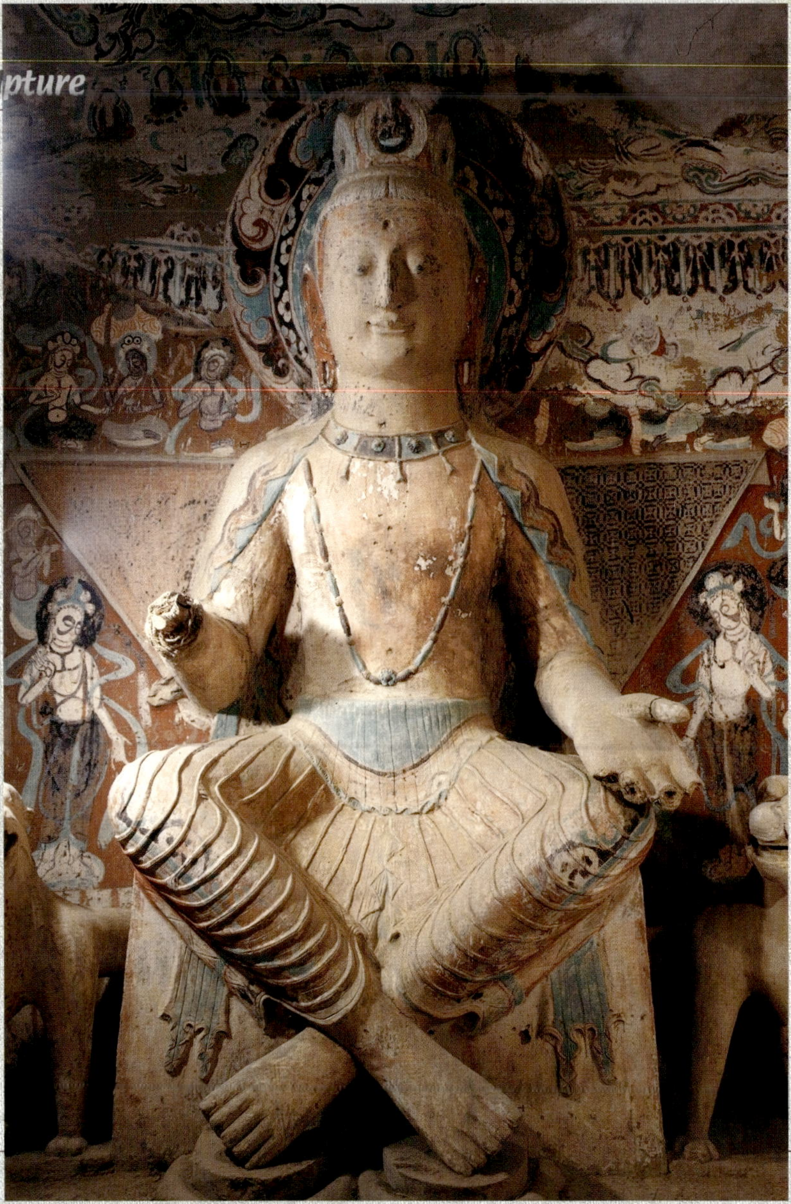

Maitreya Sitting Cross-legged, Northern Liang Dynasty. Grotto 275 of the Mogao Grottoes, Dunhuang, Gansu Province. Wearing a crown, a jeweled necklace, a long shawl and a robe, this image of Maitreya has a robust body and a solemn countenance, strongly characteristic of the Gandhara style of sculpture.

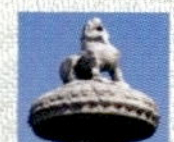

Buddha, Northern Wei Dynasty.
Grotto 259 of the Mogao Grottoes,
Dunhuang, Gansu Province.

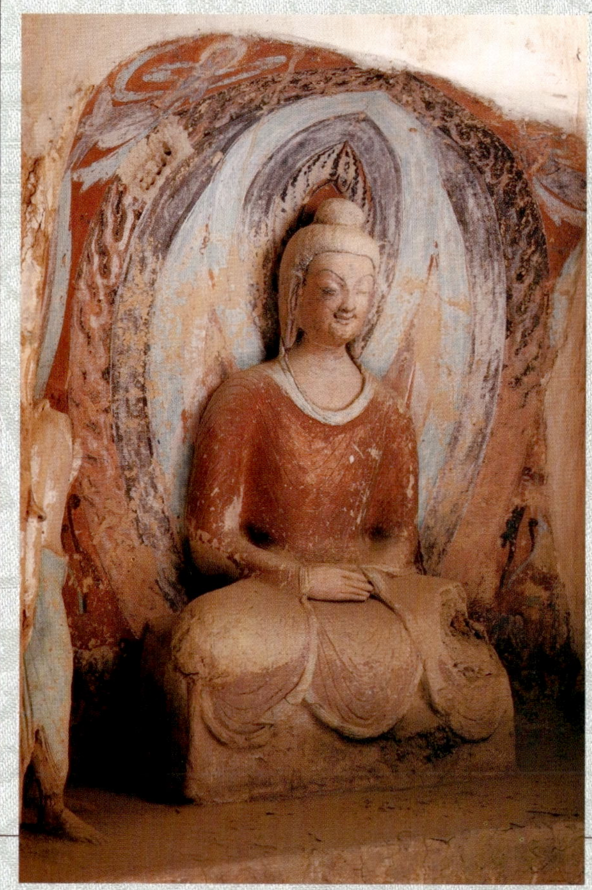

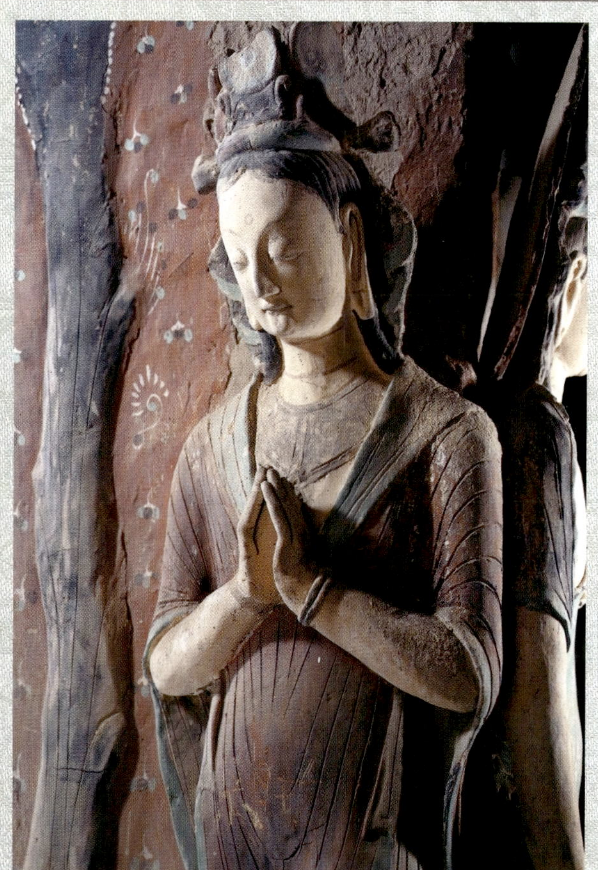

Bodhisattva, Northern Wei Dynasty. Grotto 248 of the
Mogao Grottoes, Dunhuang, Gansu Province.
Pressing his palms together before his chest, this elegant,
lifelike Bodhisattva seems to be praying.

Buddhist Monk Meditating, Western Wei Dynasty. Grotto 285 of the Mogao Grottoes, Dunhuang, Gansu Province. This Buddhist monk has fine and delicate features, and an unperturbed countenance. It seems that he is concentrating on reciting Buddhist scriptures.

Bodhisattva, Northern Zhou Dynasty. Grotto 438 of the Mogao Grottoes, Dunhuang, Gansu Province. This beautiful Bodhisattva wears a pleased, amiable look, just like an innocent girl.

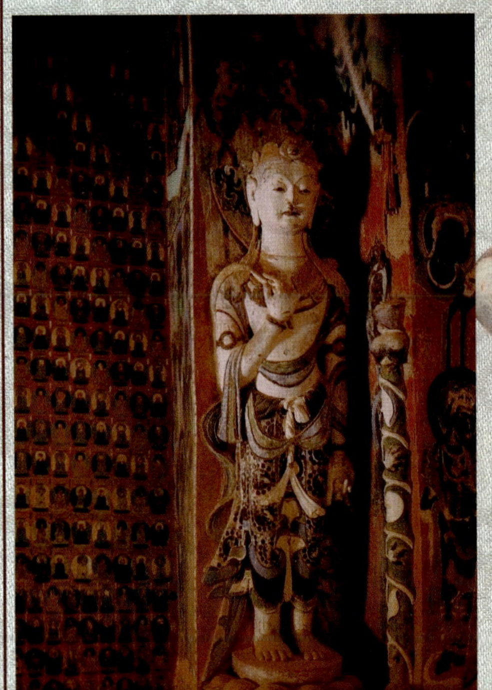

Bodhisattva, Northern Zhou Dynasty. Grotto 420 of the Mogao Grottoes, Dunhuang, Gansu Province.

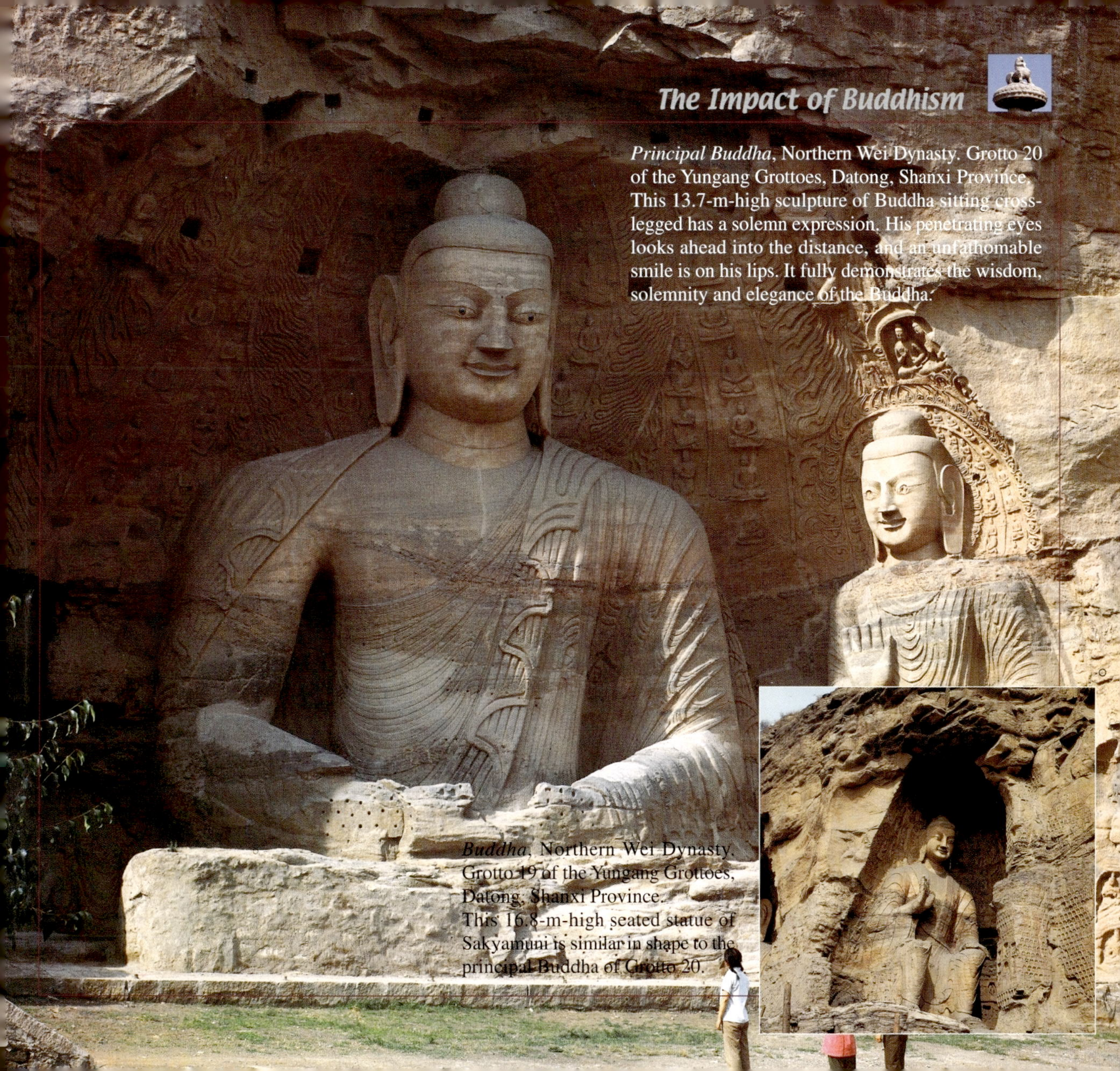

Principal Buddha, Northern Wei Dynasty. Grotto 20 of the Yungang Grottoes, Datong, Shanxi Province. This 13.7-m-high sculpture of Buddha sitting cross-legged has a solemn expression. His penetrating eyes looks ahead into the distance, and an unfathomable smile is on his lips. It fully demonstrates the wisdom, solemnity and elegance of the Buddha.

Buddha, Northern Wei Dynasty. Grotto 19 of the Yungang Grottoes, Datong, Shanxi Province. This 16.8-m-high seated statue of Sakyamuni is similar in shape to the principal Buddha of Grotto 20.

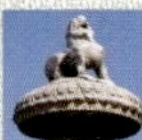

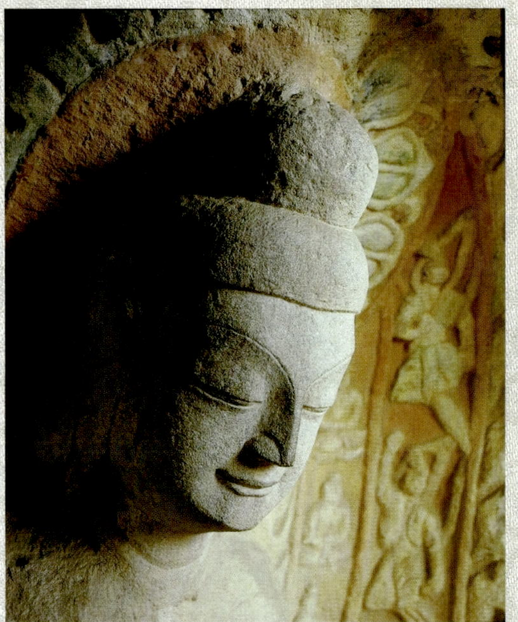

Detail of a Statue of the Buddha, Northern Wei Dynasty. Grotto 5 of the Yungang Grottoes, Datong, Shanxi Province.
This Buddha has fine and delicate features, with long willow-leaf-shaped eyebrows. His face is slightly thin, showing feminine beauty.

Kumaralabdha, Northern Wei Dynasty. Grotto 8 of the Yungang Grottoes, Datong, Shanxi Province. Kumaralabdha, which means "boy," is the son of Siva, the major god of Brahmanism. He has five heads and six arms, and rides on a strange mythological bird.

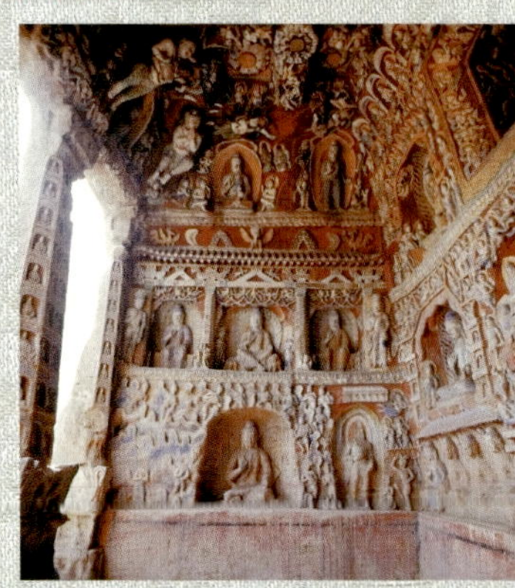

The Front Wall of Grotto 10, Northern Wei Dynasty, the Yungang Grottoes, Datong, Shanxi Province.

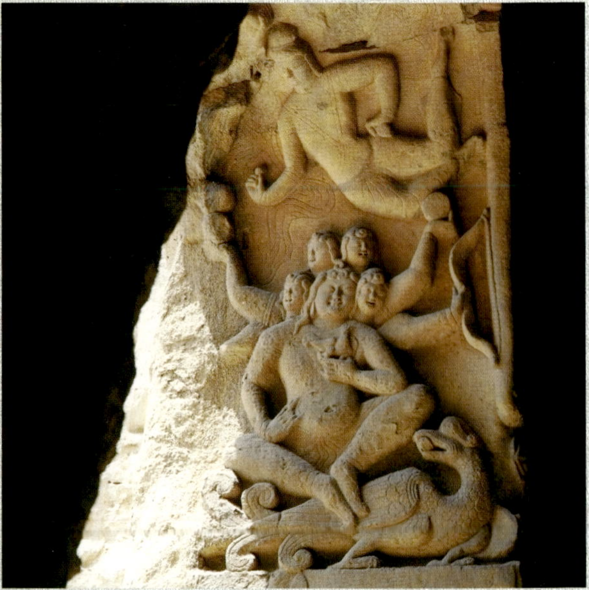

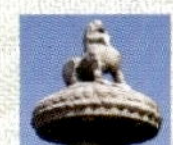

The Impact of Buddhism

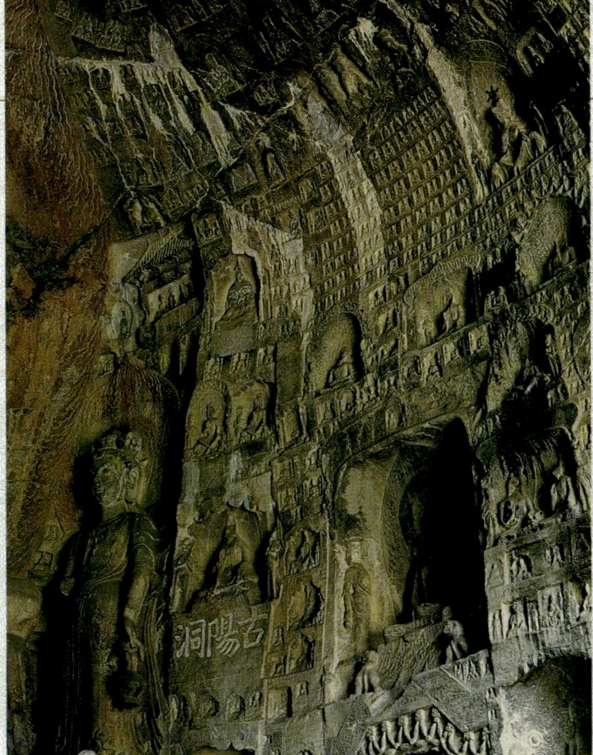

The Interior View of the Guyang Cave, Northern Wei Dynasty. Longmen Grottoes, Luoyang, Henan Province.
The carving of the Guyang Cave started in 500 and lasted three years. It was the earliest grotto carved at the order of the royal family of the Northern Wei Dynasty at Luoyang, and is also the grotto with the most complete depictions of Buddhist scripture stories of the Longmen Grottoes.

Representations of People Who Donated to the Grotto Construction, Northern Wei Dynasty. Guyang Cave, Longmen Grottoes, Luoyang, Henan Province.
The donors on the northern wall of the Guyang Grotto are basically carved in lines. Their tall and slim bodies are particularly noteworthy.

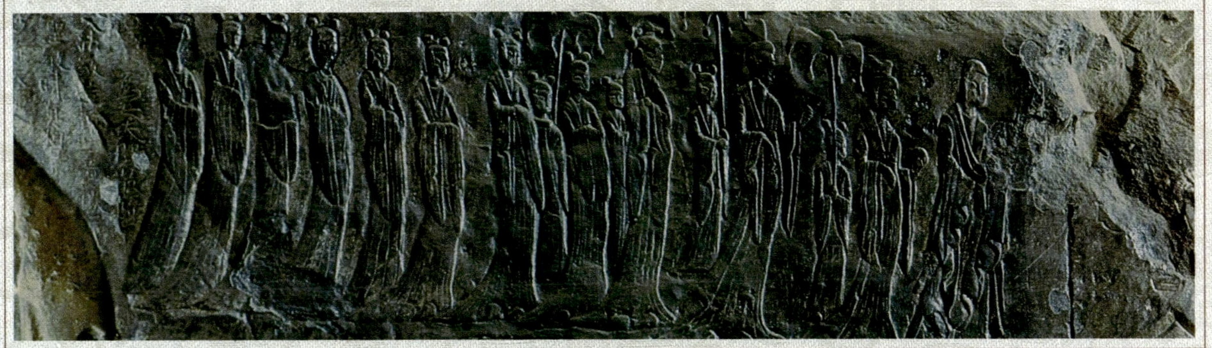

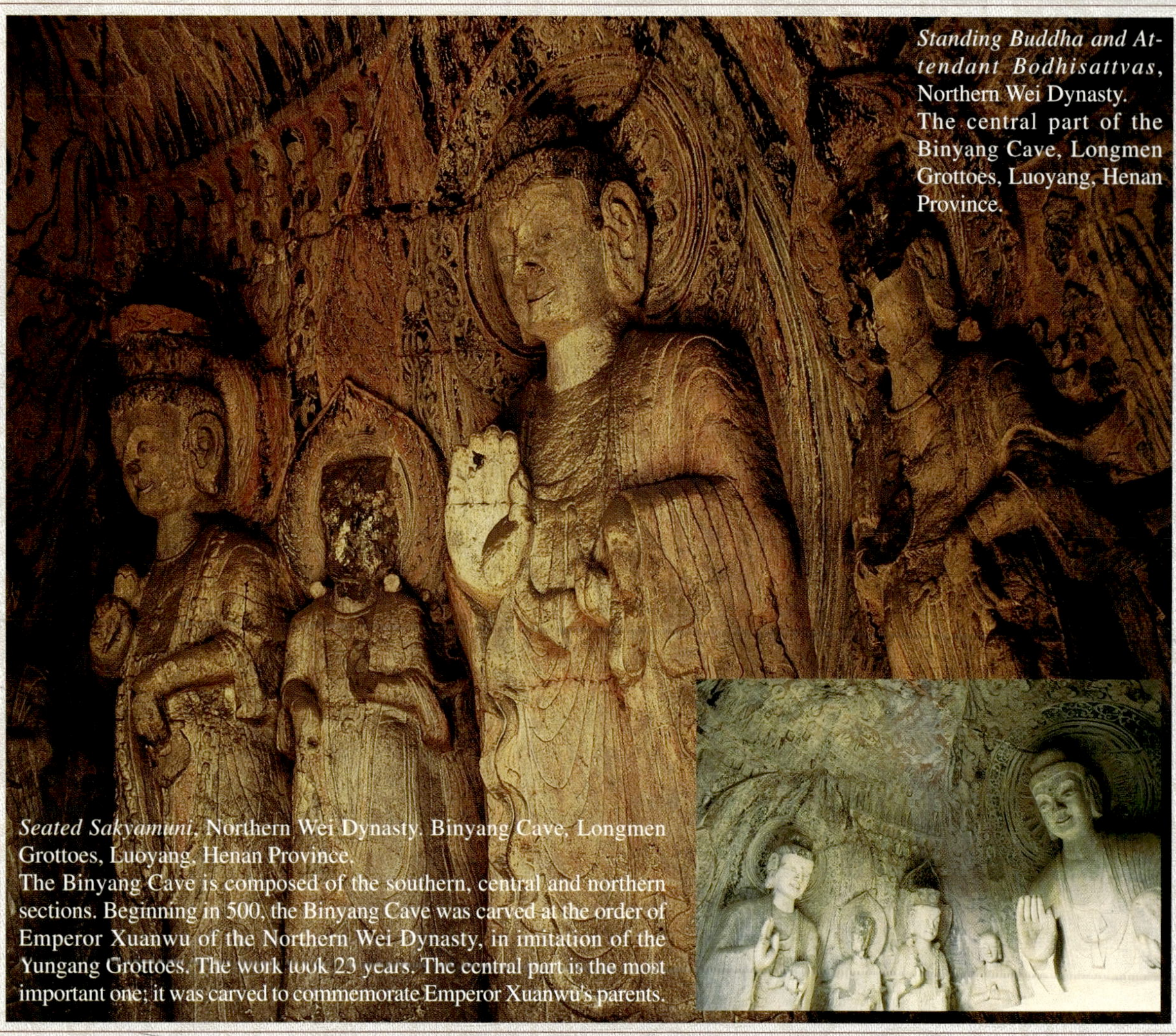

Standing Buddha and Attendant Bodhisattvas, Northern Wei Dynasty. The central part of the Binyang Cave, Longmen Grottoes, Luoyang, Henan Province.

Seated Sakyamuni, Northern Wei Dynasty. Binyang Cave, Longmen Grottoes, Luoyang. Henan Province.
The Binyang Cave is composed of the southern, central and northern sections. Beginning in 500, the Binyang Cave was carved at the order of Emperor Xuanwu of the Northern Wei Dynasty, in imitation of the Yungang Grottoes. The work took 23 years. The central part is the most important one; it was carved to commemorate Emperor Xuanwu's parents.

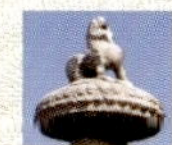

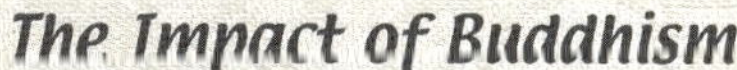

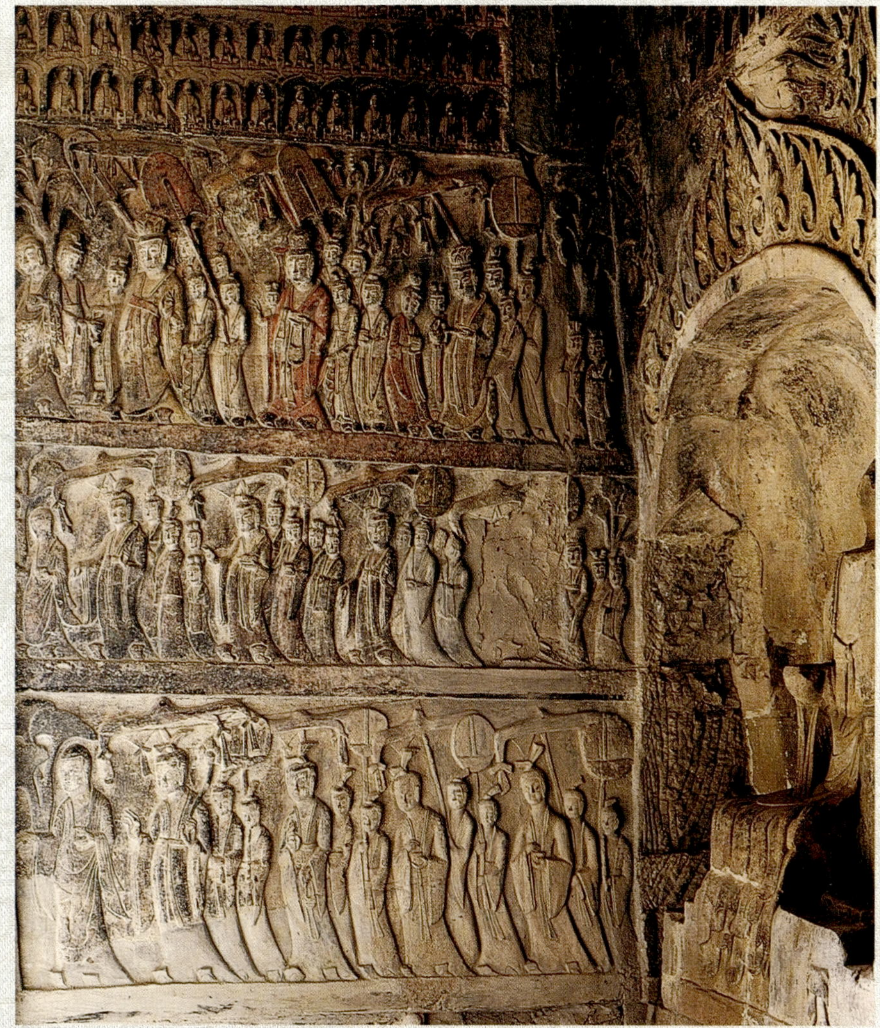

Presenting Offerings to the Buddha, Northern Wei Dynasty. Grotto 1 of the Temple of Grottoes, Gongxian County, Henan Province.

The offerings to the Buddha include lotus flowers and buds, lamps and incense burners. The Buddha sculptures are similar in style to those of the Binyang Cave, Longmen Grottoes. The figures have plump faces, and most of them are clad in scholar-official dress of the Southern Dynasties.

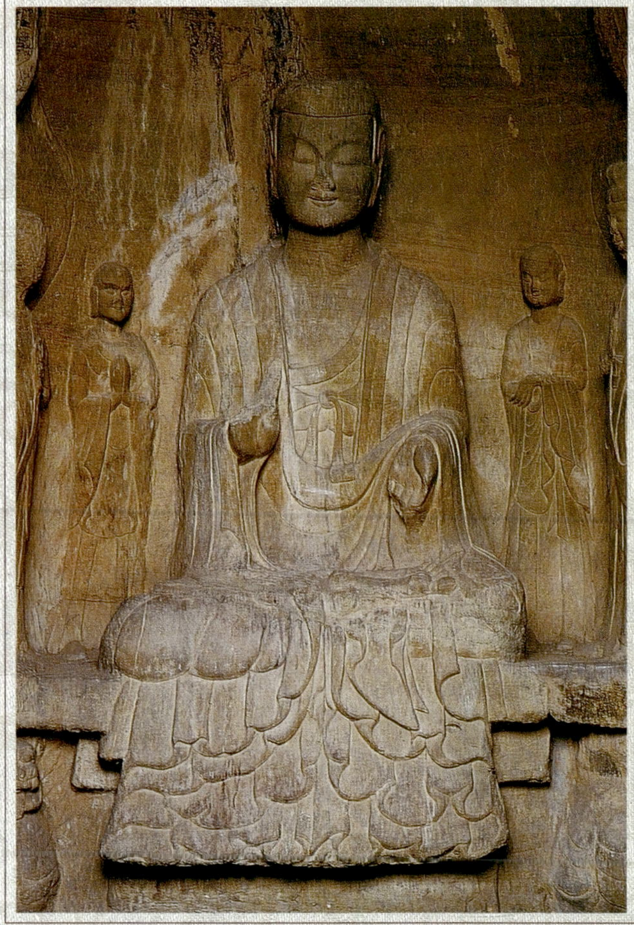

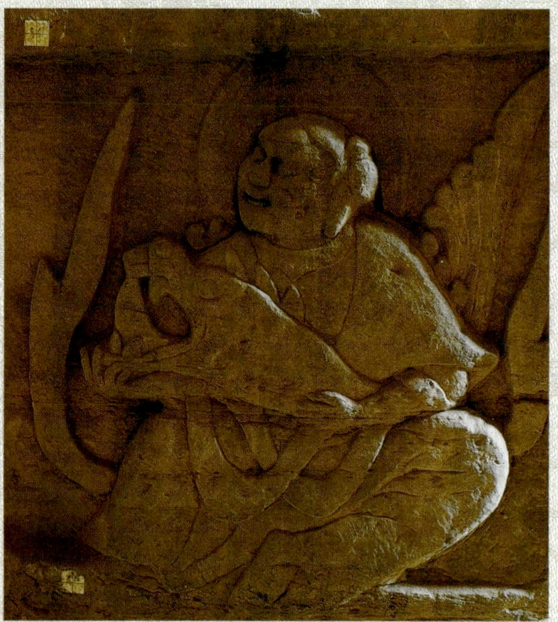

Divine King, Northern Wei Dynasty. Grotto 4 of the Temple of Grottoes, Gongxian County, Henan Province.
The third and fourth grottoes are each supported by a stone pillar in the center. There are big niches carved in the pillar on all four sides.

Buddha, Northern Wei Dynasty. Carved on the front of the central pillar of Grotto 4 of the Temple of Grottoes, Gongxian County, Henan Province.

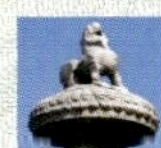

Principal Buddha, Western Wei Dynasty. Grotto 44 of the Maijishan Grottoes, Tianshui City, Gansu Province.
This is a masterpiece of the clay sculpture of the Northern Dynasty in the Maijishan Grottoes.

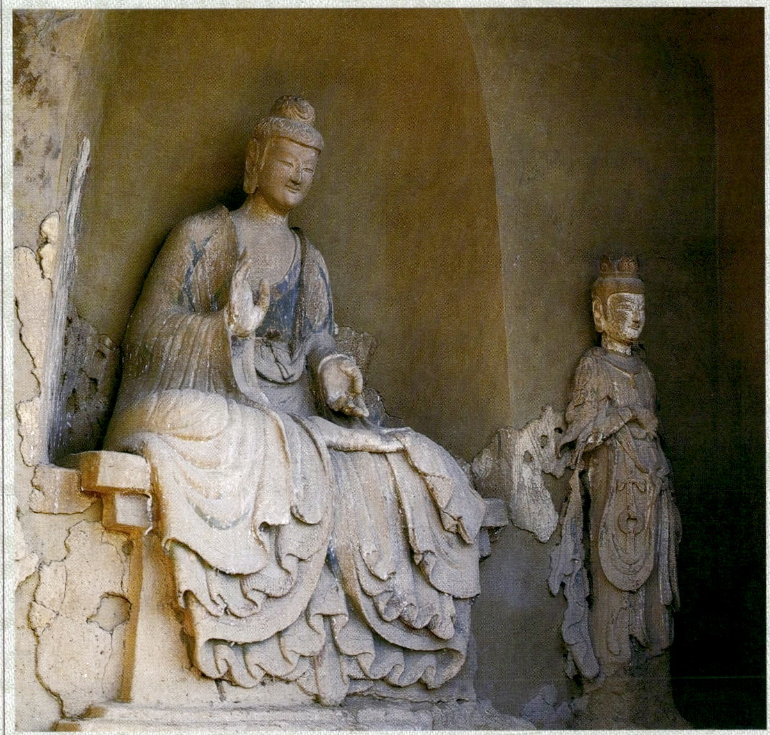

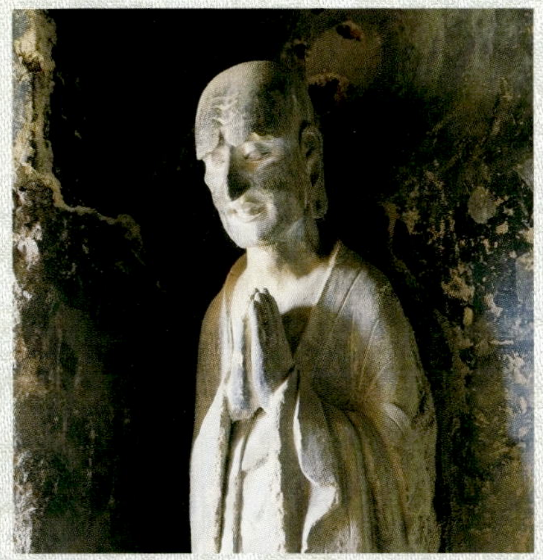

Kasyapa, Northern Wei Dynasty. Grotto 87 of the Maijishan Grottoes, Tianshui City, Gansu Province.
During the period following the removal of the Northern Wei Dynasty capital to Luoyang and throughout the Northern Qi, Northern Zhou and Sui dynasties, the Buddha sculptures of the Maijishan Grottoes became slim again, just like those of the Han Dynasty. This energetic, slim sculpture of Kasyapa Buddha has long eyebrows and deep-set eyes, a typical Indian image.

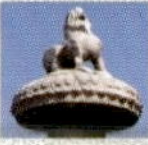

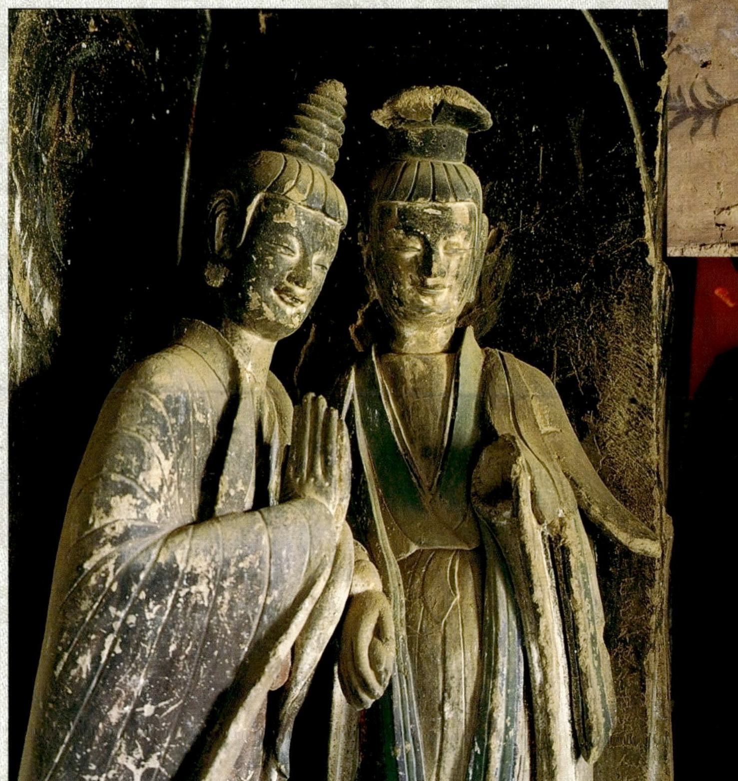

Low-relief Sculpture of an Apsara, Northern Zhou Dynasty. Grotto 4 of the Maijishan Grottoes, Tianshui City, Gansu Province. The face, breast, abdomen, arms, hands and feet were sculpted using fine clay in low relief. The robe, ribbon, flowers and cloud were painted in vivid colors.

Attendant Bodhisattva and Disciple, Northern Wei Dynasty. Grotto 121 of the Maijishan Grottoes, Tianshui, Gansu Province. The Bodhisattva is on the left. The two look as if they are whispering to each other.

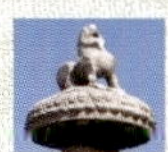

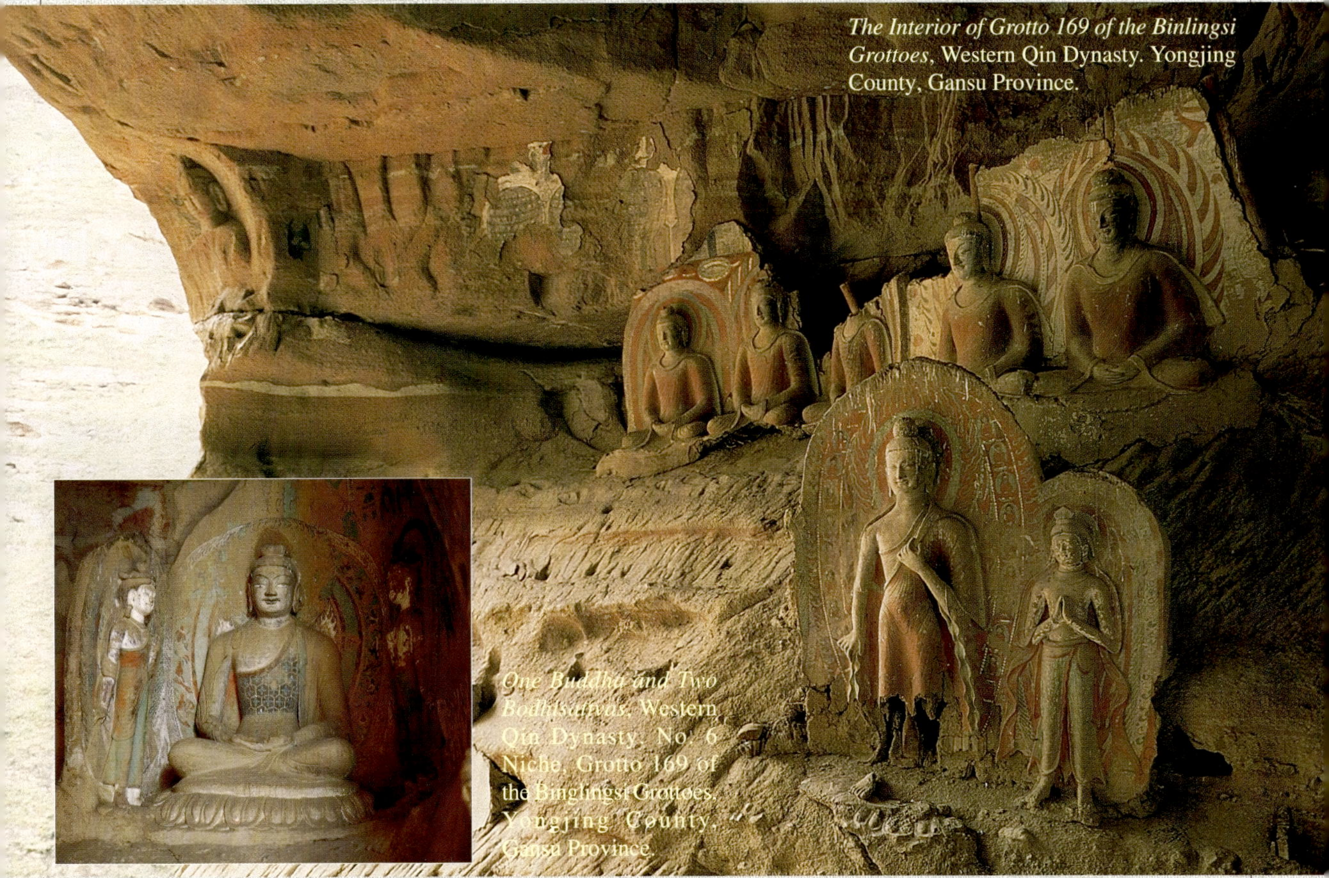

The Interior of Grotto 169 of the Binlingsi Grottoes, Western Qin Dynasty. Yongjing County, Gansu Province.

One Buddha and Two Bodhisattvas, Western Qin Dynasty, No. 6 Niche, Grotto 169 of the Binglingsi Grottoes, Yongjing County, Gansu Province.

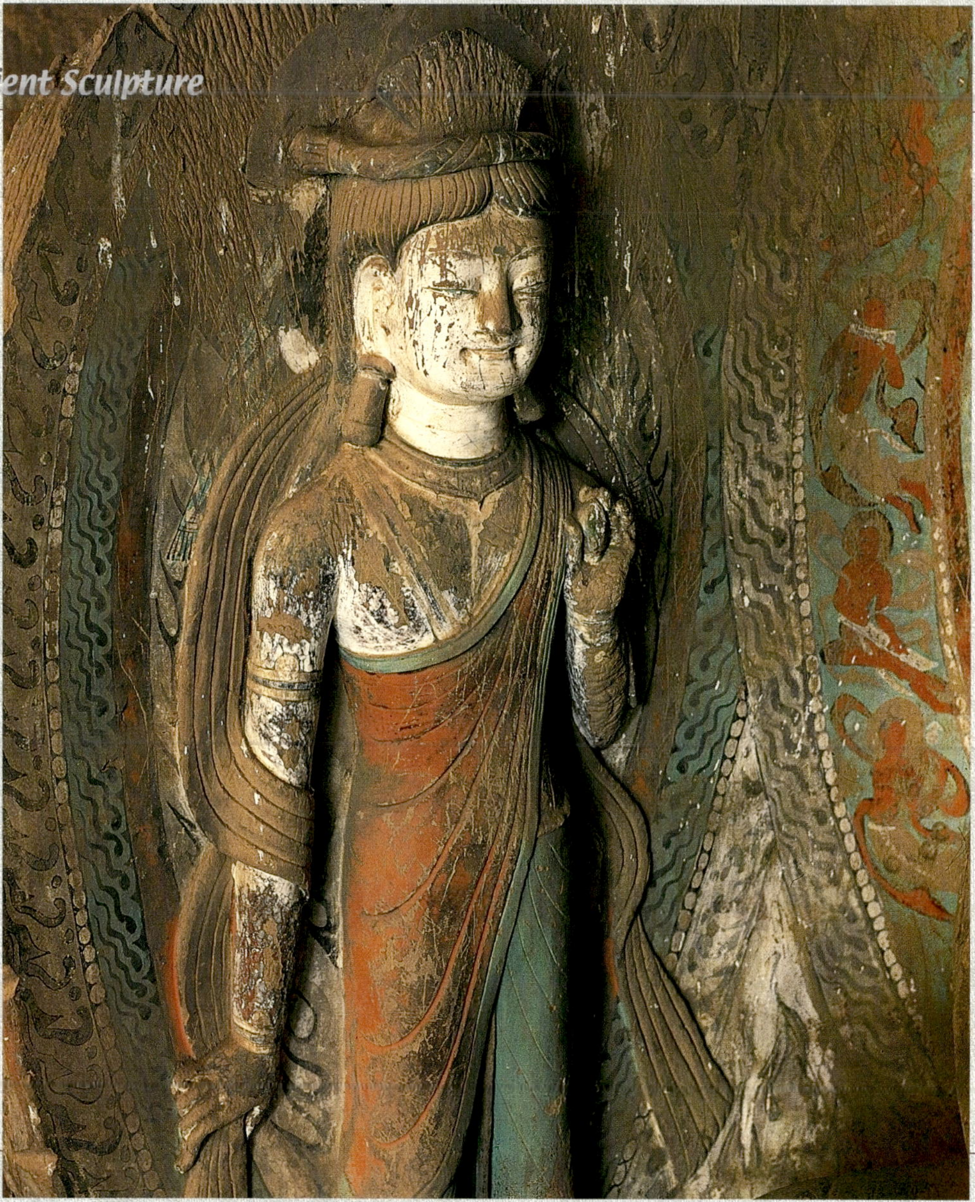

Bodhisattva, Western Qin Dynasty. Grotto 169 of the Binglingsi Grottoes, Yongjing County, Gansu Province.

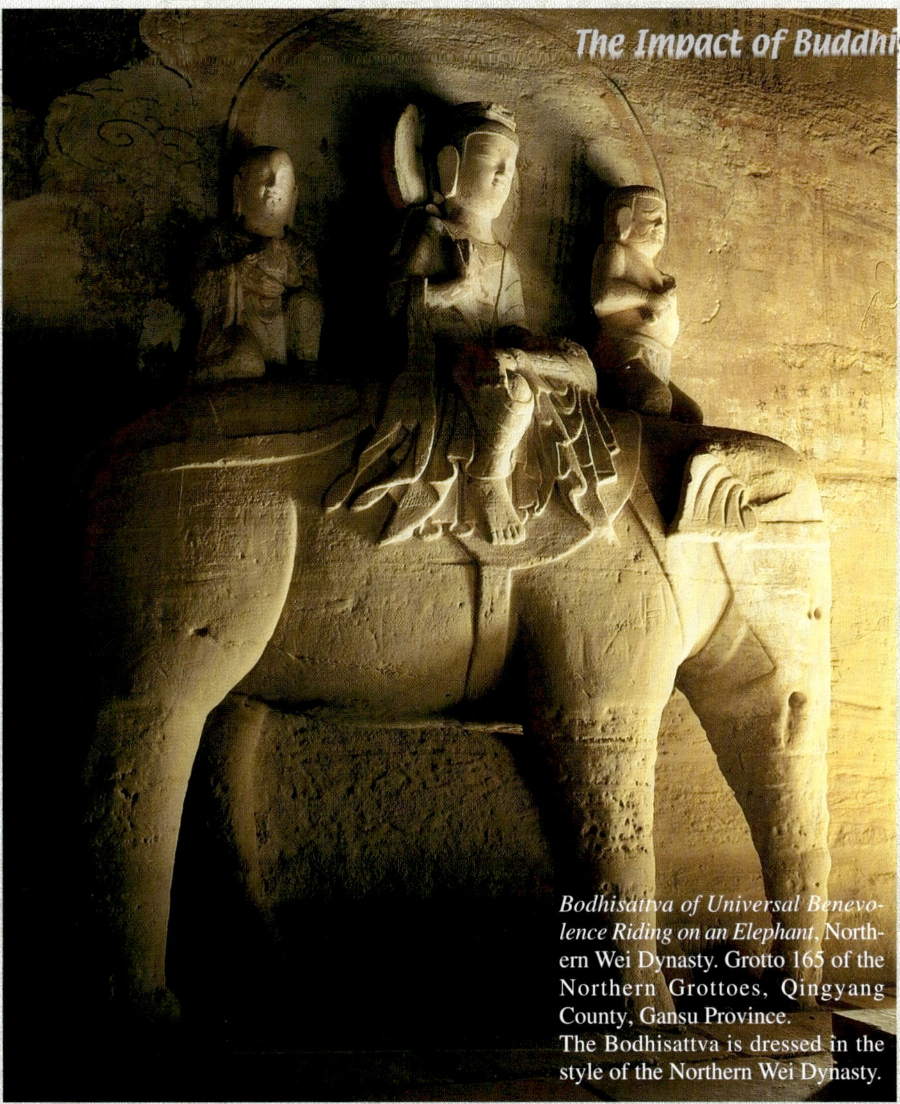

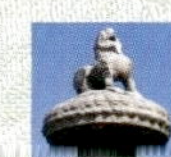

Bodhisattva of Universal Benevolence Riding on an Elephant, Northern Wei Dynasty. Grotto 165 of the Northern Grottoes, Qingyang County, Gansu Province.
The Bodhisattva is dressed in the style of the Northern Wei Dynasty.

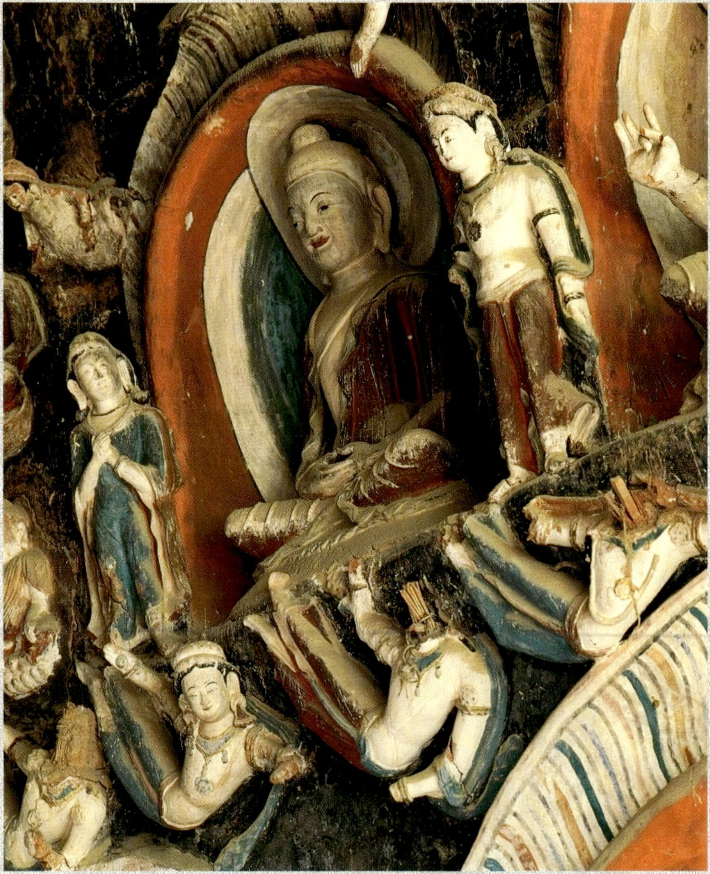

Buddha, Bodhisattvas and Apsaras, Northern
Wei Dynasty. Eastern Grottoes, Jinta Temple,
Yugn County, Gansu Province.

Three Buddhas with a Reredos, Eastern Wel Dynasty. Longxing Temple,
Qingzhou City, Shandong Province.

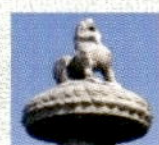

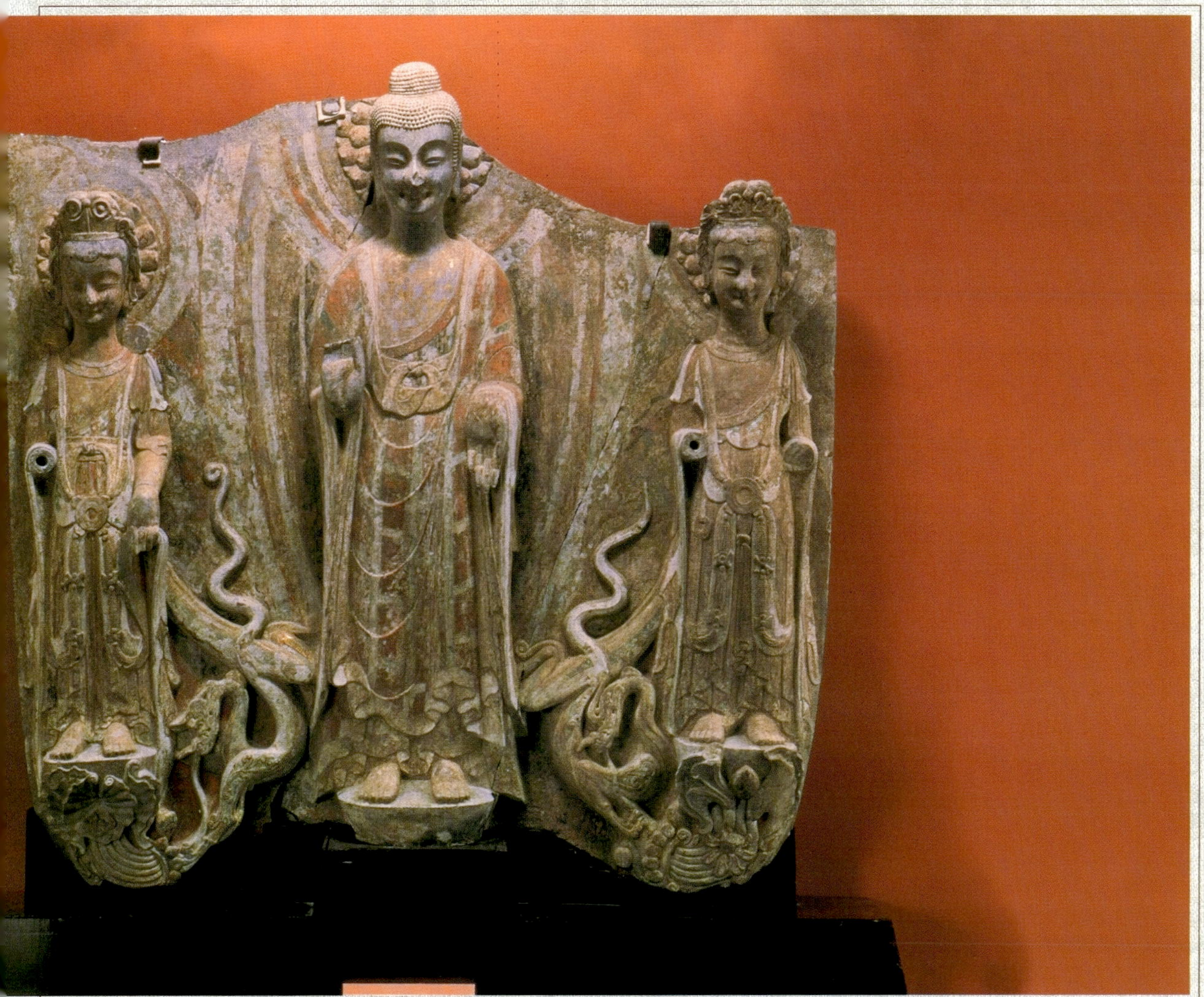

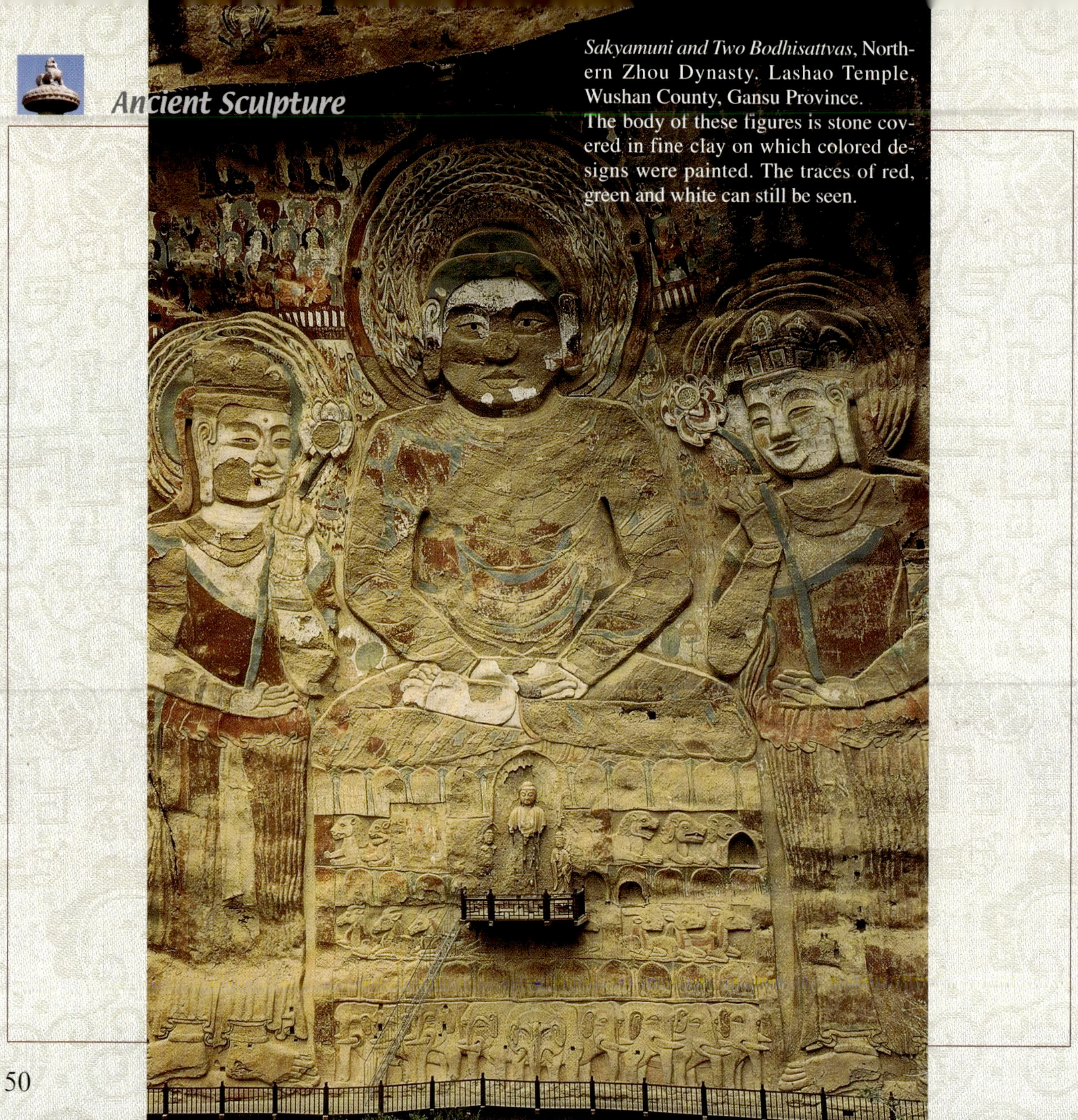

Sakyamuni and Two Bodhisattvas, Northern Zhou Dynasty. Lashao Temple, Wushan County, Gansu Province. The body of these figures is stone covered in fine clay on which colored designs were painted. The traces of red, green and white can still be seen.

The Six Steeds of the Zhaoling Mausoleum · The Statue of Vairocana

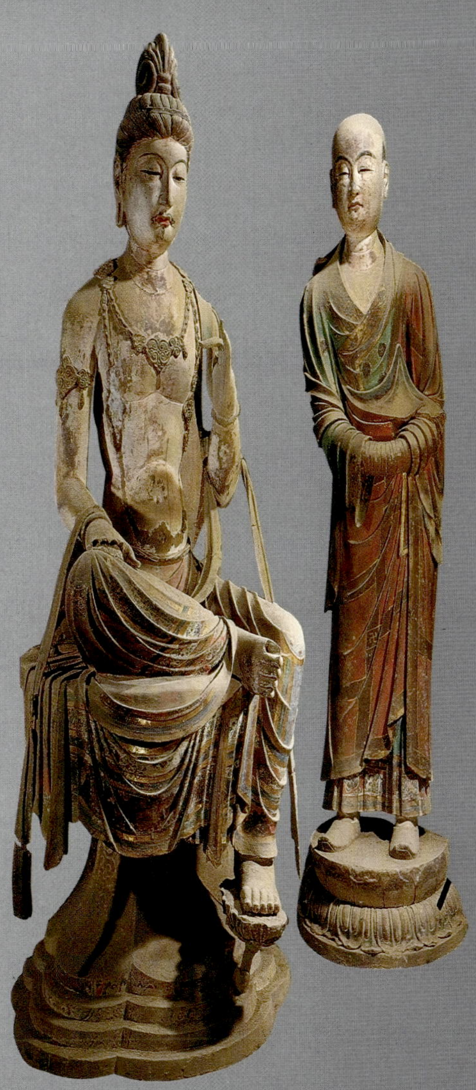

During the Sui and Tang dynasties, Chinese sculpture art reached another peak, prominently manifested in Buddhist sculptures, stone carvings on gravestones, and clay figures. Here is a brief introduction to the artistic features and achievements made in sculpture in this period. In Buddhist sculpture, the colored Tang sculptures in the Dunhuang Grottoes adopted the technique of solid, rounded sculpture, which adds realism. The clay statues of Buddhas and Bodhisattvas and the exquisite murals enhance each other's beauty. In some of these grottoes, there are sculptures of one Buddha, two disciples, two Bodhisattvas and two heavenly kings made of clay, set against wall paintings of eight classes of brave divine beings, flying Apsarases and dragon fairy maidens. The arrangement of these sculptures and paintings give an impression of harmony. The carving techniques shown in the stone Buddhist statues in the Longmen Grottoes had developed from plane carving to bulged carving, which makes the sculptures look smooth and graceful while still being elegant and imposing. The statue of Vairocana in Fengxian Temple is over 17 m tall, with an other-worldly expression on its handsome features. The statue is accompanied by eight other statues, each with a distinct identity, such as disciples, Bodhisattvas, heavenly kings or guards. All of them are first-class works of stone sculpture.

In respect of mausoleum sculpture, the themes and skills of that of the Tang Dynasty surpassed those in earlier ages, including solid, relief and line sculpture. The "The Six Steeds of the Zhaoling Mausoleum," which stand before the Zhaoling Mausoleum of Li Shimin, the second Tang emperor, is the best known Tang sculpture. The six steeds are ones which served Li Shimin with distinction. The statues are precisely shaped, vividly postured, and proficiently and penetratingly wrought. "Saluzi (Whistling Dewy Purple)", one of the steeds in the sculpture, is pure purple from head to foot. There is an arrow in its chest, and Qiu Yingong, a general, is holding the reins with one hand and trying to pull the arrow out with the other. This sculpture stresses not only the tall and sturdy bodies, vigorous limbs and solid muscles of the war-horses, but also their trappings, showing us what such accoutrements were like in the Tang Dynasty.

The pottery figurines of the Tang Dynasty, especially tri-colored glazed ones, reached the peak of ancient sculpture both in artistic level and manufacturing technique. After being heated, the roughcast was coated with green, brown, blue or white glaze. Then it was heated again, to produce a tri-colored glazed pottery product. This was possible because Tang craftsmen had mastered the art of metallic glazing.

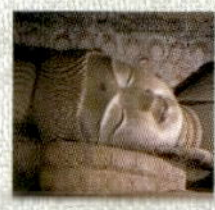

Ancient Sculpture

Bodhisattva, Sui Dynasty. Grotto 244 of the Mogao Grottoes, Dunhuang City, Gansu Province.

Attendant Bodhisattva, Sui Dynasty. Grotto 14 of the Maijishan Grottoes, Tianshui City, Gansu Province.

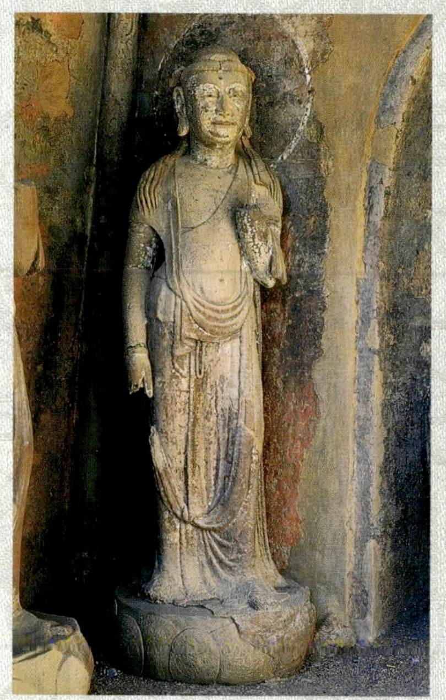

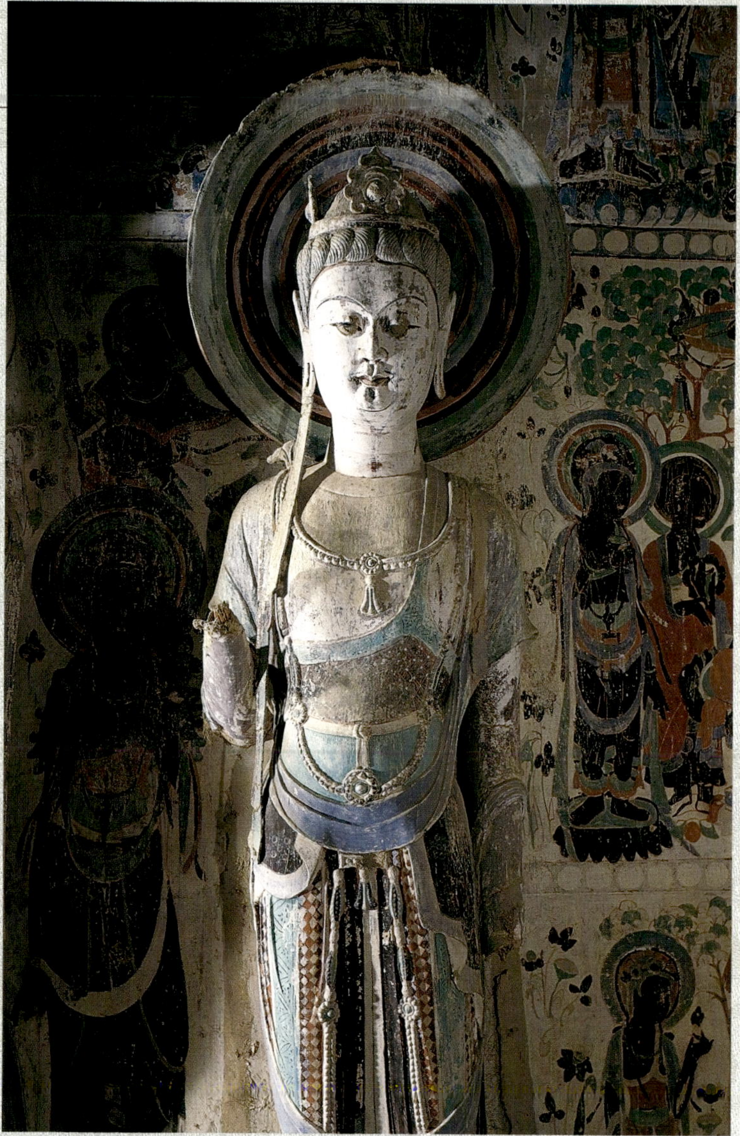

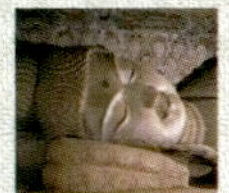

Sculpture of Deity-king Kapila, Sui Dynasty.
Part of the exterior view of Dazhusheng Grotto,
Anyang , Henan Province.

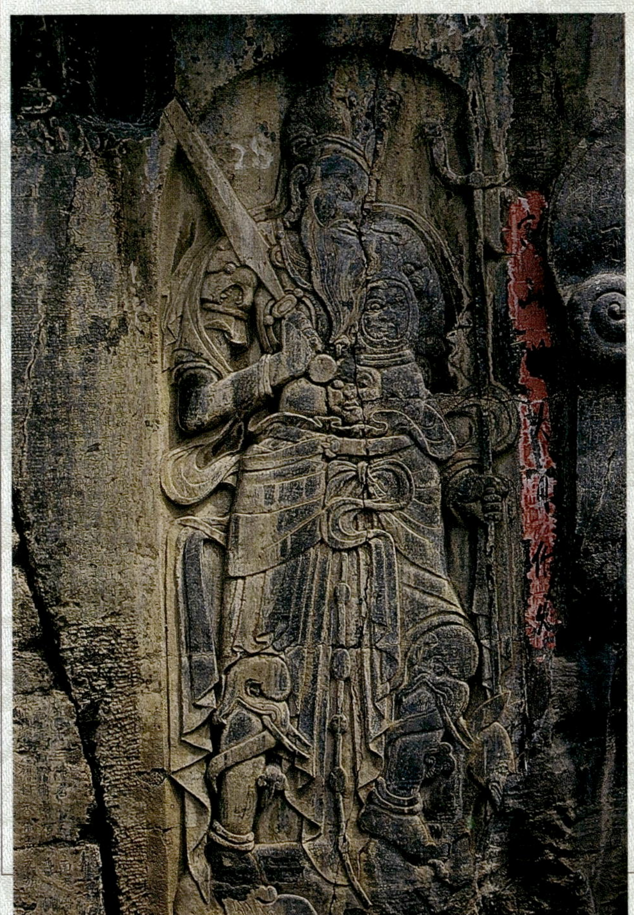

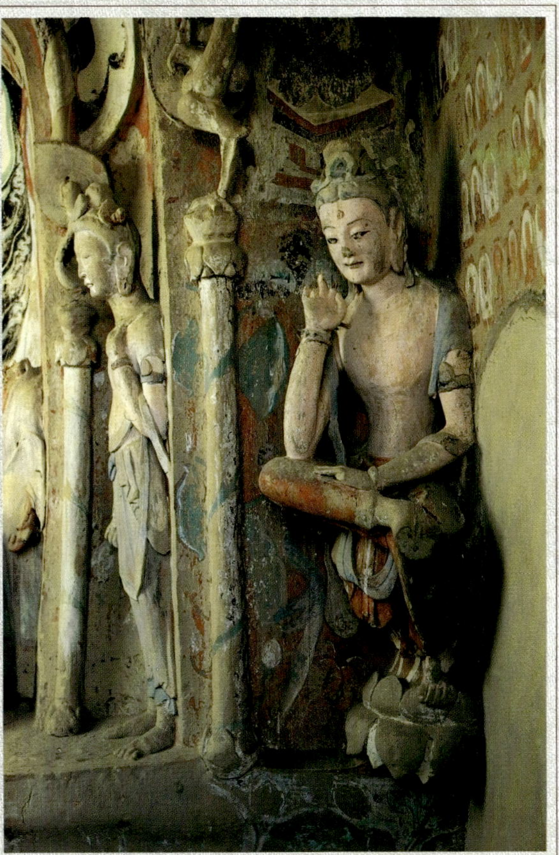

Bodhisattva, Sui Dynasty. Grotto 417 of the Mogao
Grottoes, Dunhuang City, Gansu Province.

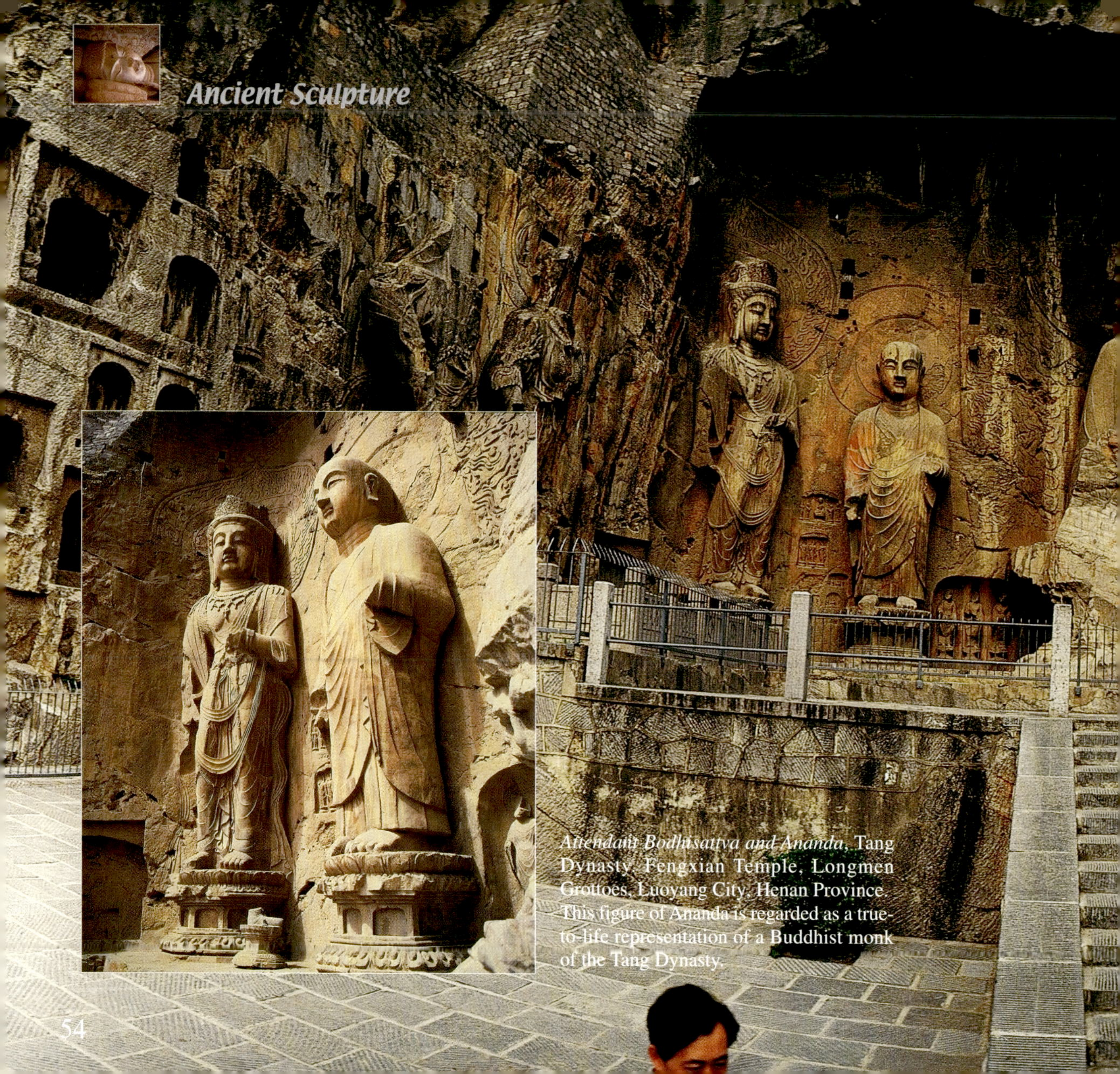

Attendant Bodhisattva and Ananda, Tang Dynasty, Fengxian Temple, Longmen Grottoes, Luoyang City, Henan Province. This figure of Ananda is regarded as a true-to-life representation of a Buddhist monk of the Tang Dynasty.

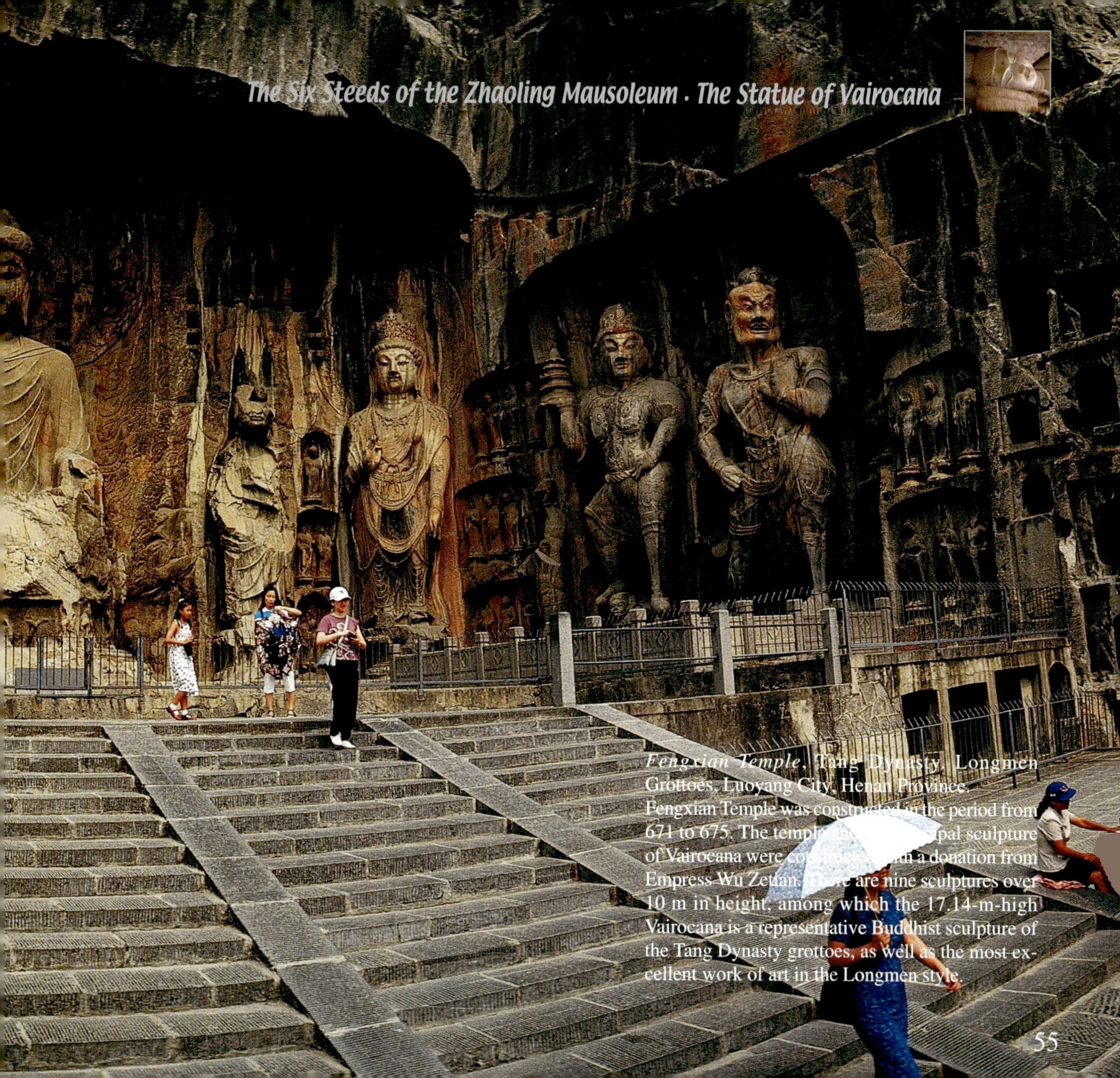

Fengxian Temple, Tang Dynasty, Longmen Grottoes, Luoyang City, Henan Province. Fengxian Temple was constructed in the period from 671 to 675. The temple and the principal sculpture of Vairocana were constructed with a donation from Empress Wu Zetian. There are nine sculptures over 10 m in height, among which the 17.14-m-high Vairocana is a representative Buddhist sculpture of the Tang Dynasty grottoes, as well as the most excellent work of art in the Longmen style.

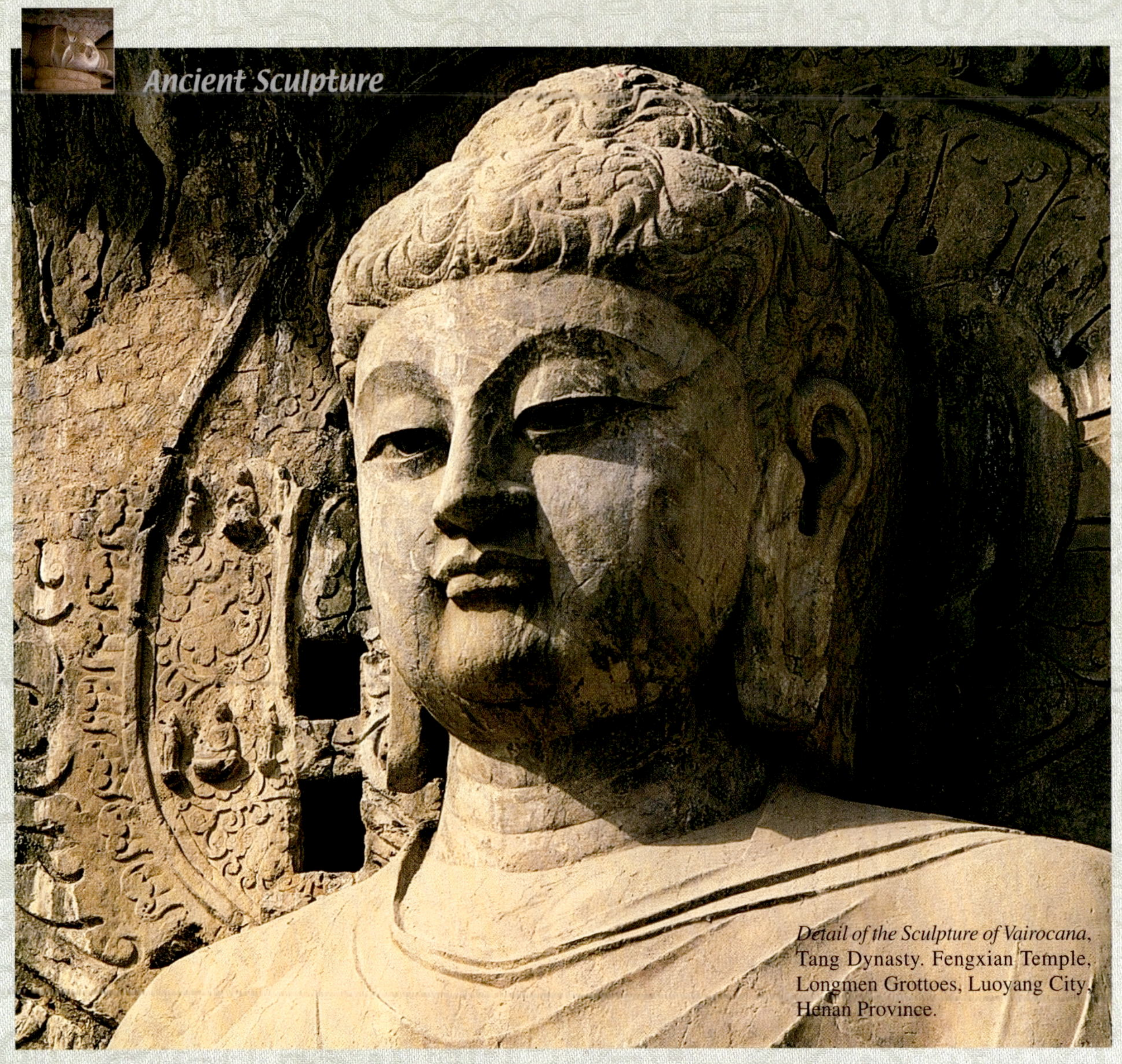

Detail of the Sculpture of Vairocana, Tang Dynasty. Fengxian Temple, Longmen Grottoes, Luoyang City, Henan Province.

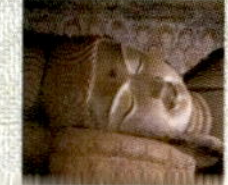

Interior View of the Ten-Thousand-Buddha Cave, Tang Dynasty. Longmen Grottoes, Luoyang City, Henan Province.
With Amitabha as the principal Buddha, on the cave's walls there is a total of over 15,000 small Buddha statues, accounting for one seventh of the total sculptures in the Longmen Grottoes.

Arhats, Tang Dynasty. Kanjing Temple, Longmen Grottoes, Luoyang City, Henan Province.

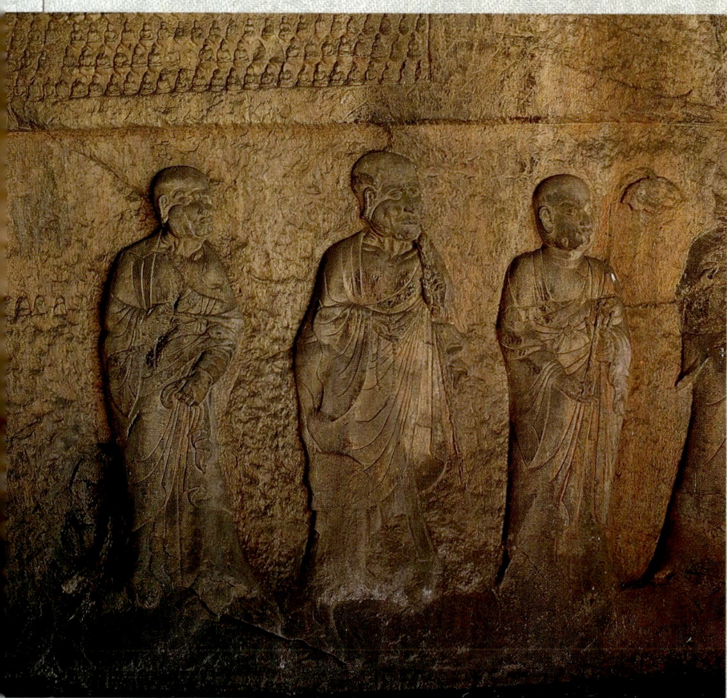

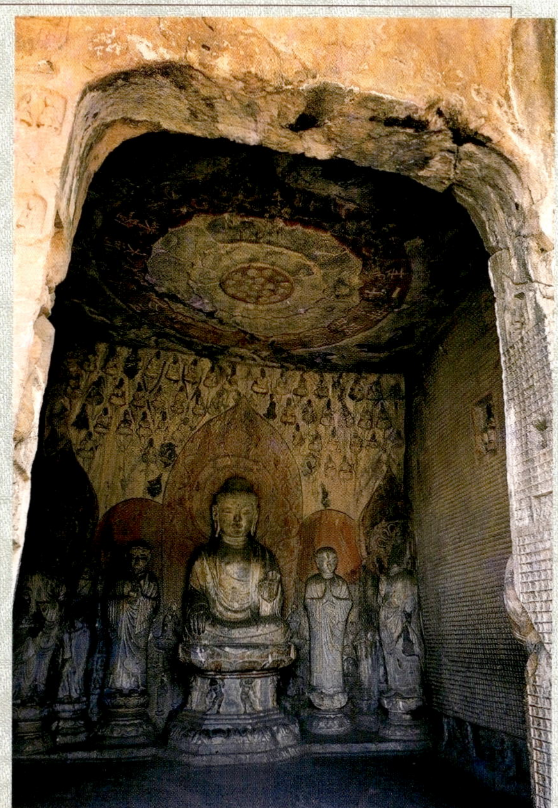

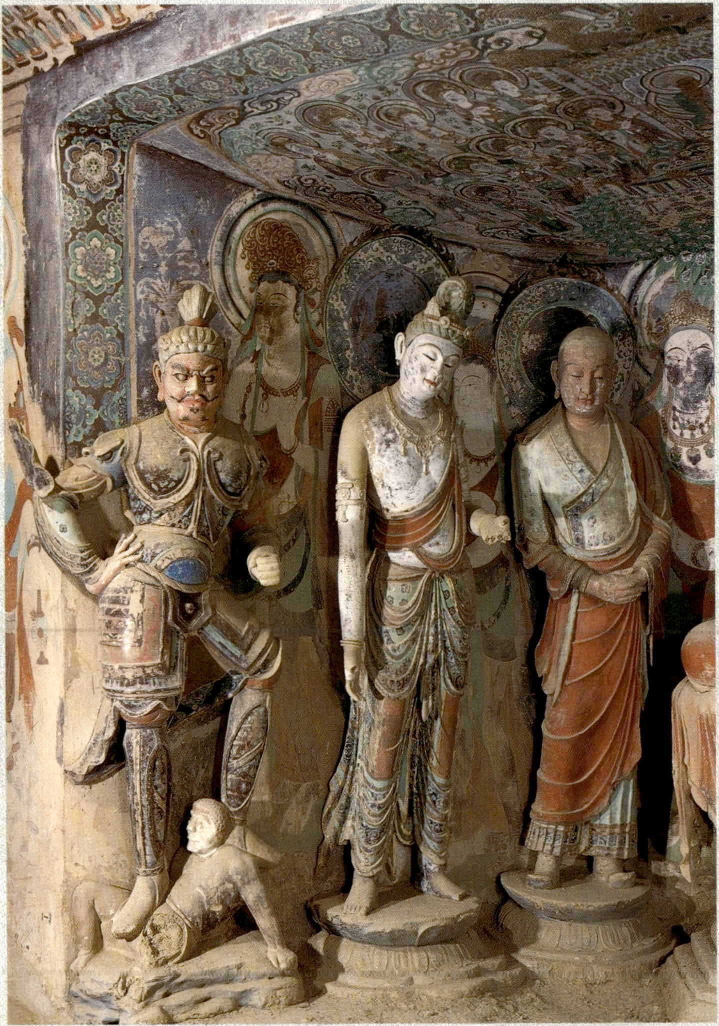

Bodhisattva, Ananda and Heavenly King, Tang Dynasty. Grotto 45 of the Mogao Grottoes, Dunhuang City, Gansu Province. These are excellent examples of the painted clay sculpture of the Tang Dynasty.

Head Sculpture of a Bodhisattva, mid-Tang Dynasty. Grotto 159, Mogao Grottoes, Dunhuang, Gansu Province.

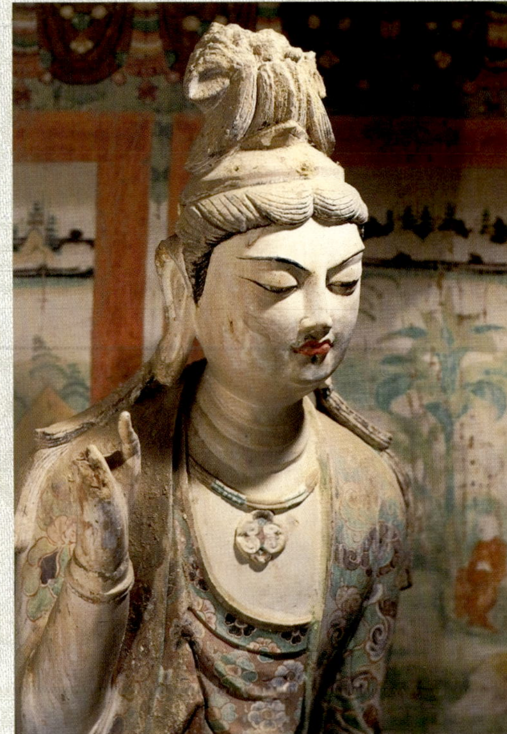

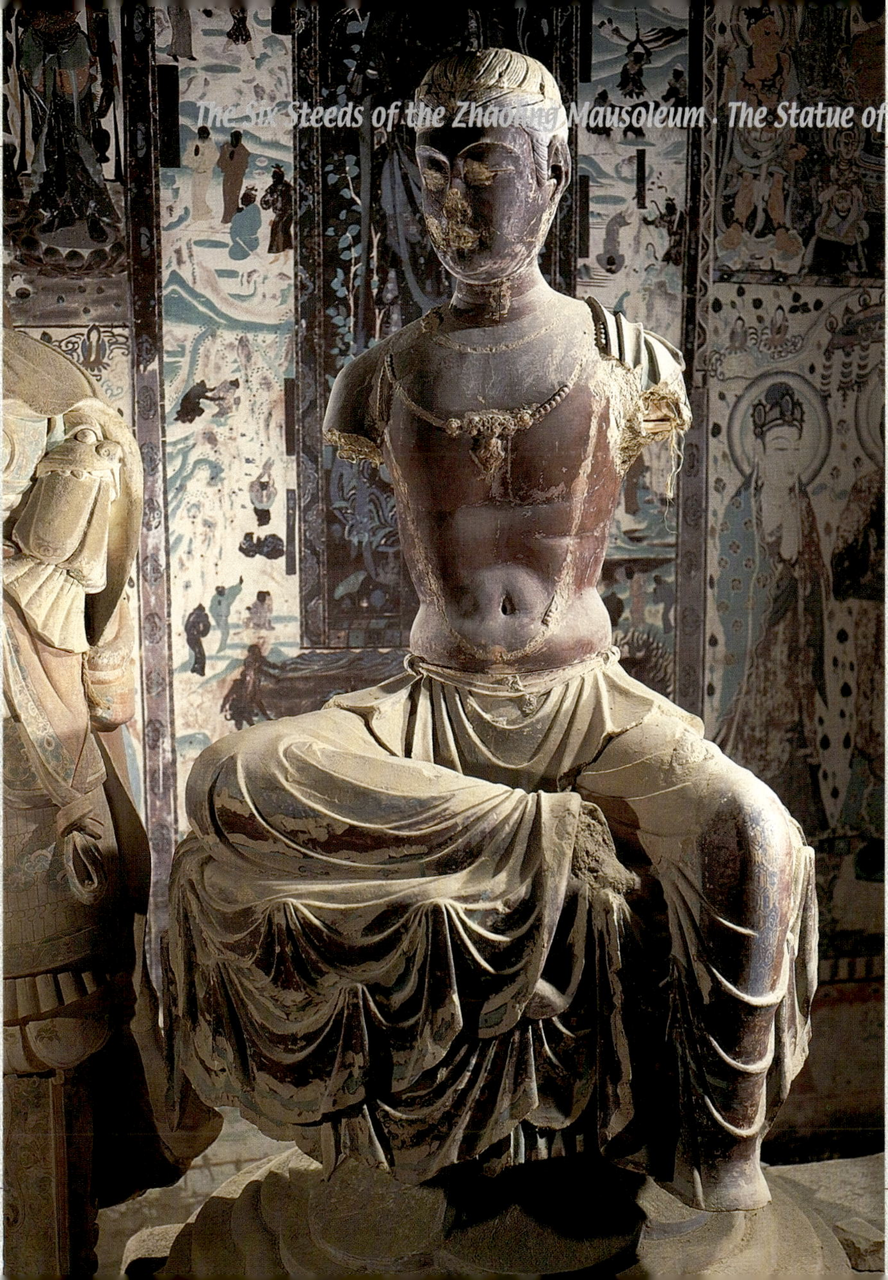

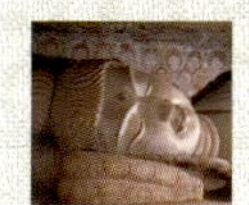

Bodhisattva, early Tang Dynasty. Grotto 205 of the Mogao Grottoes, Dunhuang, Gansu Province.
The shape of the body of this Bodhisattva is unusual among the sculptures in the Mogao Grottoes. The chest and abdomen are close to realistic, and the proportion of the head to the body is roughly accurate.

59

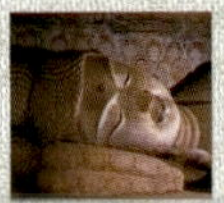

Ancient Sculpture

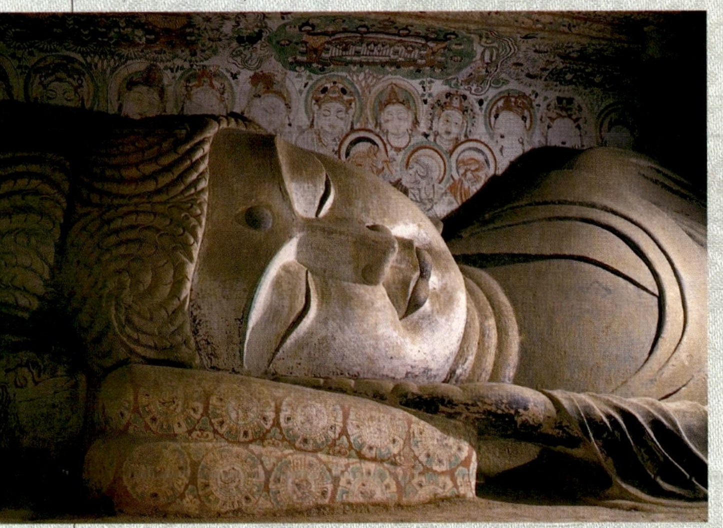

Head of Reclining Sakyamuni, mid-Tang Dynasty. Grotto 158, Mogao Grottoes, Dunhuang, Gansu Province. The reclining Buddha is 16 m long.

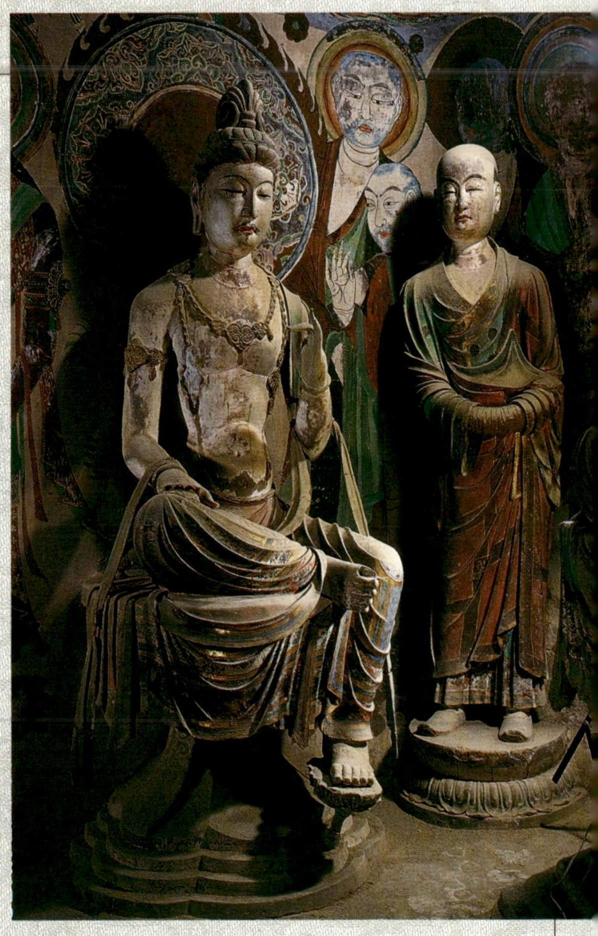

Bodhisattva and Disciple, Tang Dynasty. Grotto 328, Mogao Grottoes, Dunhuang, Gansu Province.

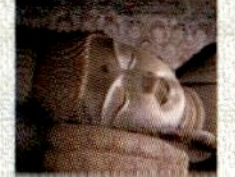

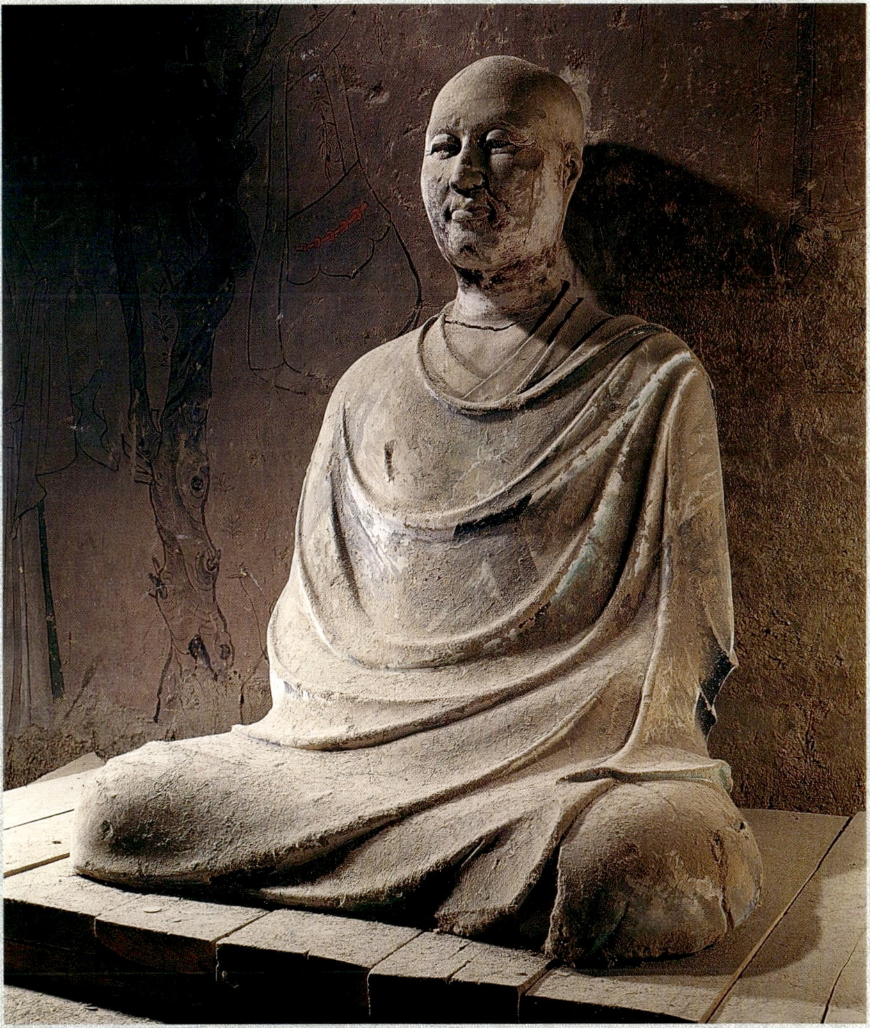

Sculpture of Hong Gong, late Tang Dynasty. Grotto 147, Mogao Grottoes, Dunhuang City, Gansu Province.
The sculpture of Hong Gong, a prominent monk of the Tang Dynasty, is one of the earliest sculptures of famous monks of China.

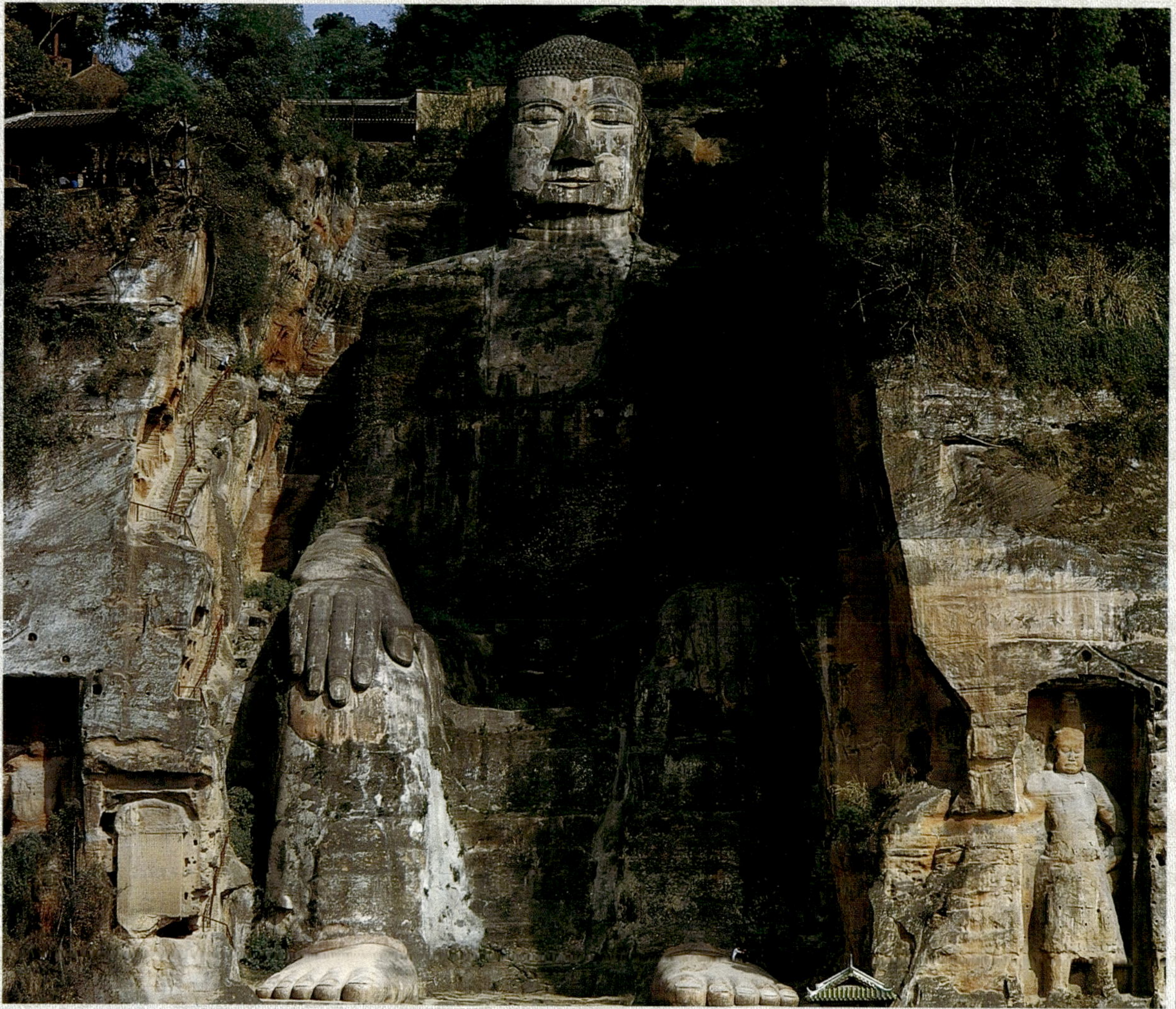

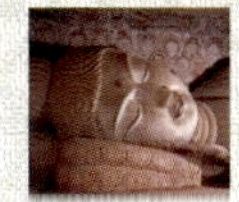

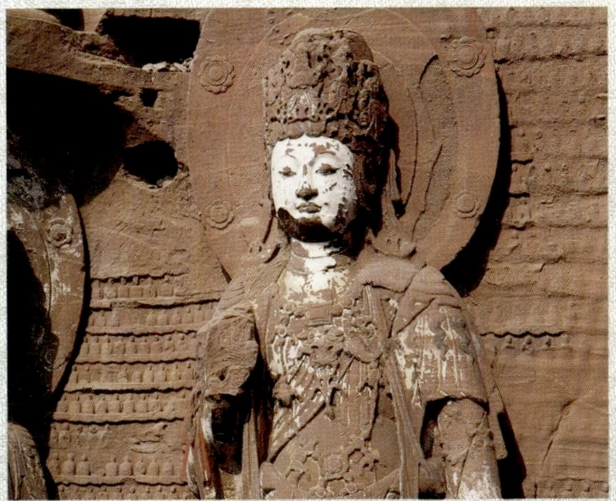

Goddess of Mercy, late Tang Dynasty. No. 56 Grotto, Qianfo Village, Anyue County, Sichuan Province.

Interior View of the Buddha Cave, early Tang Dynasty. Grotto 10, Huangze Temple, Guangyuan City, Sichuan Province.
This grotto is seven m high, 5.85 m wide and 3.59 m deep. Five sculptures of Buddha are over four m high, and three, over three m high. It is the largest grotto at the Huangze Temple, and is an outstanding model for the study of the stone sculptures of the early Tang Dynasty.

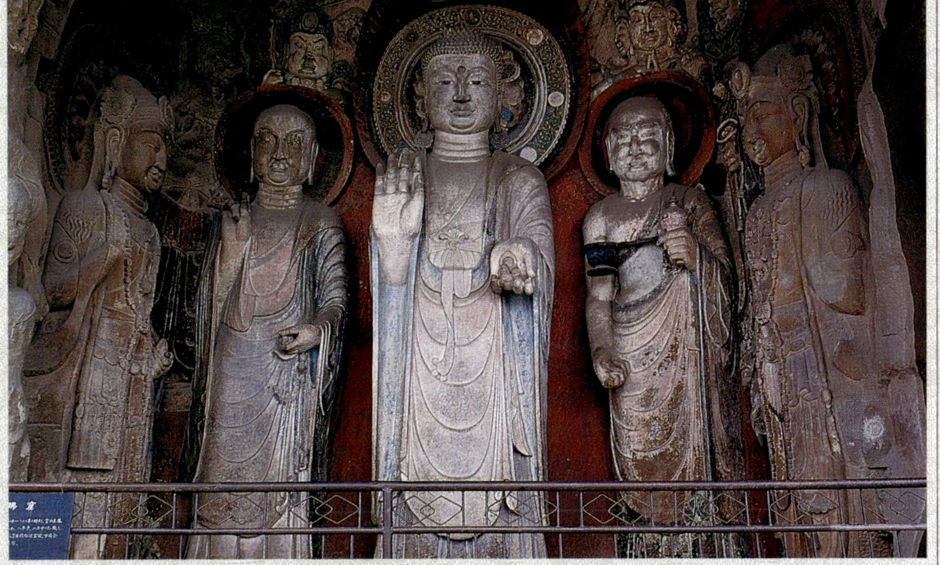

Leshan Giant Buddha, Tang Dynasty. Leshan City, Sichuan Province. Carved out of a sheer cliff face, the Leshan Giant Buddha faces the confluence of the Minjiang, Qingyi and Dadu rivers. It is 71 m high. Its construction began in 713, and was finished in 803.

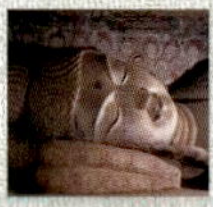

Ancient Sculpture

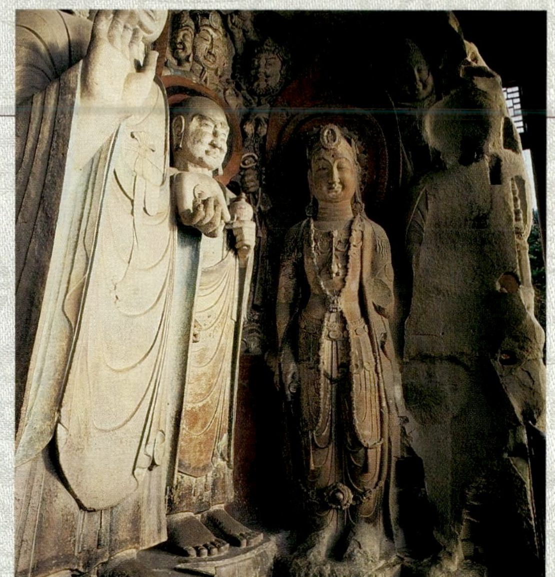

Attendant Bodhisattva, early Tang Dynasty. Buddha Cave in the Huangze Temple, Guangyuan City, Sichuan Province.

Reclining Buddha, Tang Dynasty. Reclining Buddha Valley, Anyue County, Sichuan Province.
The statue is 23 m long, of which the head is three m long. Behind it, there is a depiction of the Buddha preaching to some 20 disciples and Bodhisattvas in deep relief.

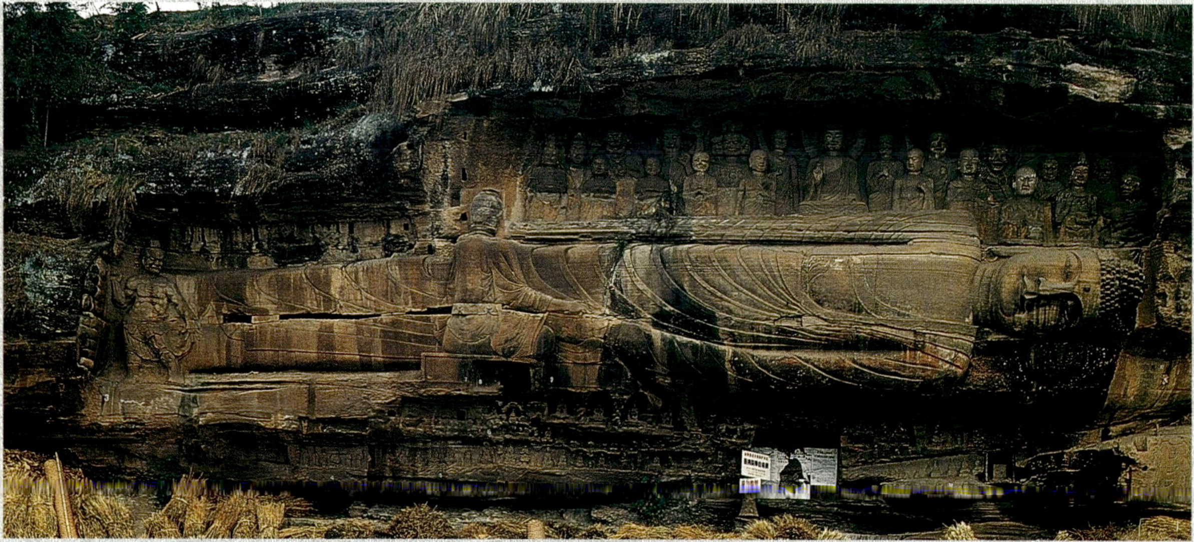

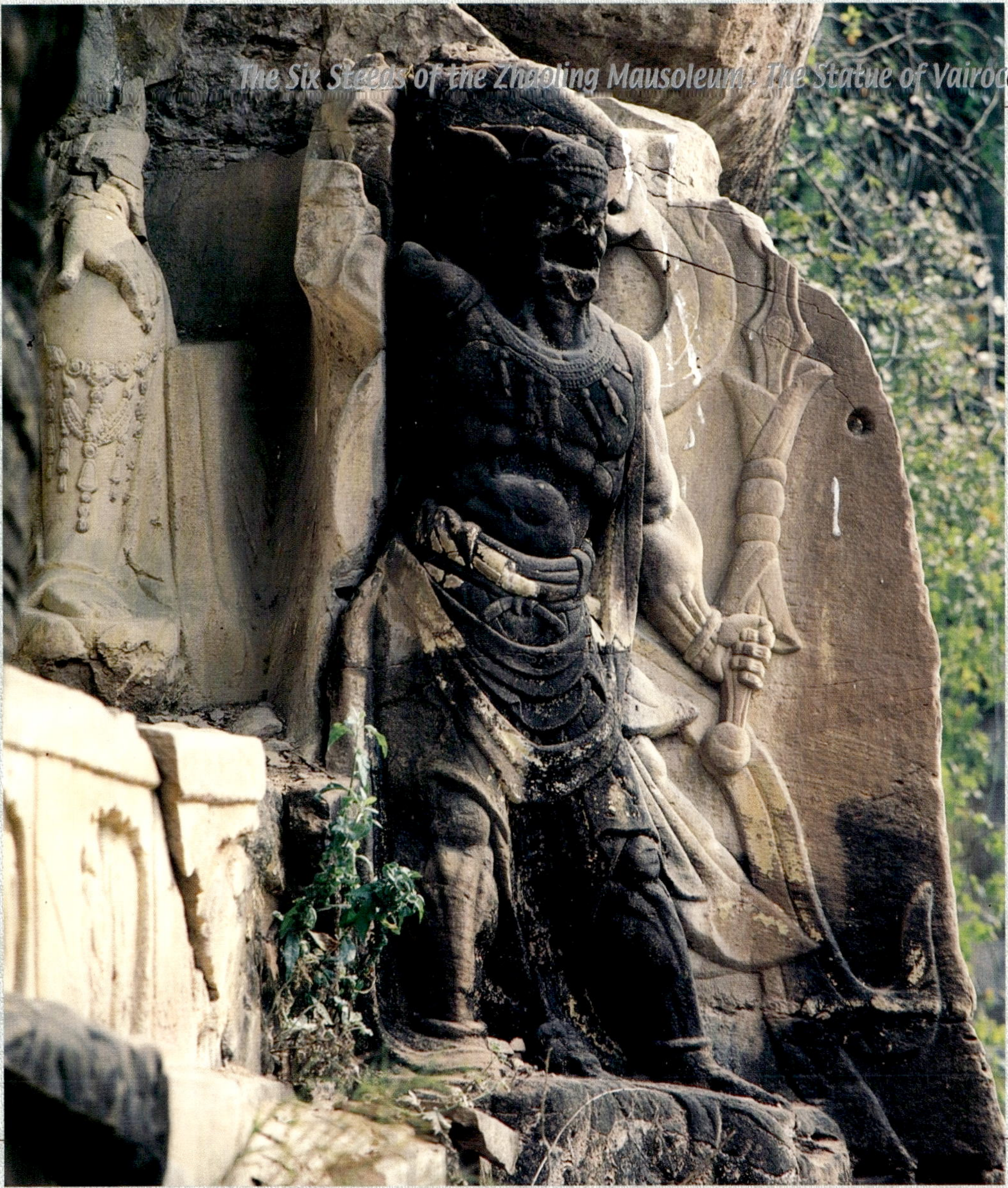

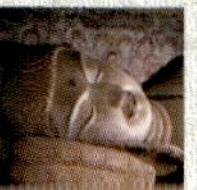

Warrior, mid-Tang Dynasty. Mount Shixun, Qionglai County, Sichuan Province.

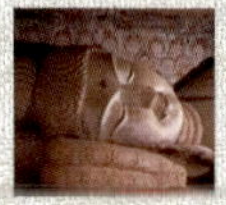

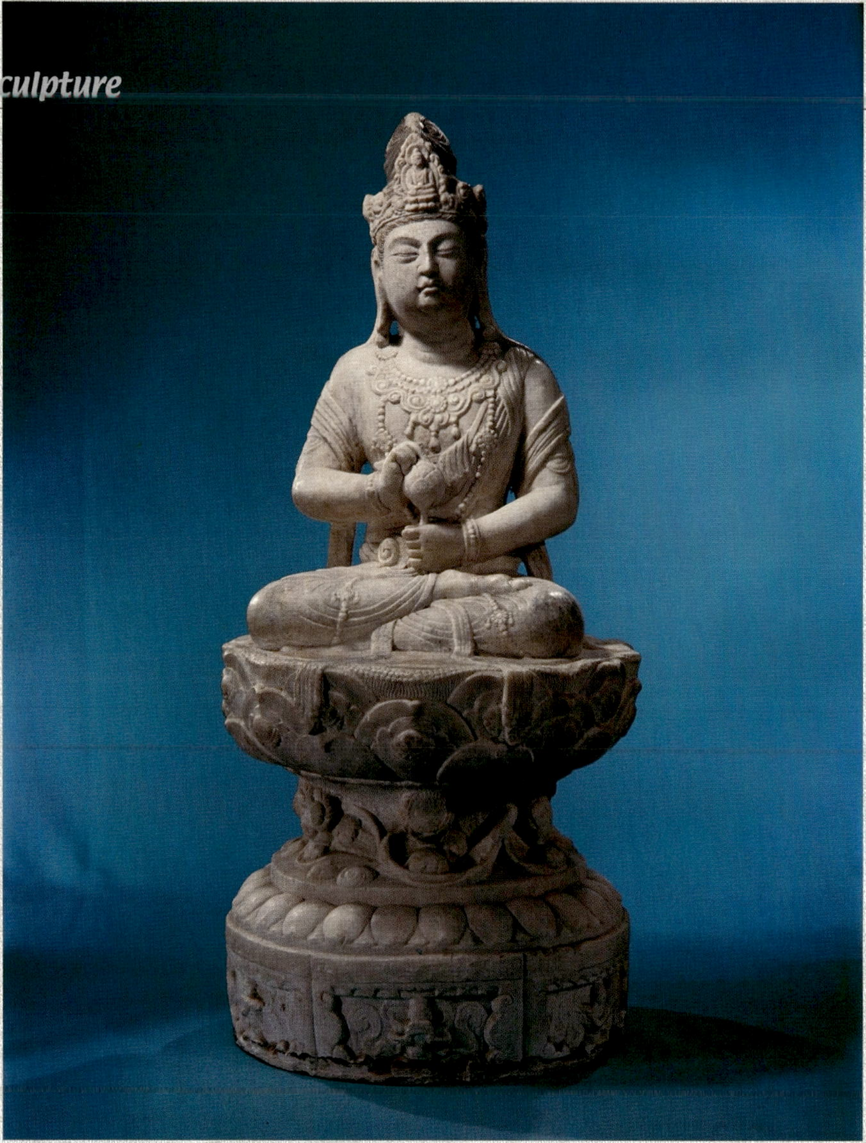

Goddess of Mercy Holding a Lotus Flower Bud, Tang Dynasty. Unearthed from the Anguo Temple, Xi'an, Shaanxi Province. Now in the collection of the Shaanxi Provincial Museum.

This white marble sculpture is 73 cm high. The Bodhisattva sits on a lotus flower throne, wearing a crown and a jeweled necklace, and holding a lotus flower bud.

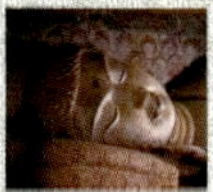

Bodhisattva of Universal Benevolence, Tang Dynasty. Nanchan Temple, Mount Wutai, Shanxi Province.

Nanchan Temple was constructed in 782. The principal Buddha is seated in the center of the spacious altar: There are a total of 17 sculpted figures in the temple, including the Bodhisattva of Wisdom, Bodhisattva of Universal Benevolence, Heavenly King, disciples and donors, varying in height. Among them, the three-meter-high plump, elegant Bodhisattva of Universal Benevolence riding an elephant and the Bodhisattva of Wisdom riding a lion are the most eye-catching.

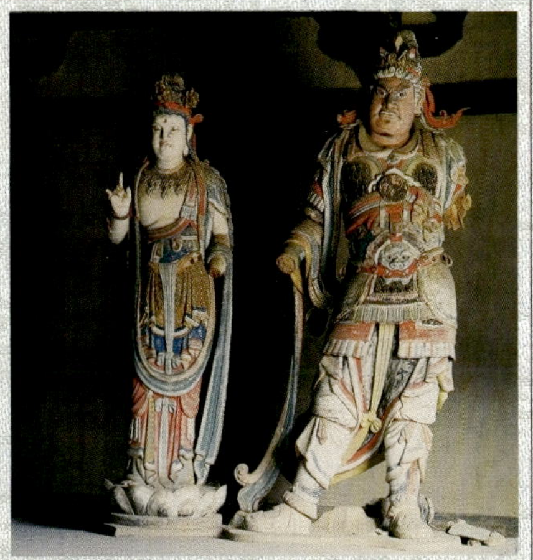

Bodhisattva and Heavenly King, Tang Dynasty. Nanchan Temple, Mount Wutai, Shanxi Province.

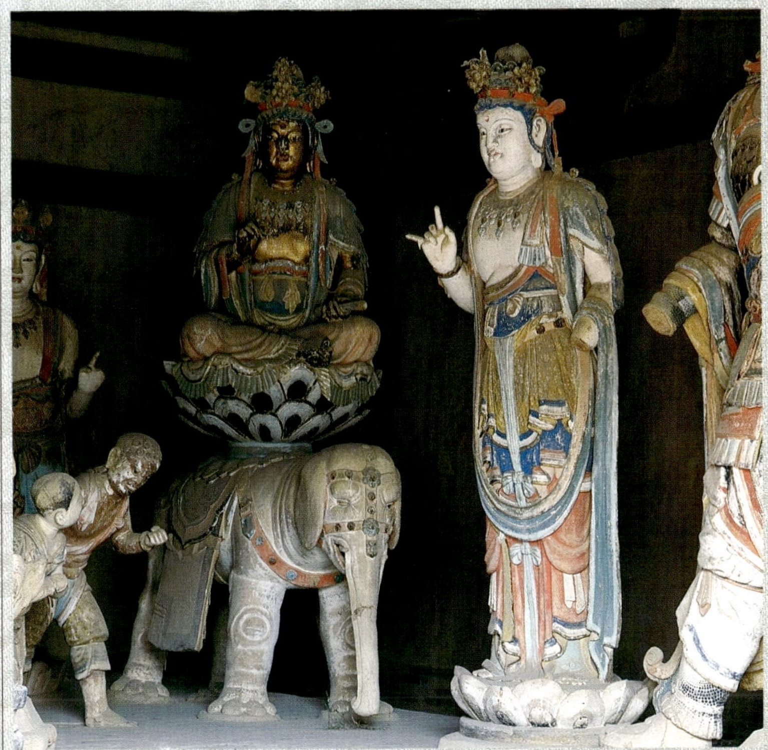

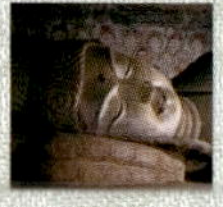

Tricolor Pottery Women Figurines, Tang Dynasty. Unearthed from a site in Xi'an, Shaanxi Province. In the collection of the Shaanxi Provincial Museum.

Typical Tang Dynasty sculptures of women show them as being plump. However, in the south of Shaanxi such sculptures are usually slim and lithe.

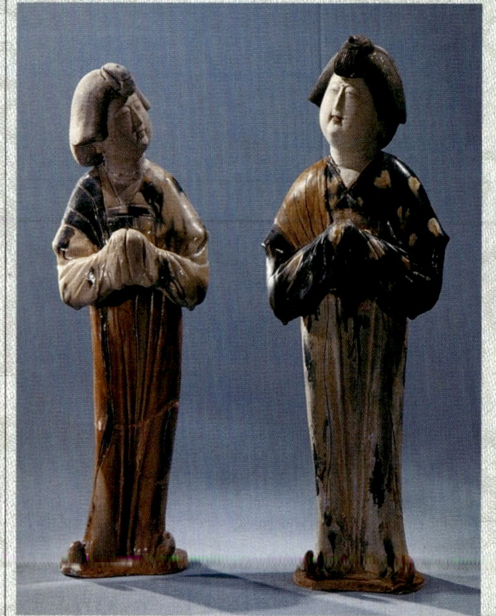

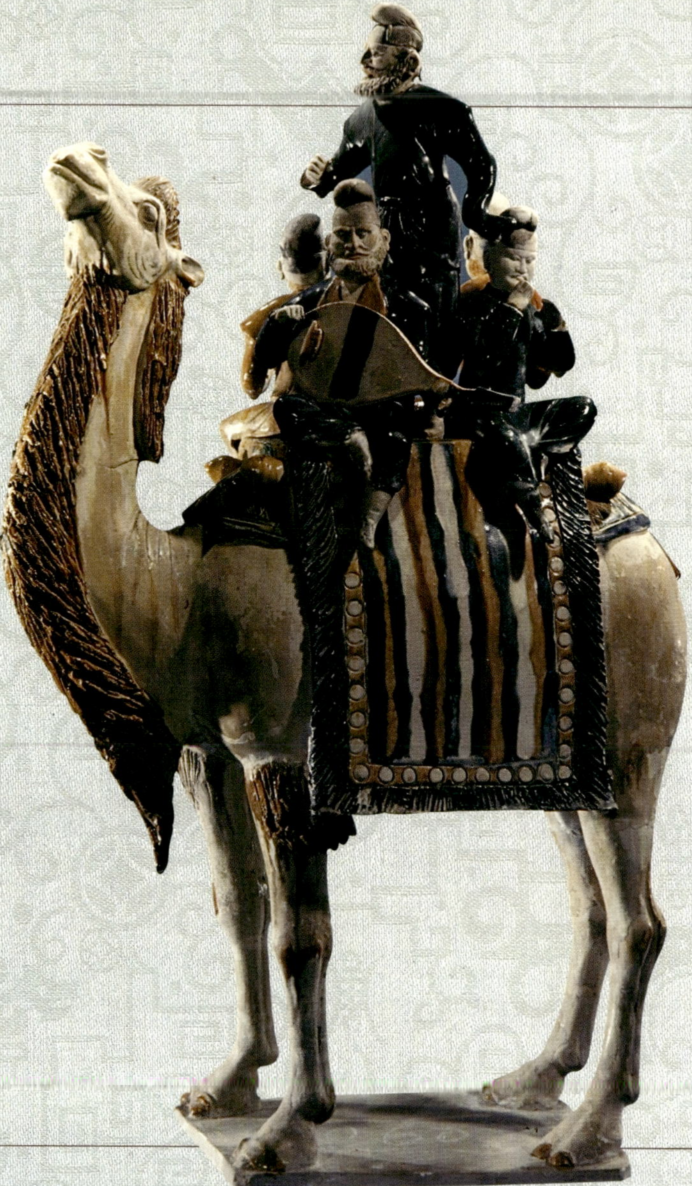

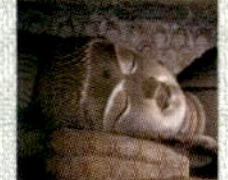

Tricolor Glazed Camel Carrying Musicians, Tang Dynasty. Unearthed from a site in Xi'an, Shaanxi Province. In the collection of the Shaanxi Provincial Museum.

Interior View of Foguang Temple, Mount Wutai, Shanxi Province. Foguang Temple fell into disrepair when Emperor Wuzong of the Tang Dynasty banned Buddhism in 845. It was reconstructed in 847. The faces of the seated sculptures of Sakyamuni, Maitreya, Amitabha, the Bodhisattva of Universal Benevolence and the Bodhisattva of Wisdom on the altar are overlaid with gold leaf.

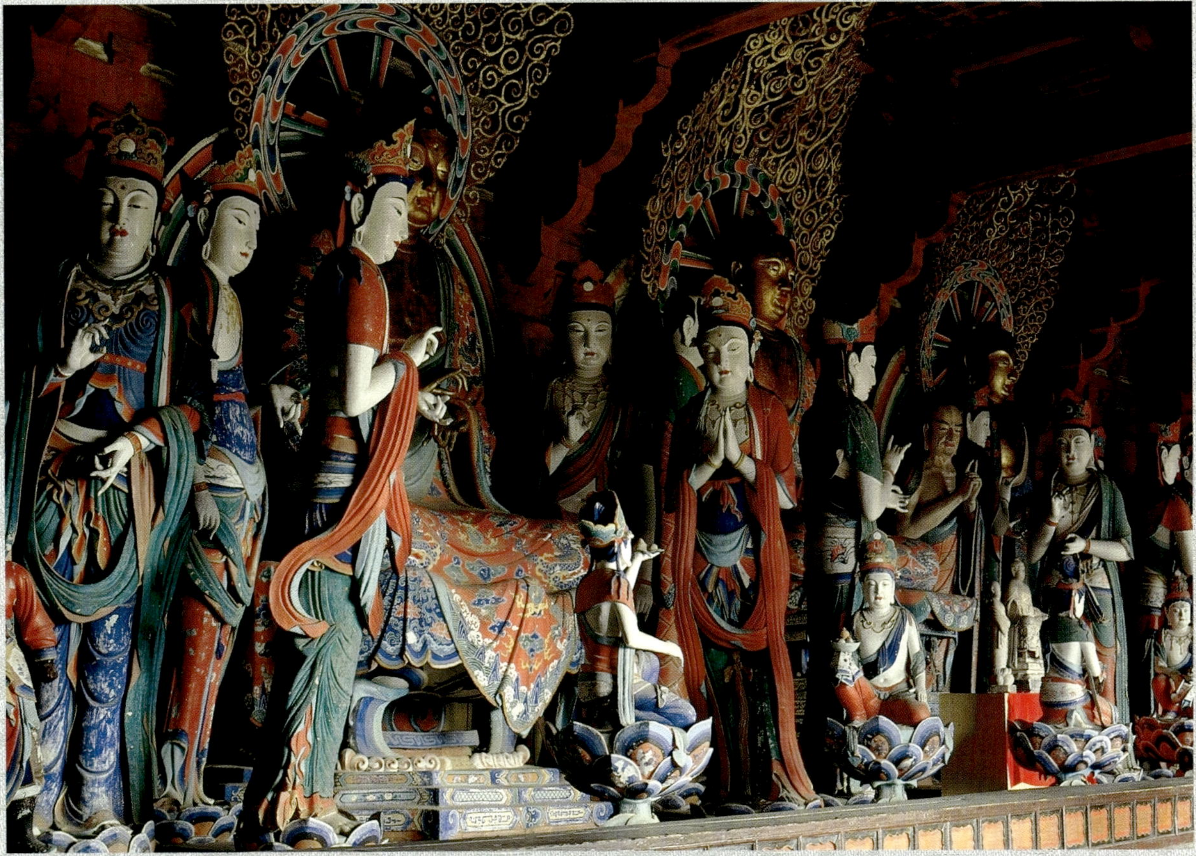

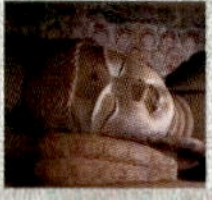

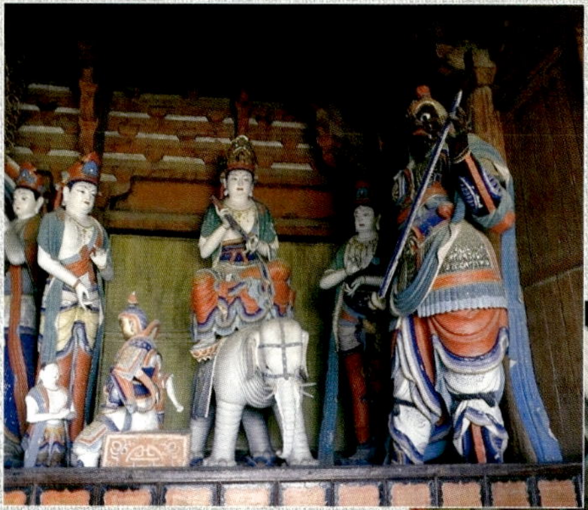

Bodhisattva Personifying Offerings, Tang Dynasty. Foguang Temple, Mount Wutai, Shanxi Province.

Bodhisattvas and Heavenly King, Tang Dynasty. Foguang Temple, Mount Wutai, Shanxi Province.

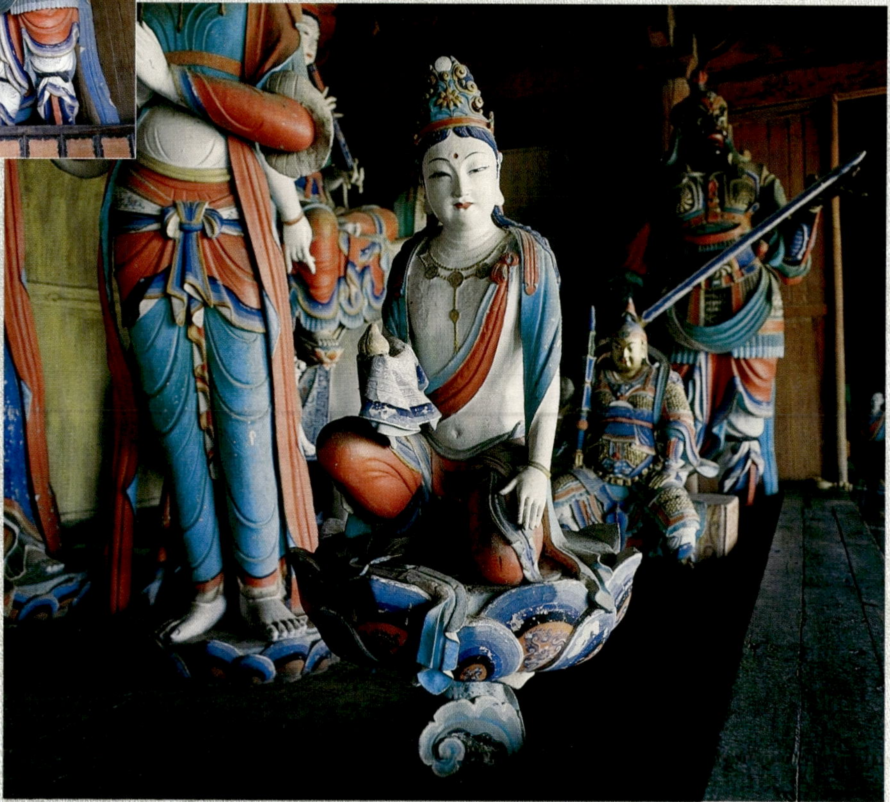

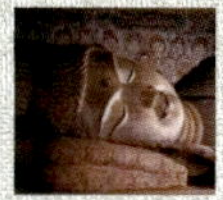

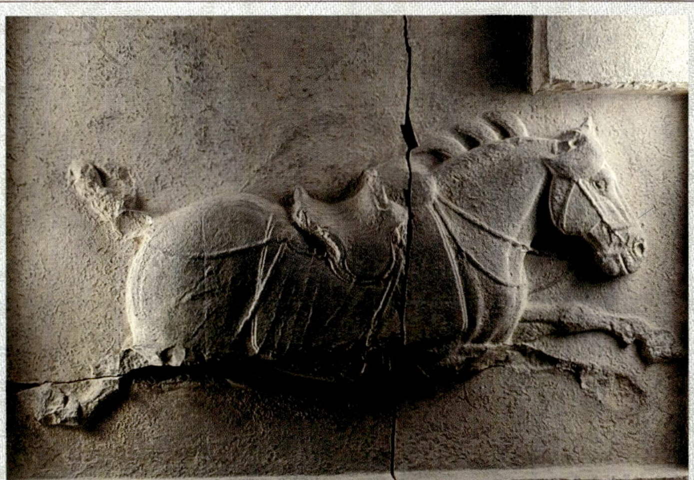

The Warhorse Shifachi, Tang Dynasty. Unearthed from the Zhaoling Mausoleum, Liquan County, Shaanxi Province. Now in the collection of the Xi'an Forest of Steles Museum.

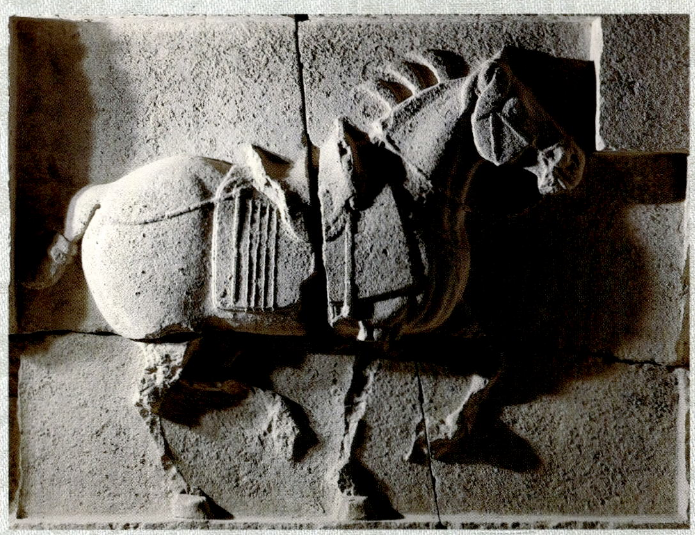

The Warhorse Telebiao, Tang Dynasty. Unearthed from the Zhaoling Mausoleum in Liquan County, Shaanxi Province. Now in the collection of the Xi'an Forest of Steles Museum. Shifachi and Telebiao were two of the six horses on which Li Shimin, Emperor Taizong, rode as he fought to establish the Tang Dynasty.

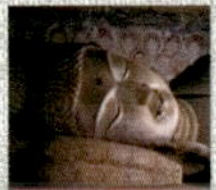

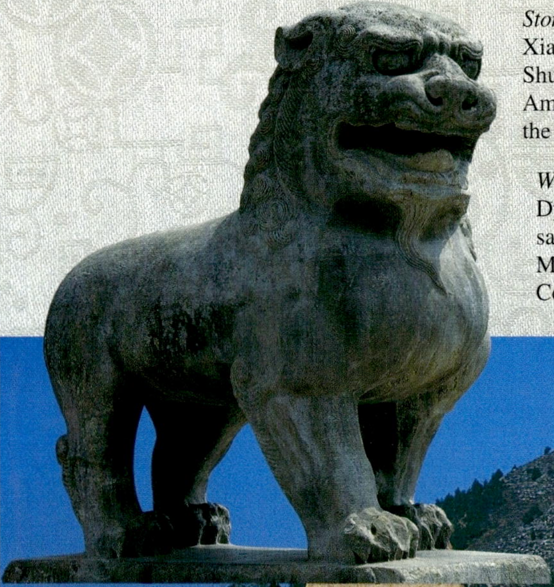

Ancient Sculpture

Stone Lion, Tang Dynasty. Excavated from the Shunling Mausoleum, Xianyang, Shaanxi Province.
Shunling Mausoleum is the tomb of Empress Wu Zetian's mother. Among the stone sculptures found in the tomb, the most famous is the stone lion.

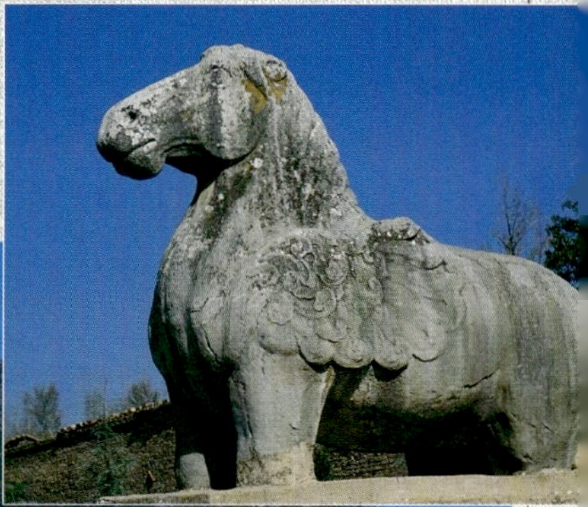

Winged Horse, Tang Dynasty. Placed by the passage leading to the Qianling Mausoleum, Qianxian County, Shaanxi Province.

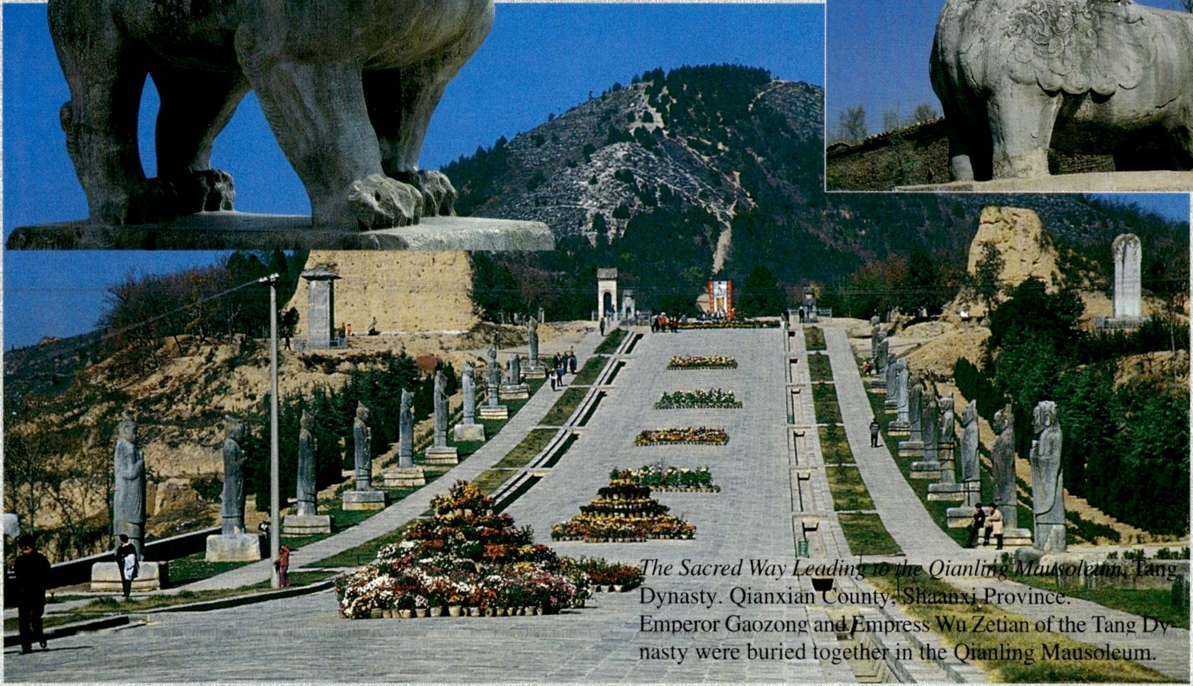

The Sacred Way Leading to the Qianling Mausoleum, Tang Dynasty. Qianxian County, Shaanxi Province.
Emperor Gaozong and Empress Wu Zetian of the Tang Dynasty were buried together in the Qianling Mausoleum.

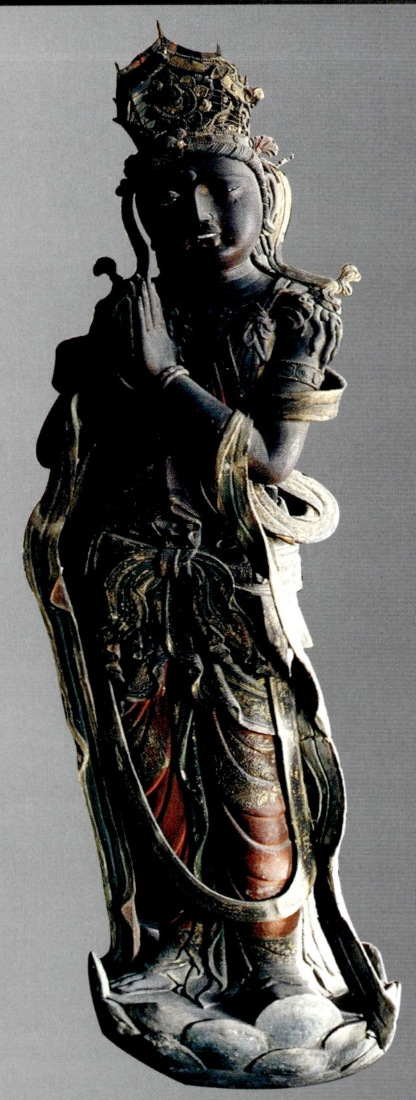

Secularized Buddhist Statues · Long Series of Stone Buddhas

A noticeable feature of the Buddhist temples and statues in the Five Dynasties, and Song, Liao, Kin and Yuan dynasties periods is the decrease of spiritual elements and the increase of secular elements. In the 1,000 Buddha Hall of Lingyan Temple in Changqing, Shandong Province, the 40 colored clay statues of Buddhist arhats are life-size, with various traits of appearance according to their supposed different ages, experiences and dispositions, and lively and subtle expressions. These figures demonstrate the highly realistic level of Song Dynasty sculptures, and exude little spirituality. In the Holy Mother Hall in the Jin Memorial Shrine, Taiyuan, capital of Shanxi Province, the 33 colored clay statues of the Holy Mother's attendant maids look like any group of pretty young girls.

In the Mount Baoding Grottoes in Dazu County, Sichuan, there are thousands of statues sculpted in the Southern Song Dynasty. They are grouped, instead of being placed in separate niches, and tell the story of the Buddha's life and enlightenment.

The stone carvings in the Mausoleum of Emperor Wang Jian of the Former Shu Dynasty of the Five Dynasties period are the best of this kind. In the main tomb chamber, there is a stone coffin platform with reliefs of musical performers carved on all four sides. They are lifelike, and provide important reference material for the study of ancient Chinese music. In the rear chamber is an 86-cm-high seated statue of Emperor Wang Jian, whose features accord with those described in historical documents. This statue is of great value, for it is the only statue of a Chinese emperor made in his times that has ever been discovered. In this connection should be mentioned the imperial mausoleums of the Northern Song Dynasty in Gongxian County, Henan Province.

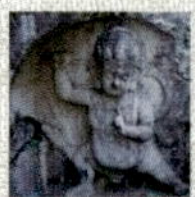

Ancient Sculpture

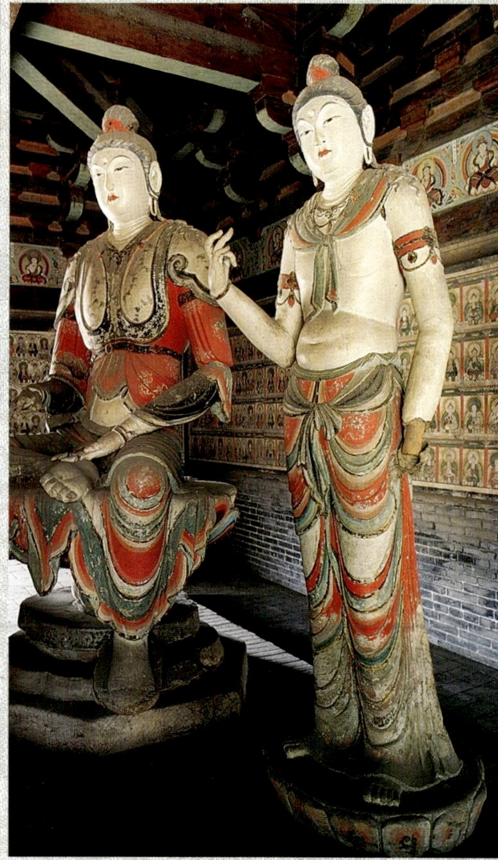

Buddha, Bodhisattva, Heavenly King and Disciples, Five Dynasties. Zhenguo Temple, Pingyao County, Shanxi Province.

There are 11 painted sculptures made in 963 in the Zhenguo Temple. The sculpture of the Buddha has a dignified expression, the Bodhisattva has round cheeks and looks graceful, the disciples look wise, sincere and honest, and Heavenly King looks powerful and splendid.

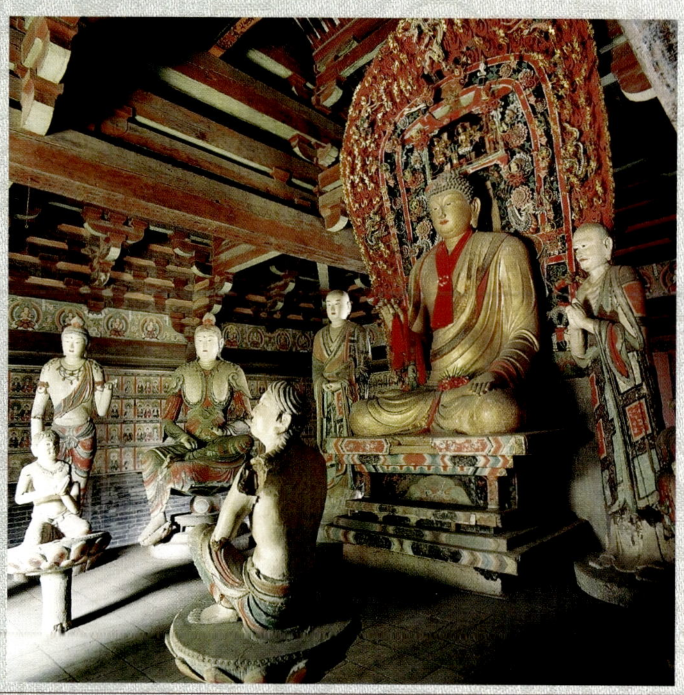

Bodhisattva, Five Dynasties. Zhenguo Temple, Pingyao County, Shanxi Province.

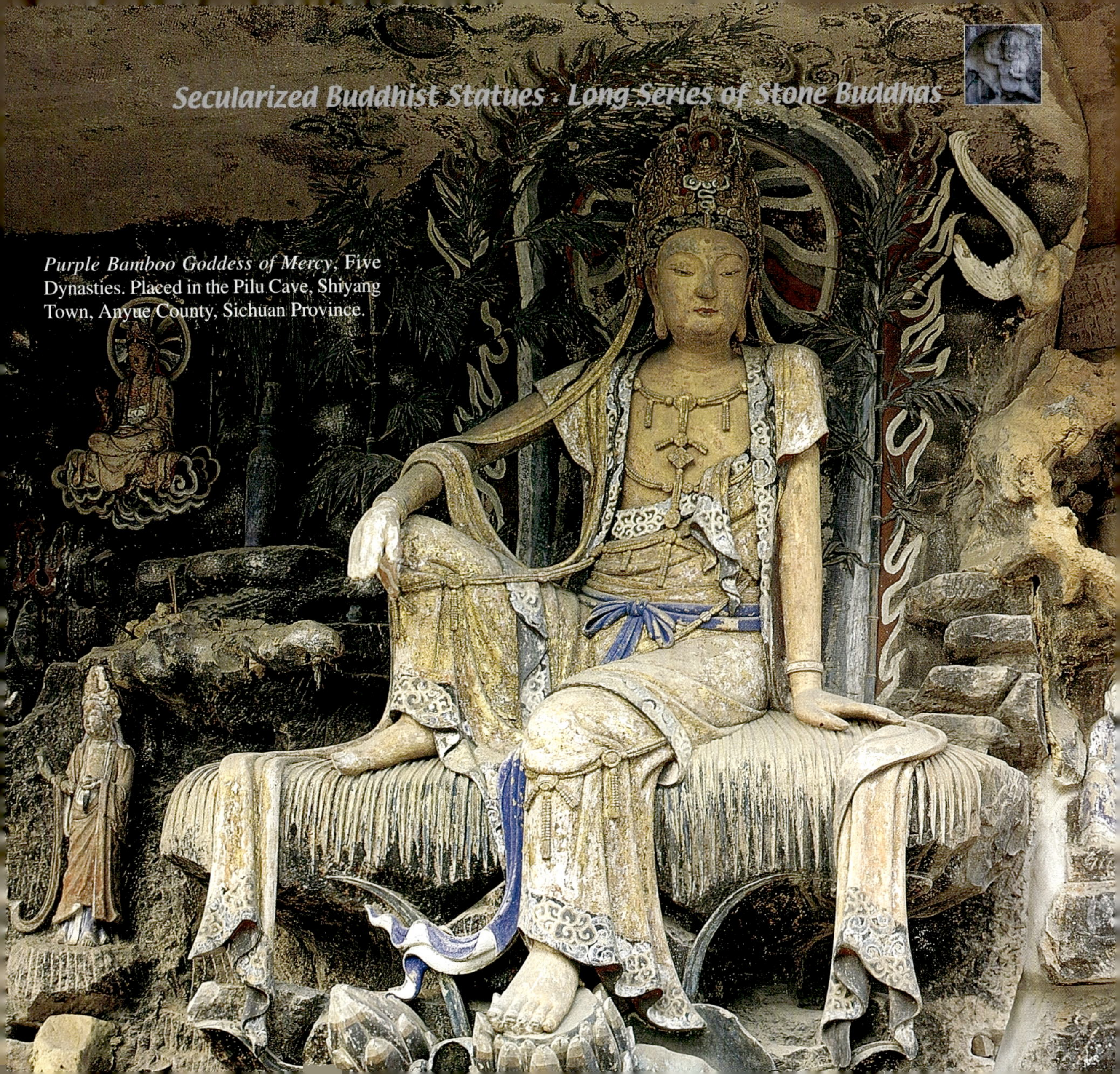

Purple Bamboo Goddess of Mercy, Five Dynasties. Placed in the Pilu Cave, Shiyang Town, Anyue County, Sichuan Province.

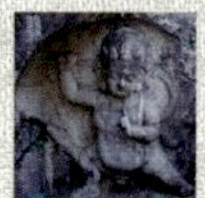

Ancient Sculpture

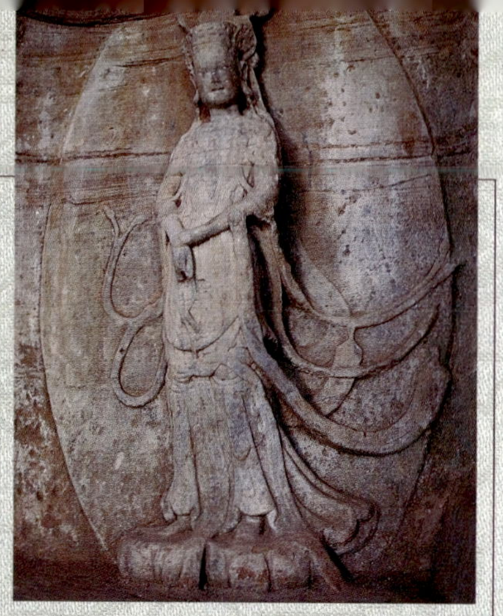

Bead-counting Goddess of Mercy, Song Dynasty. Grotto 125 of Beishan, Dazu Grottoes, Chongqing.

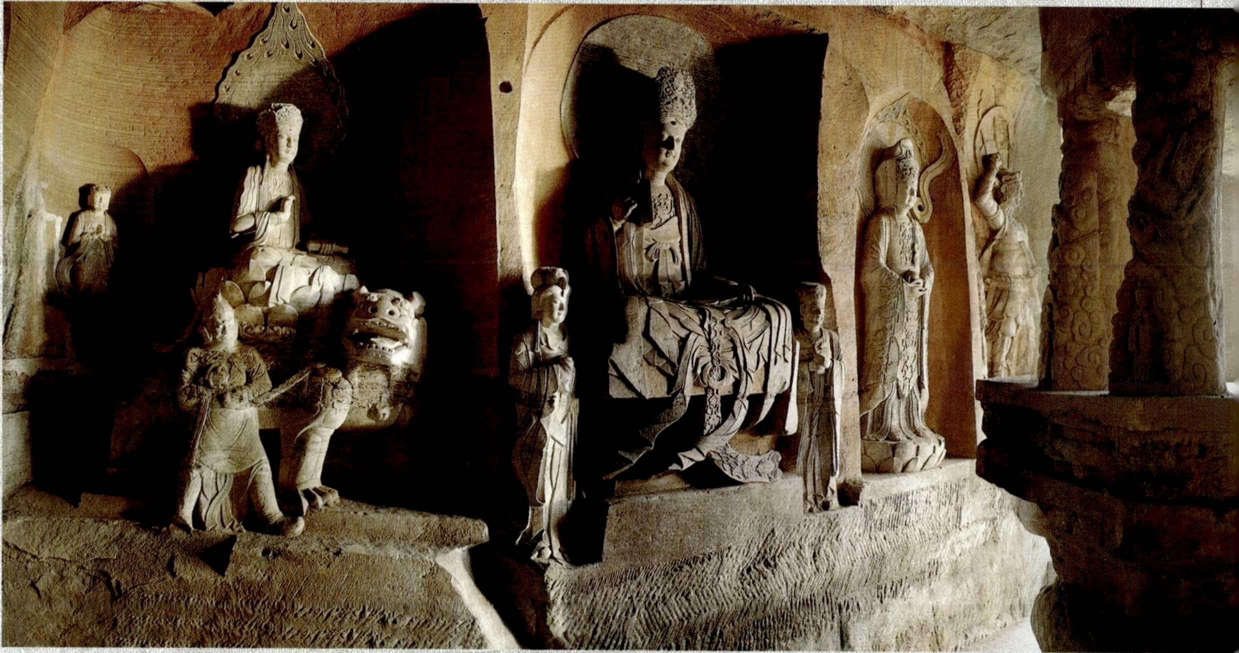

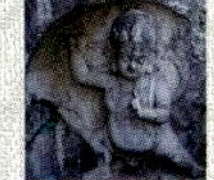

Full View of the Cave of the Revolving Wheel. Grotto 136 of Beishan, Dazu Grottoes, Chongqing. The sculptures in this grotto are of different characters and in various postures, showing dexterous, concise carving techniques. They can be rated as representative stone sculptures of the Song Dynasty.

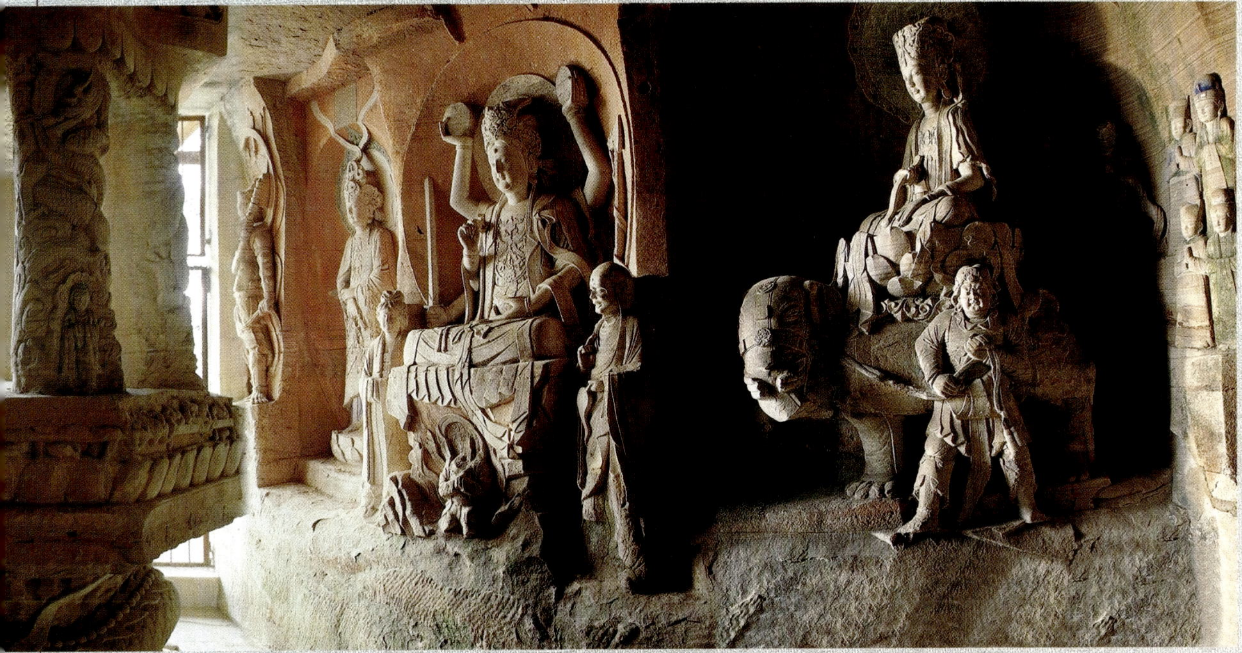

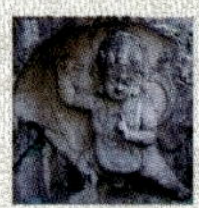

Ancient Sculpture

Brightness Kings, Song Dynasty. No. 22 Cliffside Sculpture. Mount Baoding, Dazu County, Chongqing. Most of the sculptures of the ten great Brightness Kings, or messengers of Vairocana, in Mount Baoding are unfinished works, which might have been left by Liao invaders. Each of the Brightness Kings has three heads, and four or six arms, and all are fierce-looking. Though incomplete, these sculptures are regarded as art treasures.

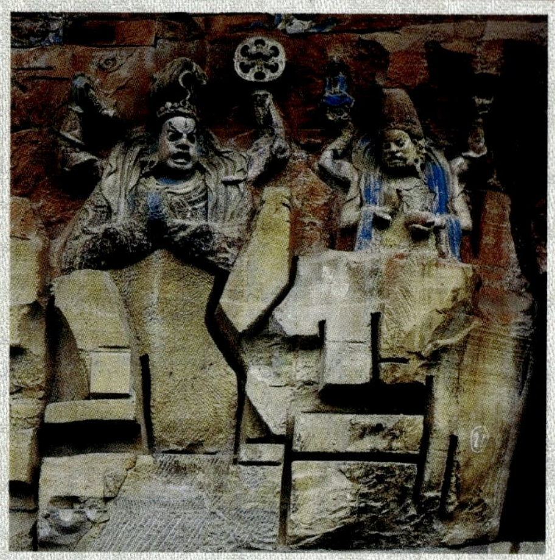

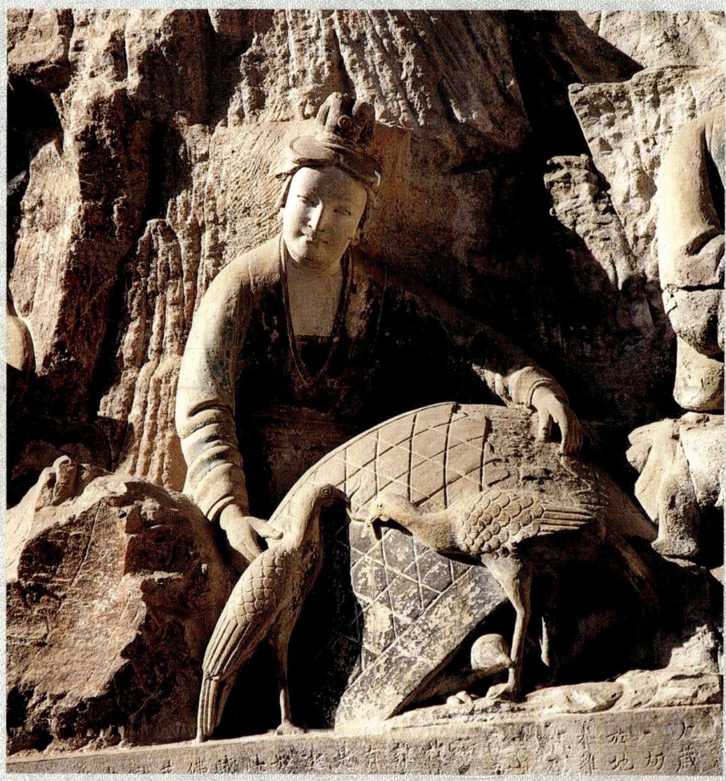

Girl Feeding Chickens, Song Dynasty. No. 20 Cliffside Sculpture. Daodingshan, Dazu Grottoes, Chongqing.

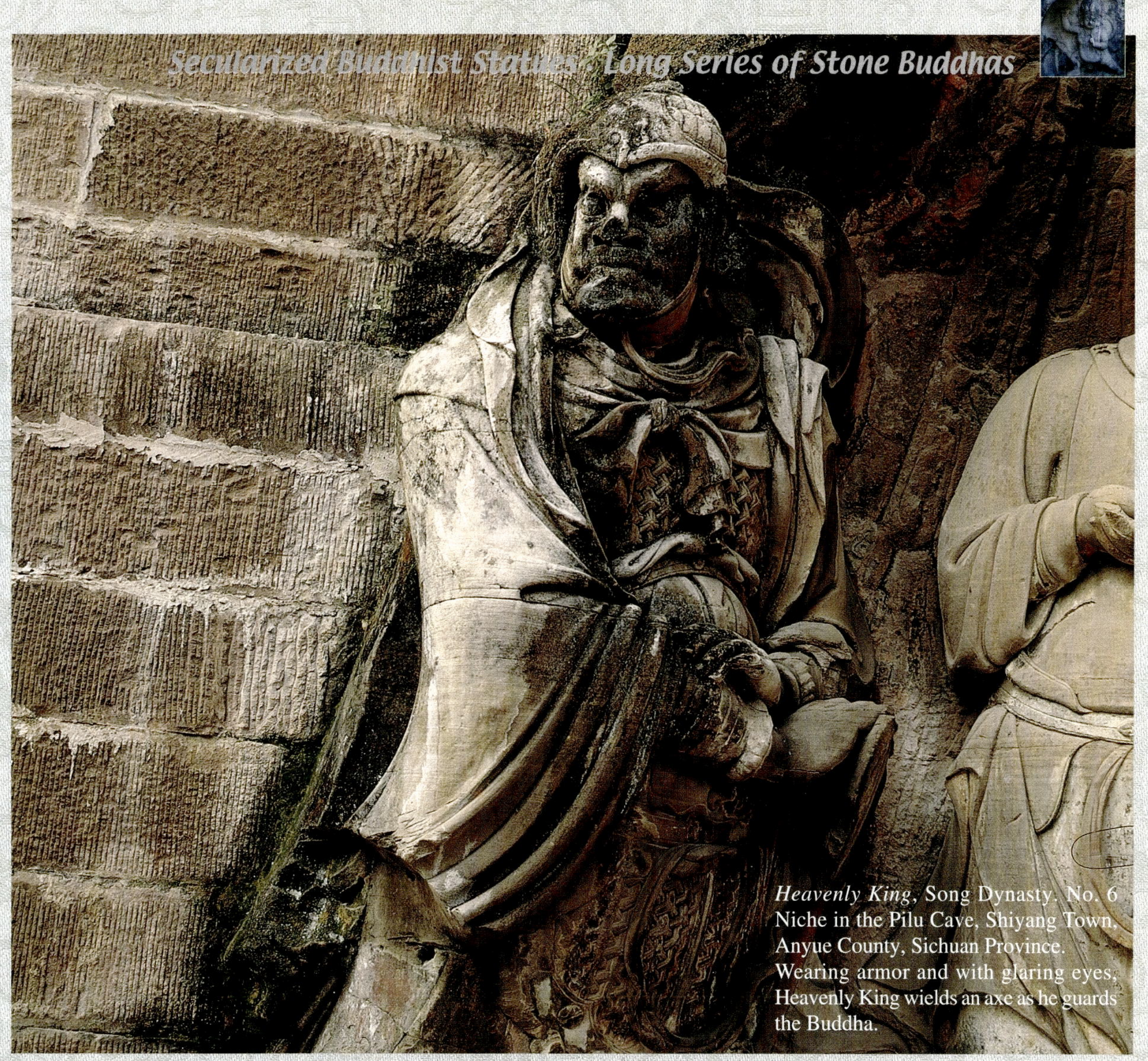

Heavenly King, Song Dynasty. No. 6 Niche in the Pilu Cave, Shiyang Town, Anyue County, Sichuan Province. Wearing armor and with glaring eyes, Heavenly King wields an axe as he guards the Buddha.

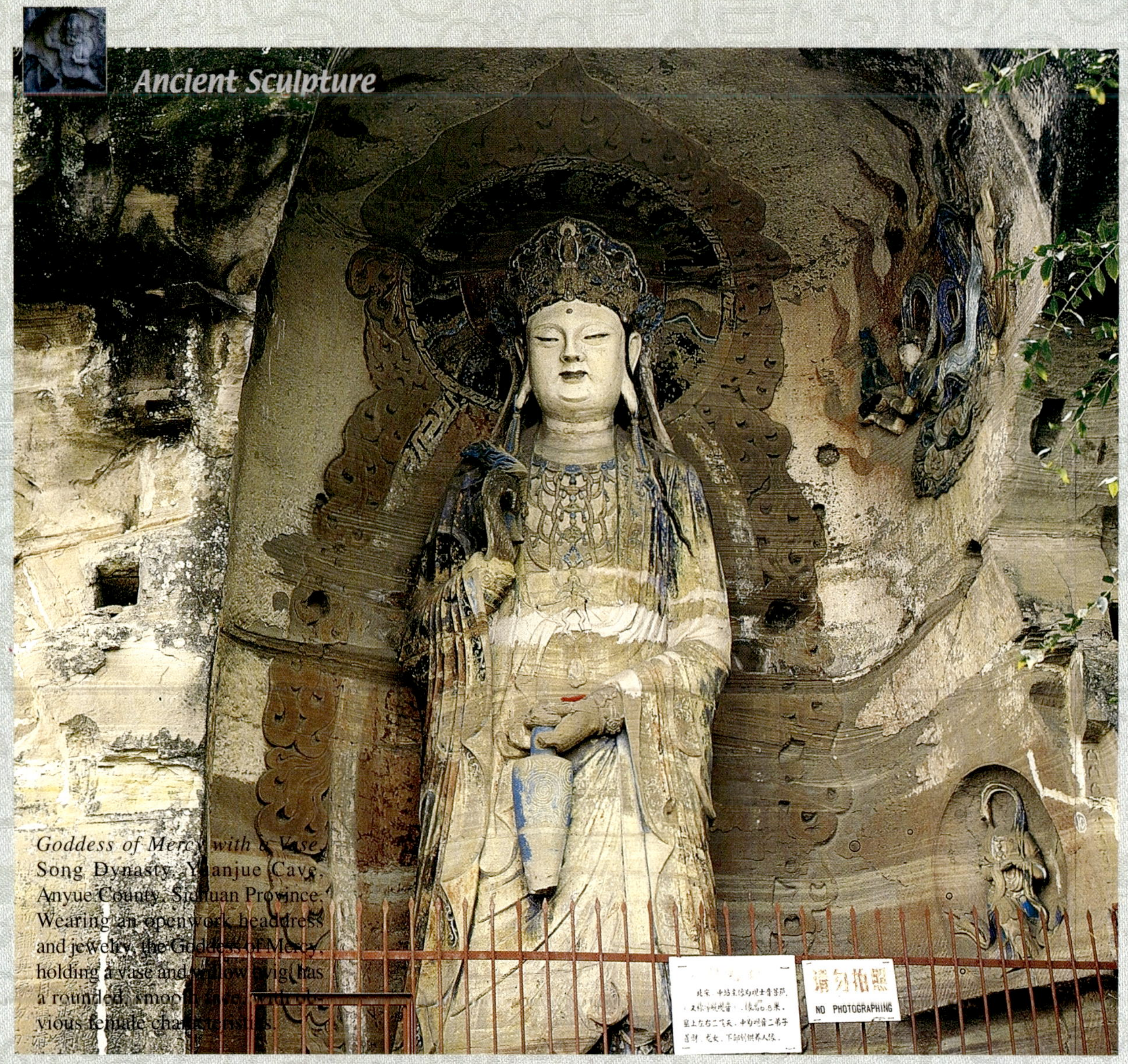

Goddess of Mercy with a Vase
Song Dynasty, Yuanjue Cave, Anyue County, Sichuan Province. Wearing an openwork headdress and jewelry, the Goddess of Mercy, holding a vase and willow twig, has a rounded, smooth face with obvious female characteristics.

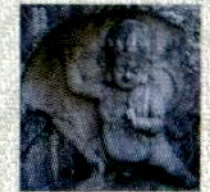

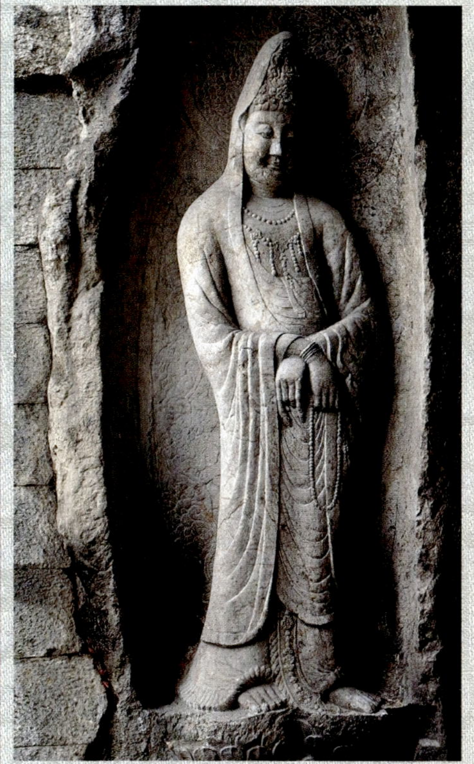

Man Holding Books on the Clouds, Song Dynasty. Yanxia Cave, Hangzhou City, Zhejiang Province.

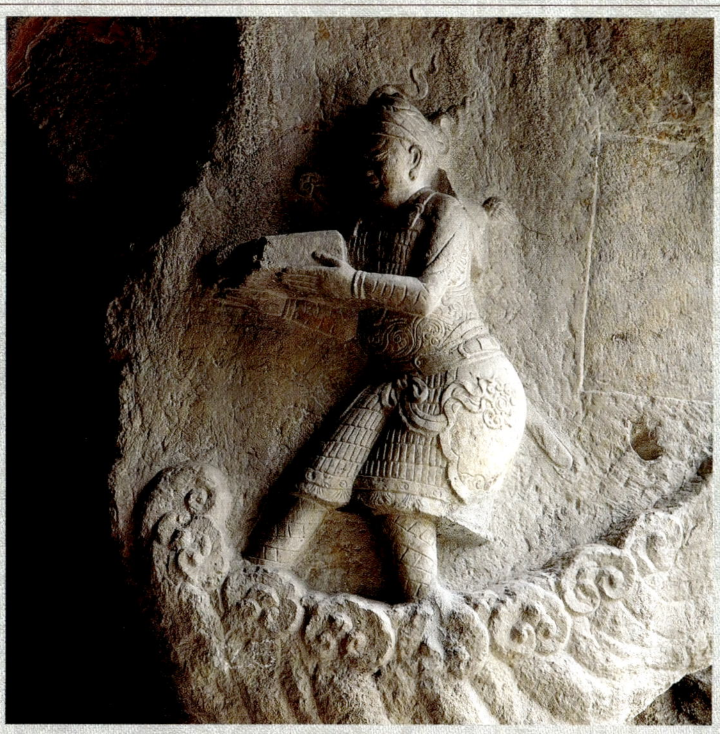

Goddess of Mercy, Song Dynasty. Yanxia Cave, Hangzhou City, Zhejiang Province.

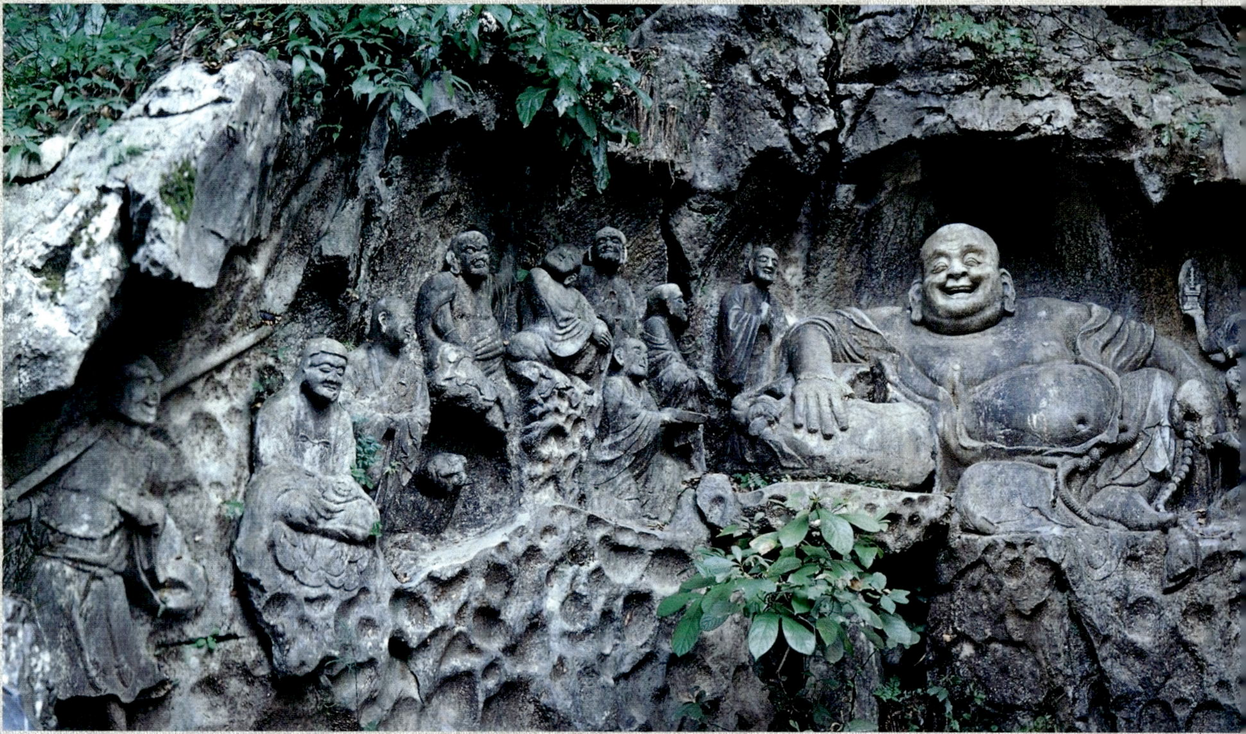

Maitreya, Song Dynasty. One of Feilai Peak cliffside sculptures, Hangzhou City, Zhejiang Province.
It is said that the big-bellied Maitreya wearing a broad smile placed at the gate to a Buddhist temple is a portrait of Qi Ci, an eminent monk of the Five Dynasties period, who was regarded as the incarnation of Maitreya. This statue, carved in 966, together with the 18 arhats carved later, is the most obvious manifestation of the secularization of the art of Buddhist sculpture during the Song Dynasty.

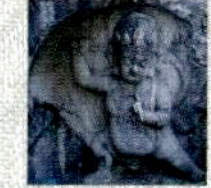

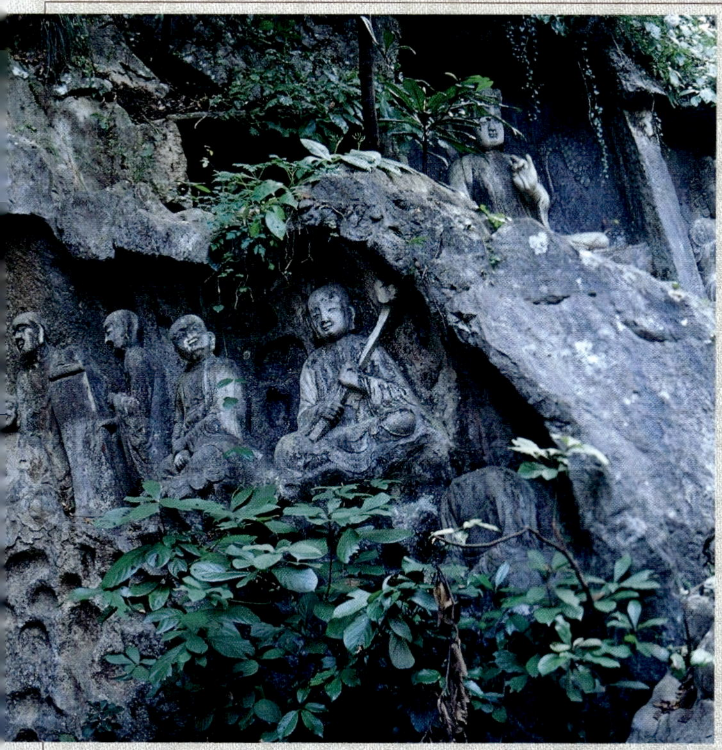

Seated Image of Lao Zi, Song Dynasty. Mount Qingyuan, Quanzhou City, Fujian Province.
The sculpture is six m high. It employs exaggerated realism and fine freehand brushwork, paying attention to the contrast of the scantiness and density of the lines.

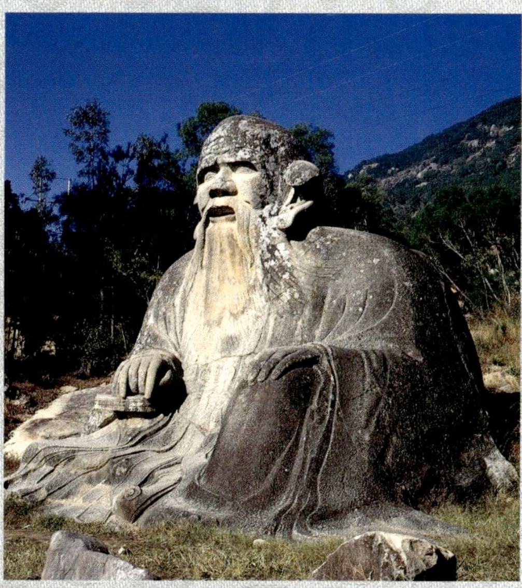

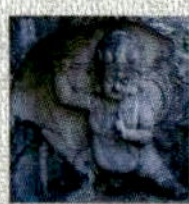

Sculpture of an Arhat (II), Song Dynasty. Lingyan Temple, Changqing County, Shandong Province.

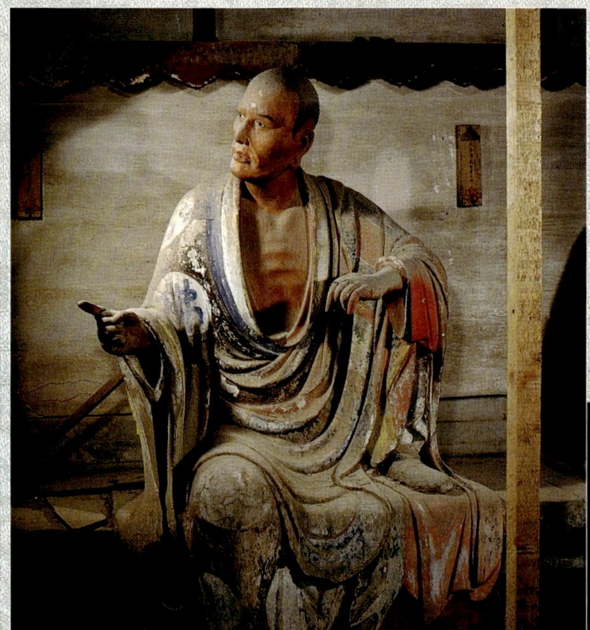

Sculpture of an Arhat (I), Song Dynasty. Lingyan Temple, Changqing County, Shandong Province.
Northwest of Mount Taishan, in Shandong Province, Lingyan Temple boasts 40 painted sculptures of arhats, which are praised as "the most outstanding sculptures in China." The life-sized sculptures, 1.5 m in height, vary in appearance and countenance, and are very lifelike.

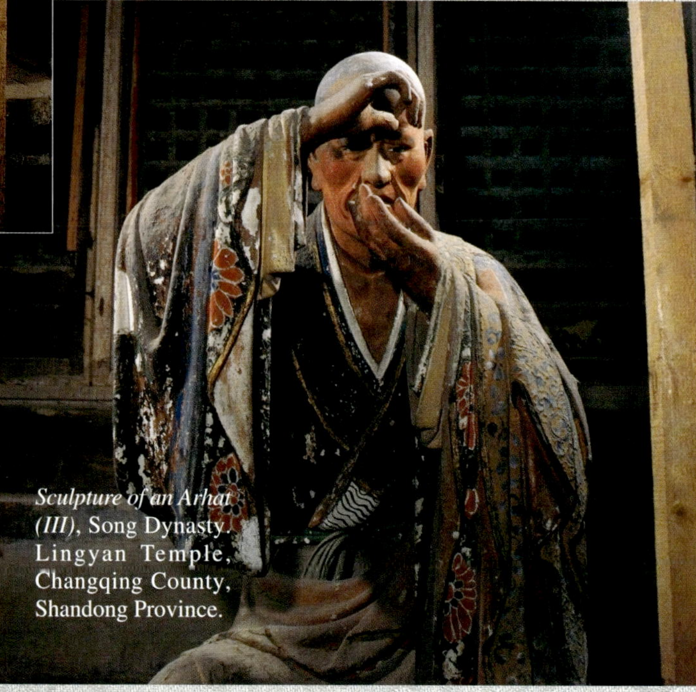

Sculpture of an Arhat (III), Song Dynasty. Lingyan Temple, Changqing County, Shandong Province.

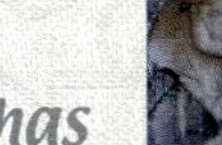

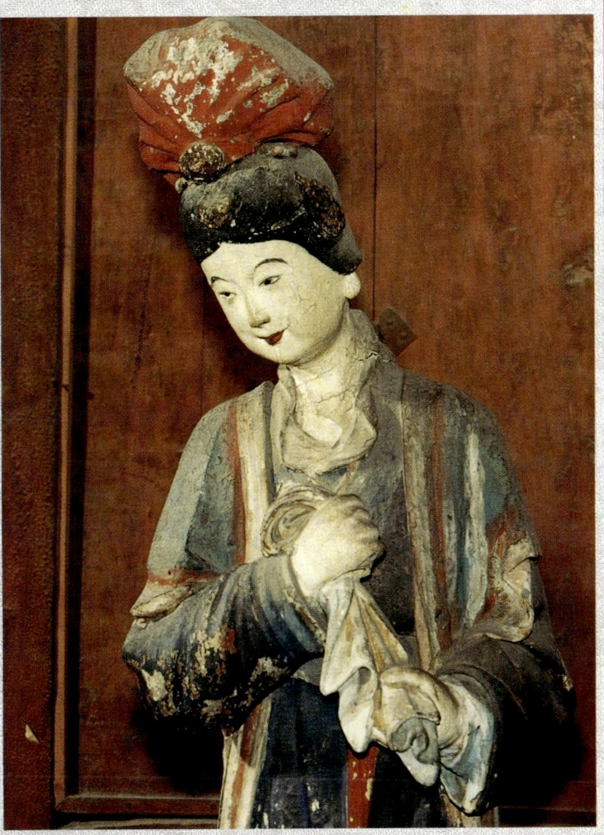

Statue of a Maid (I), Song Dynasty. Holy Mother Hall, Jin Memorial Shrine, Taiyuan City, Shanxi Province.
The maids in the Jin Memorial Shrine show various characters and bearings. Some seem to be arrogant and calculating, some open-minded and amiable, some honest and obedient, some naive and vivacious, and some prudent and cool-headed.

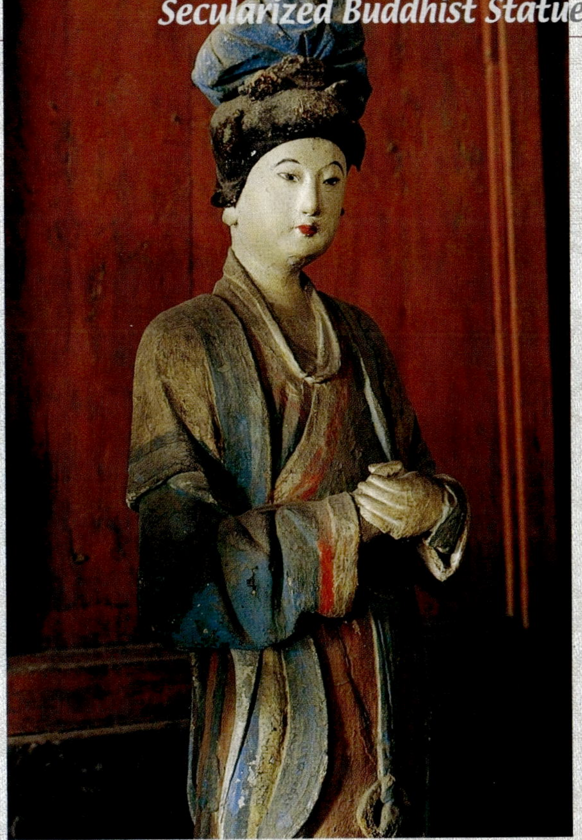

Statue of a Maid (II), Song Dynasty. Holy Mother Hall, Jin Memorial Shrine, Taiyuan City, Shanxi Province.

Stone Sculptures Lining the Sacred Way, Song Dynasty, Gongxian County, Henan Province.
The imperial tombs of the Northern Song Dynasty are located between Mount Songshan and the Luoshui River in Gongxian County, where many emperors had been buried since the Eastern Han Dynasty.

Elephant and Its Tamer, Song Dynasty, Gongxian County, Henan Province.
Before the Song Dynasty, elephants were never included among the stone sculptures guarding imperial tombs. It was probably due to closer contacts between the Northern Song Dynasty and South Asia and Africa that images of elephants began to appear at the imperial tombs of the Song Dynasty.

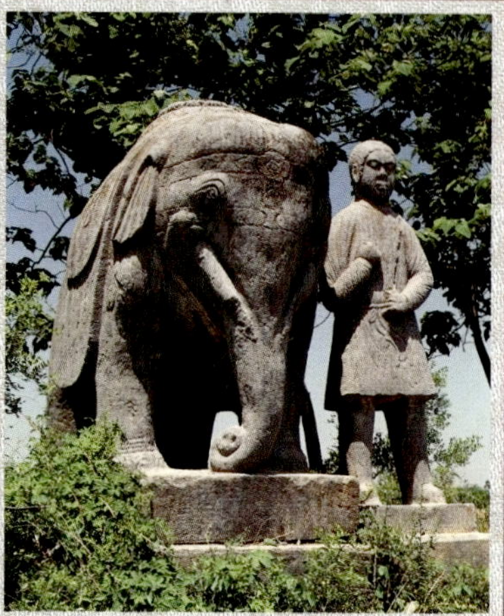

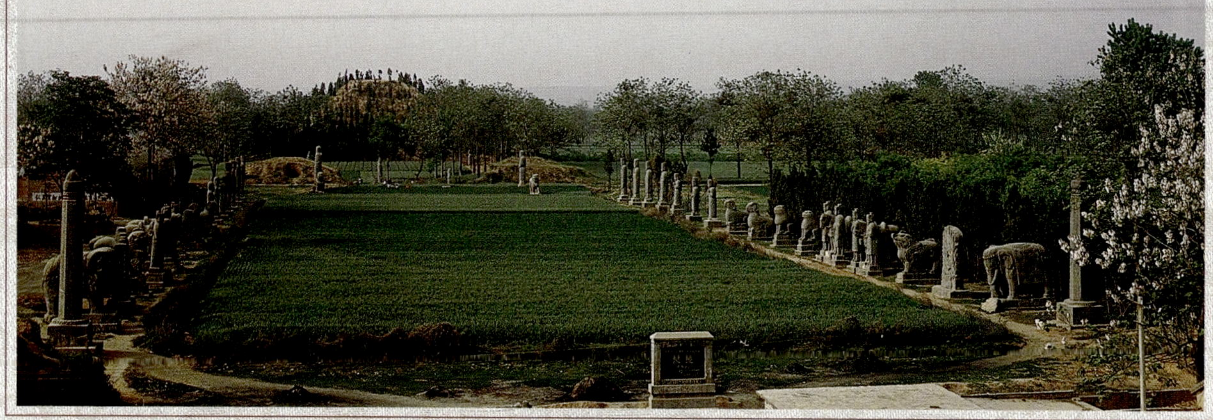

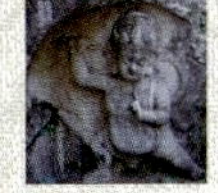

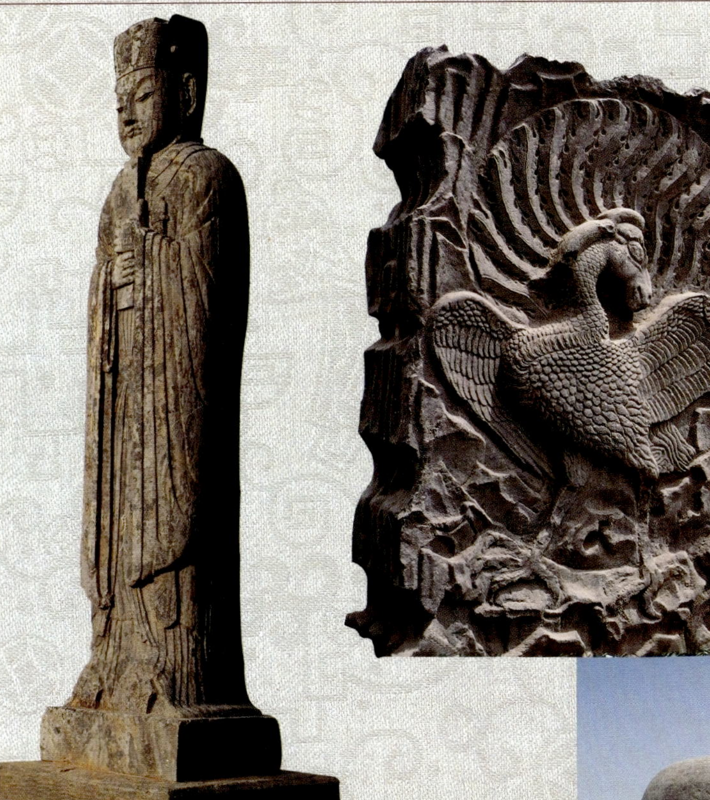

Statue of a Civil Official, Song Dynasty. Gongxian County, Henan Province. The carving technique used on the face is mature, the structure is accurate, and the figure is well proportioned.

Horse-headed Bird, Song Dynasty. Gongxian County, Henan Province.
Judging from the image, it is probably a combination of the "celestial horse" found in imperial tombs of the Tang Dynasty and the ostrich.

Jiaoduan, Song Dynasty. Gongxian County, Henan Province.
Auspicious mythical beasts, mainly Jiaoduan, first appeared in the imperial tombs of the Song Dynasty to praise the emperors' virtues and achievements. Jiaoduan is a mixture of the features of various animals.

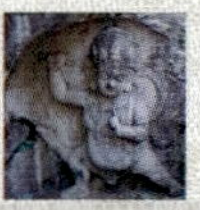

Bronze Bodhisattva of Universal Benevolence Riding an Elephant, Song Dynasty. Wannian Temple, Mount Emei, Sichuan Province. The statue plus the lotus flower throne is 7.4 m high and 4.7 m long, and weighs 62 tons. The bronze Bodhisattva is 2.65 m in height.

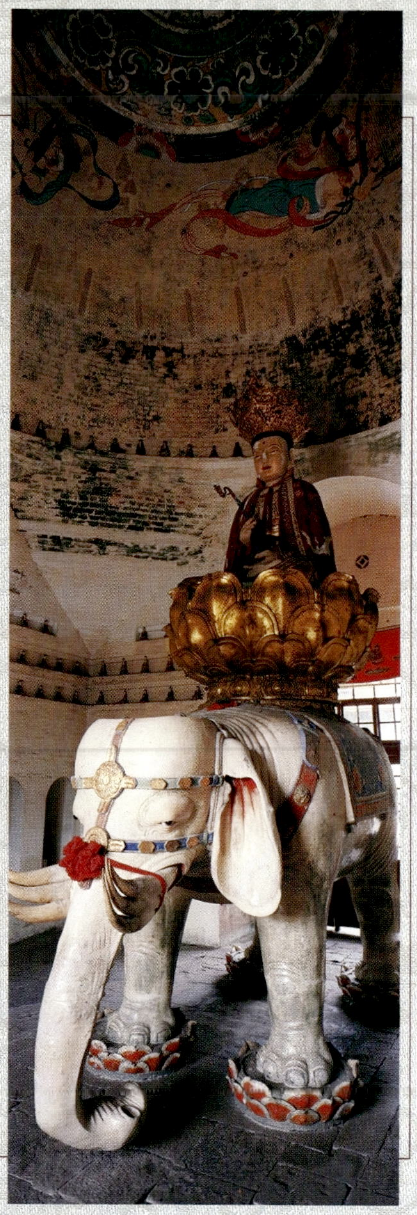

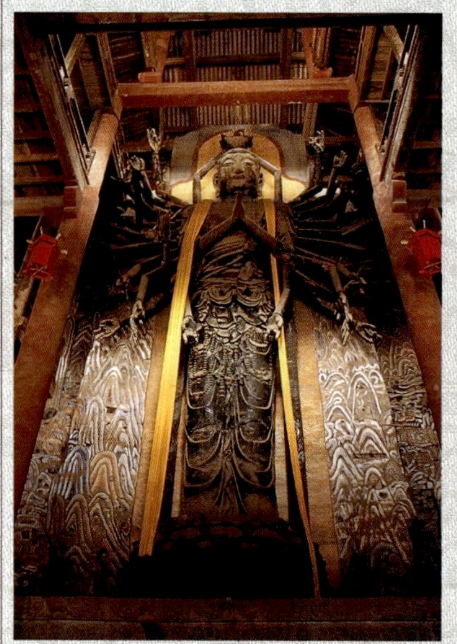

Thousand-armed Goddess of Mercy, Song Dynasty. Longxing Temple, Zhengding County, Hebei Province. This 22.5-m-high bronze statue cast in 971, the fourth year of the Kaibao reign period of the Northern Song Dynasty, is the largest and oldest bronze Buddhist statue in China. Standing on the lotus flower throne, the well-proportioned goddess is gorgeously dressed, and wears a solemn expression. She has 42 arms, with an eye in each palm, and is thus also known as the "Goddess of Mercy with a Thousand Arms and a Thousand Eyes."

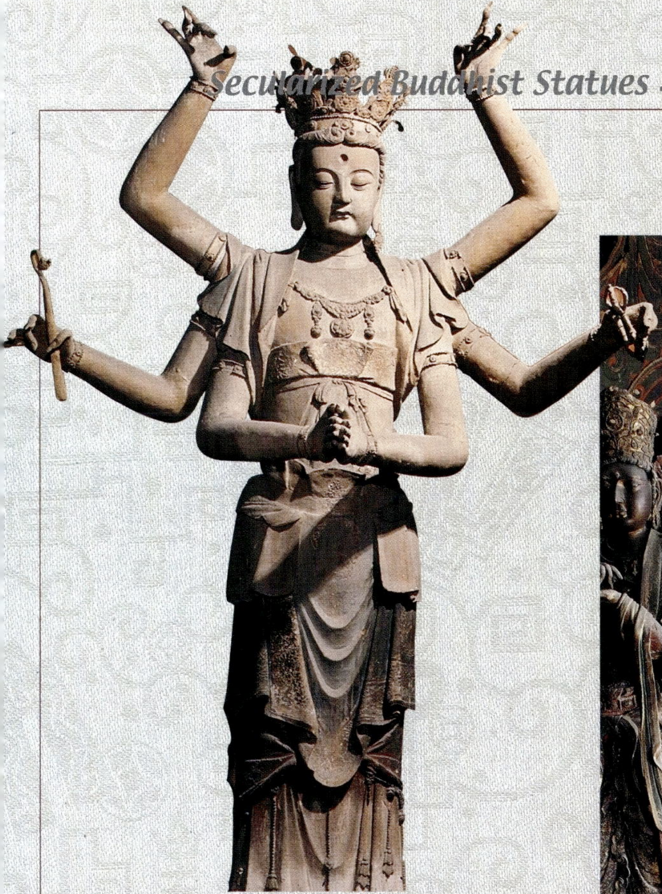

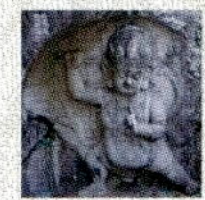

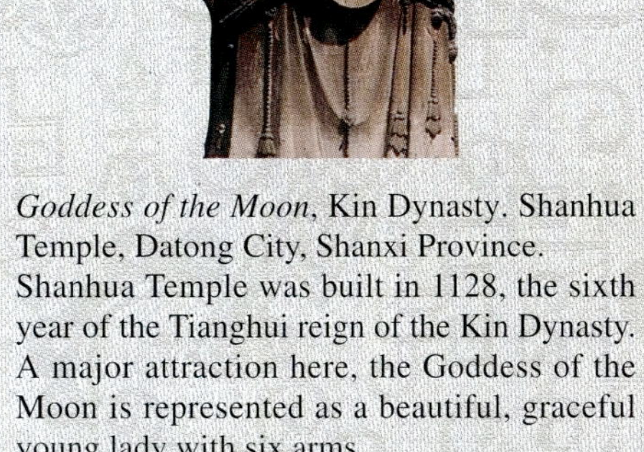

Goddess of the Moon, Kin Dynasty. Shanhua Temple, Datong City, Shanxi Province. Shanhua Temple was built in 1128, the sixth year of the Tianghui reign of the Kin Dynasty. A major attraction here, the Goddess of the Moon is represented as a beautiful, graceful young lady with six arms.

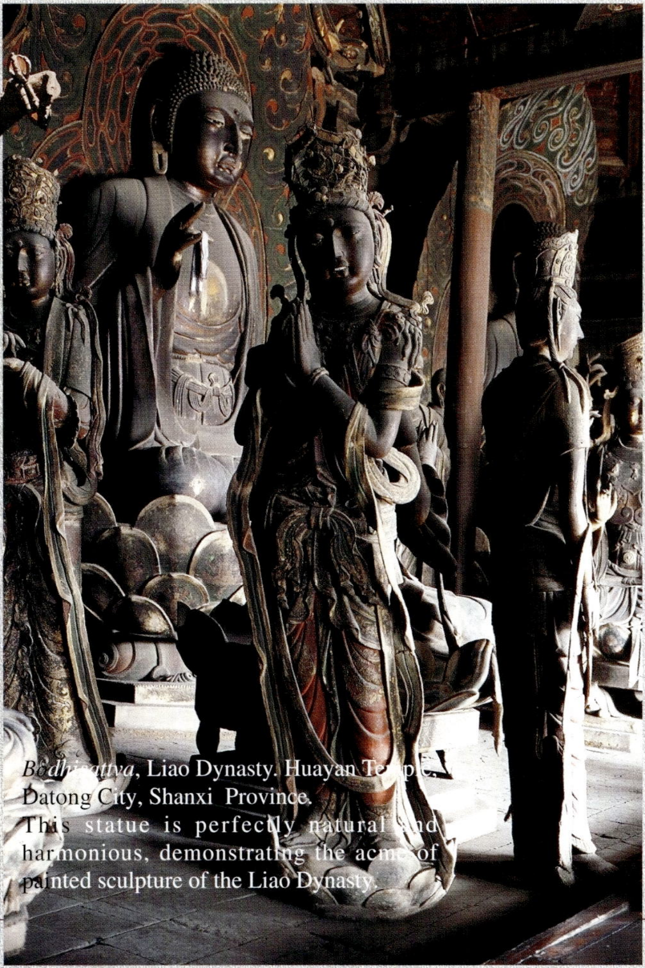

Bodhisattva, Liao Dynasty. Huayan Temple, Datong City, Shanxi Province. This statue is perfectly natural and harmonious, demonstrating the acme of painted sculpture of the Liao Dynasty.

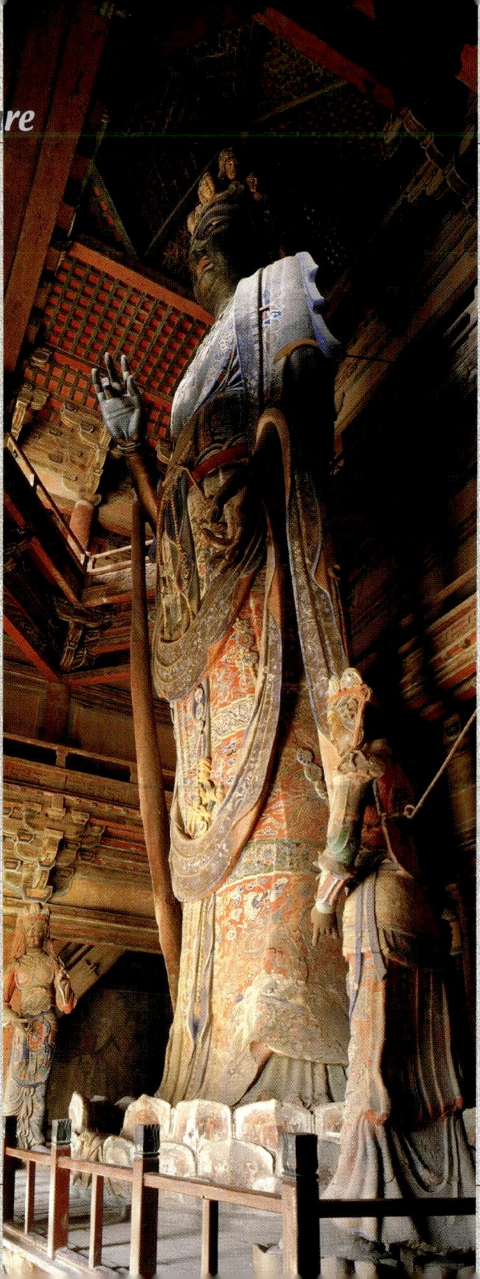

Goddess of Mercy, Liao Dynasty. Dule Temple, Jixian County, Tianjin. The Goddess is 16 m high, and has 10 small heads on the top of her head, so the statue is also called the "Goddess of Mercy with Eleven Heads." The Goddess is well proportioned, and looks gentle and graceful. This is the tallest extant clay sculpture in China.

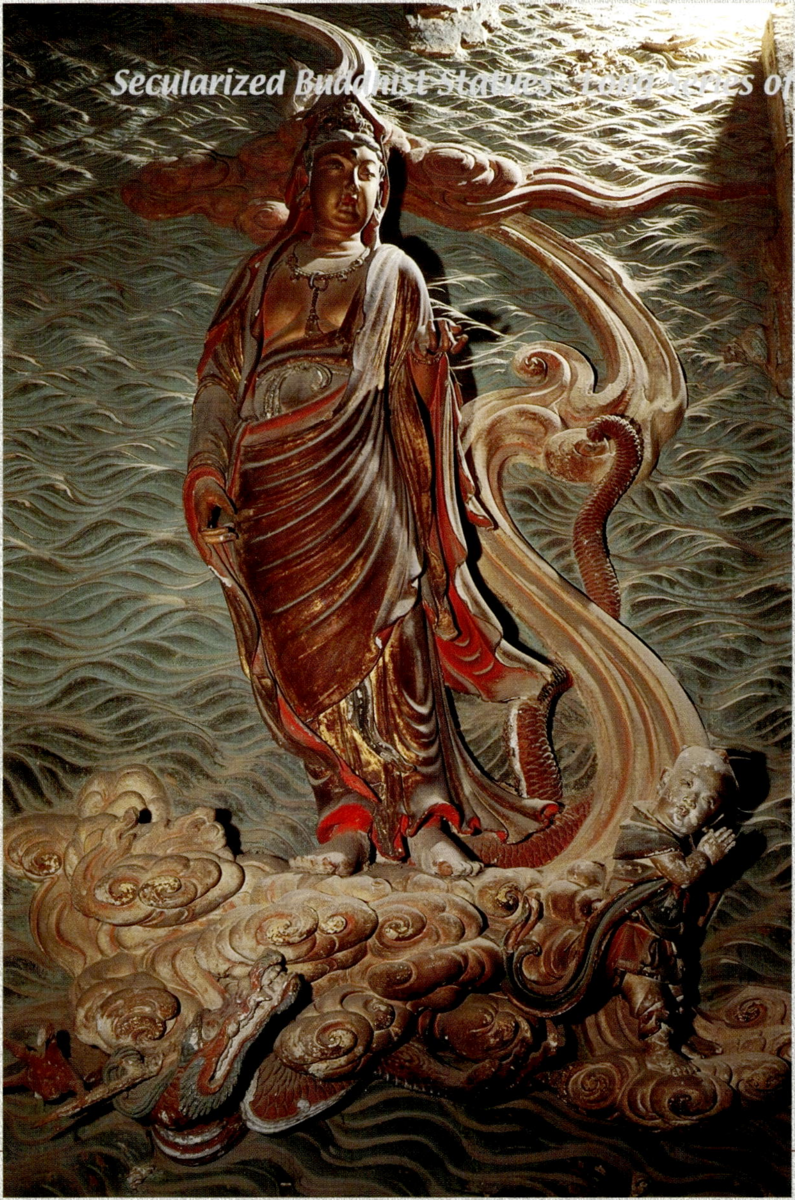

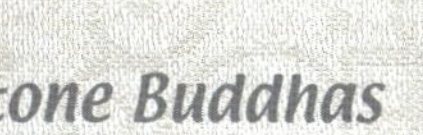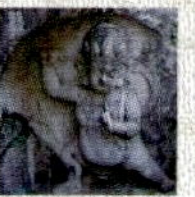

Goddess of Mercy Crossing the Sea, Yuan Dynasty. Fusheng Temple, Xinjiang County, Shanxi Province. Wearing a cowl and a cloak, the Goddess has a well-rounded figure and looks serene. The true-to-life figure, clouds and the sea combine into a harmonious whole.

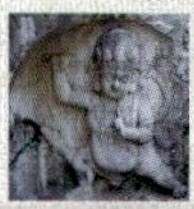

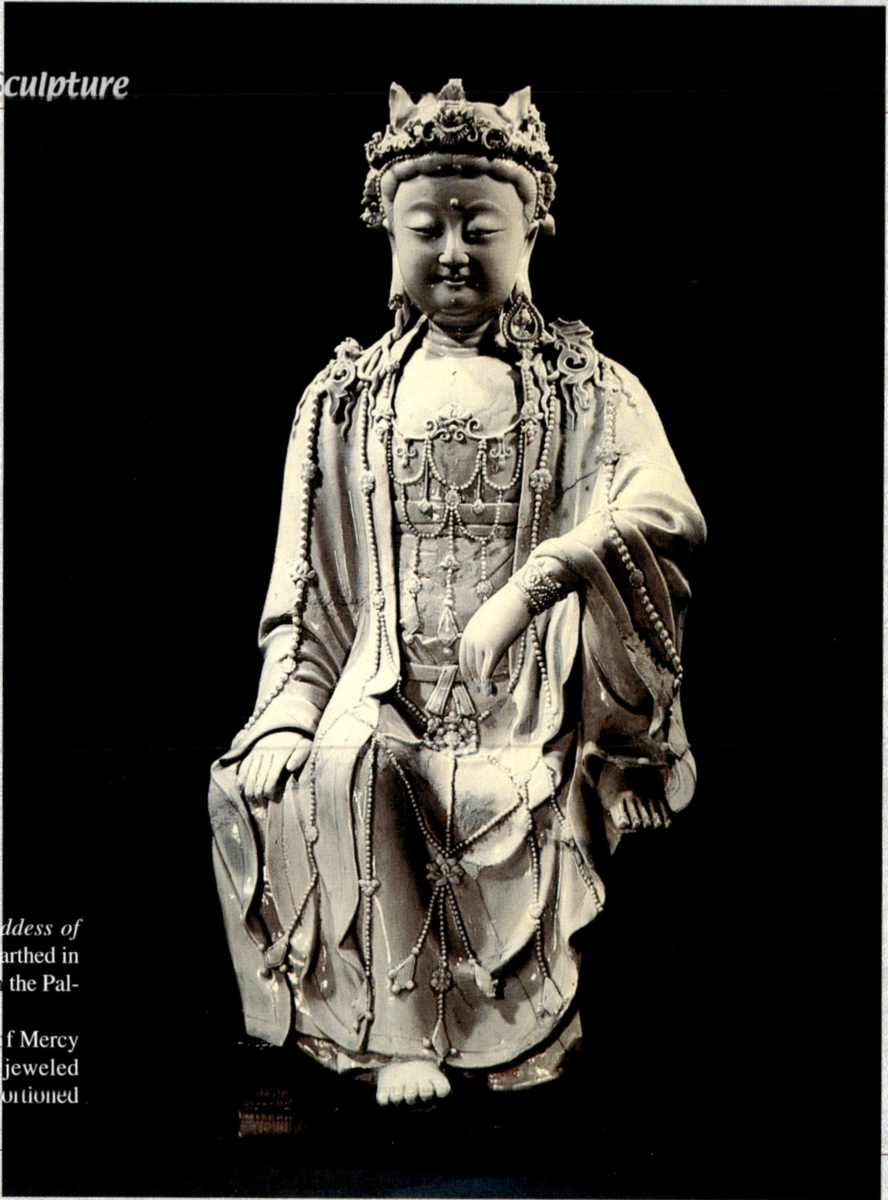

Misty Blue Porcelain Goddess of Mercy, Yuan Dynasty. Unearthed in Beijing in 1955 and now in the Palace Museum collection.
The 66-cm-high Goddess of Mercy wears a crown, robe and jeweled necklace. She is well proportioned and has a graceful bearing.

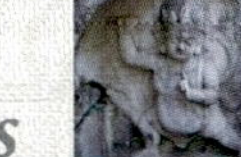

Virudhaka, Yuan Dynasty. Juyong Pass, Changping County, Beijing.

The four Heavenly kings on the pedestal of a ruined stone pagoda are carved in deep and low relief, combining realistic and exaggerated styles. The vivid expressions, postures and ornaments and accurate proportion fully demonstrate the consummate skills of the craftsmen of the Yuan Dynasty.

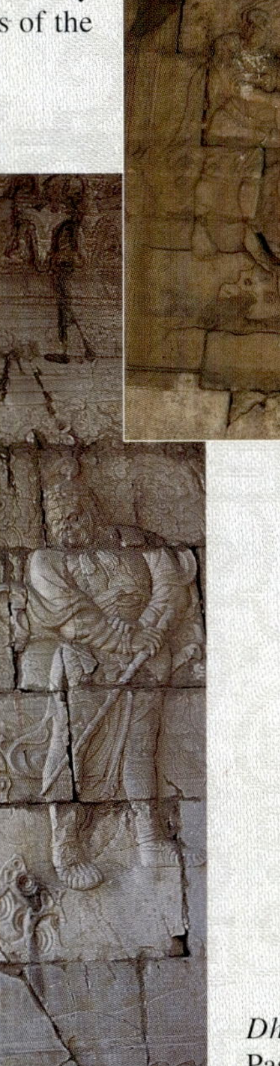

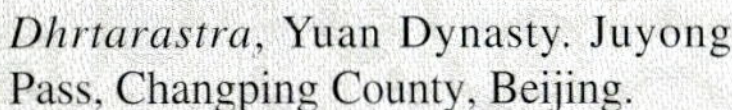

Dhrtarastra, Yuan Dynasty. Juyong Pass, Changping County, Beijing.

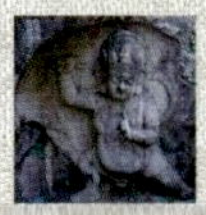

Vajrapani Bodhisattva, Yuan Dynasty. Feilai Peak Cliffside Sculptures, Hangzhou, Zhejiang Province The stone carvings on the cliffs of Feilai Peak were started in the Southern Dynasties, but unfortunately none of them remains. The extant carvings were mainly carved in the Five Dynasties, and during the Song and Yuan dynasties. Of the Yuan Dynasty carvings, many look bizarre, and are executed in the styles of Mongolian and Tibetan Buddhism.

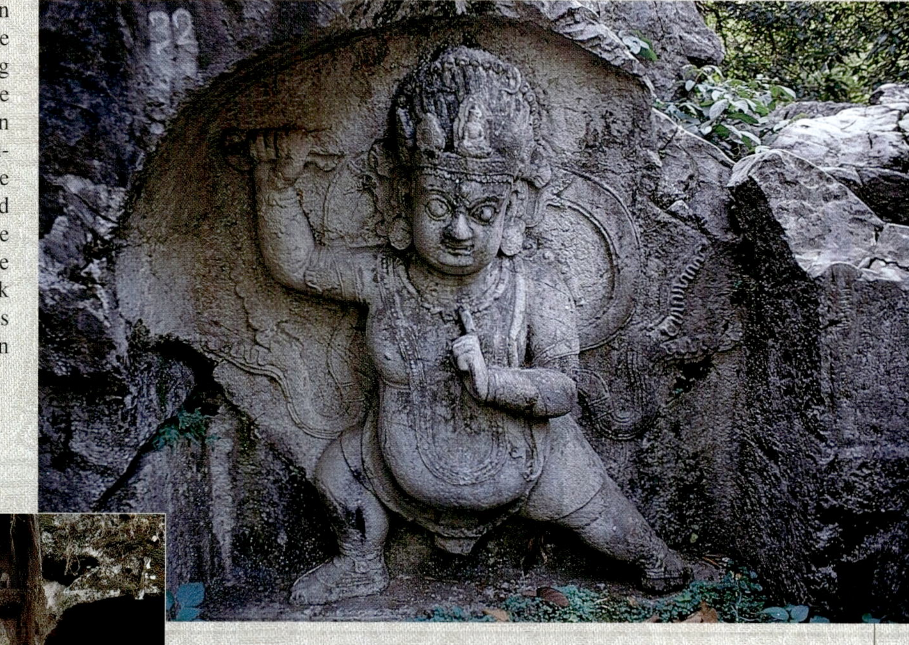

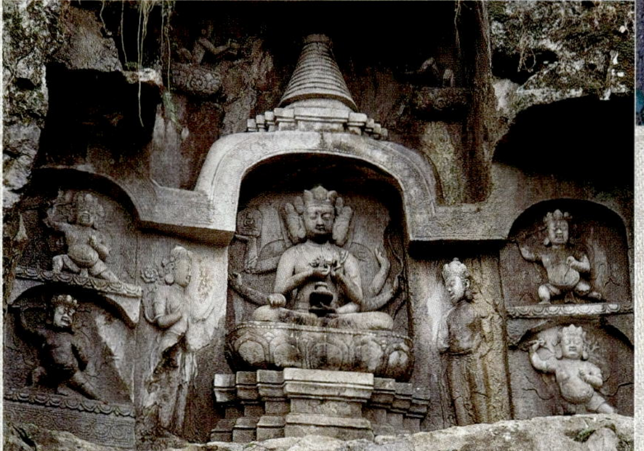

Goddess of Mercy with Three Heads and Eight Arms, Yuan Dynasty, Feilai Peak, Hangzhou, Zhejiang Province

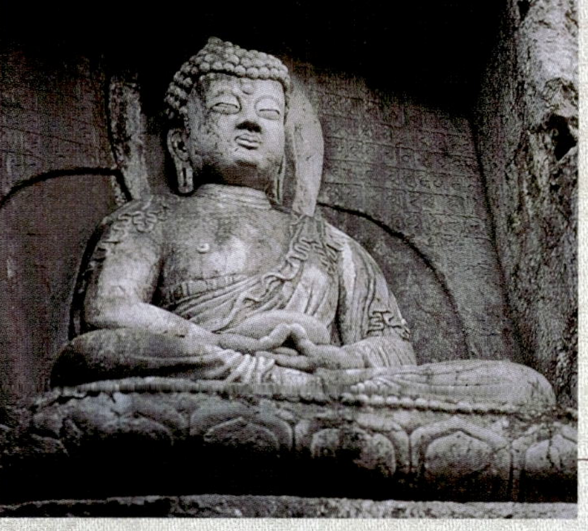

Buddha of Infinite Life, Yuan Dynasty. Feilai Peak, Hangzhou, Zhejiang Province.

Statues of Tibetan Buddhism · Stone Carvings in the Ming and Qing Imperial Mausoleums

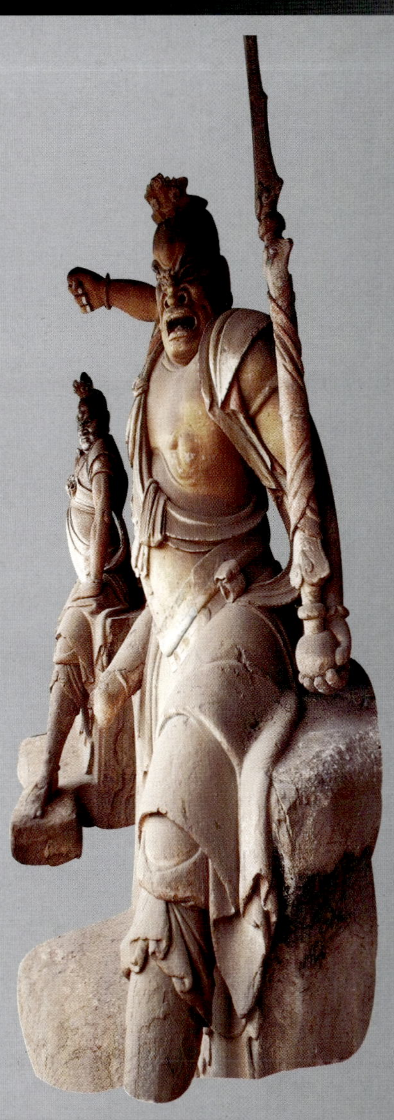

Tibetan Buddhist sculpture in the Ming and Qing dynasties has its own unique characteristics.

The sculpture "Mountain of 500 Arhats" carved out of purple sandalwood, the Buddhist niche carved out of nanmu wood and the Grand Buddha carved out of white sandalwood in the Yonghe Lamasery in Beijing are praised as the "three matchless pieces of wood sculpture." The Grand Buddha is carved out of a single log of white sandalwood, with 18 m of it above the ground and the other eight meters below ground. The "Mountain of 500 Arhats" is nearly five m high, 3.5 m wide and 30 cm thick. The 500 arhats, each 10 cm high, are made of gold, silver, bronze, iron and tin.

Statues of the Buddha in the tradition of Tibetan Buddhism (also known as Lamaism) are mostly made of gilded bronze, but some are made of gold or silver. In the collections of artistic works in the Palace Museum, there are many precious pieces, such as the standing statue of Maitreya and the seated statue of Sakyamuni (the founder of Buddhism), both made of pure gold. The seated statue of Sakyamuni is 45 cm tall; together with the halo and the lotus-throne pedestal, the statue is 90.5 cm high in total. With his right shoulder exposed Sakyamuni is rotating the "wheel of the law" (an emblem of the power of the Buddhist doctrine, which crushes all delusions and superstitions just as a wheel crushes anything it passes over). The simplicity of the statue itself forms a distinct contrast with the splendor of the halo and lotus throne.

The imperial mausoleums of the Ming and Qing dynasties are guarded by monumental stone animals. In the Xiaoling Mausoleum of the Ming Dynasty in Nanjing, on each side of the tomb passage are lined up 12 pairs of six stone animals, namely, lions, *xiezhi* (a fabulous animal reputed to be able to distinguish between good and evil), camels, elephants, *qilin* (Chinese unicorn) and horses, and two pairs of civil officials and military officers. The Ming Tombs near Beijing cover an area of about 40 sq km. Eighteen pairs of grandiose stone civil and military officials and animals line the approach to the mausoleum.

Miniature carvings using jade, stone, ivory, bamboo, horn, wood and clay materials were quite well developed in the Ming and Qing dynasties. There was a special jade workshop installed in the former Imperial Palace during the Ming Dynasty. A masterpiece of the reign of Emperor Qianlong of the Qing Dynasty is a huge jade carving weighing seven tons, titled, "Yu the Great (the reputed founder of the Xia Dynasty) Harnessing the Floods." In addition, the wood carvings of Dongyang, Zhejiang Province, and the clay figurines of Huqiu in Suzhou, Huishan in Wuxi, Jiangsu Province, are quite famous, but most of them were made by unknown artisans. The colored clay figures made by "Zhang the Clay-figurine Master" of Tianjin in the late Qing Dynasty are vivid and lively, demonstrating the extraordinary workmanship of folk sculptors.

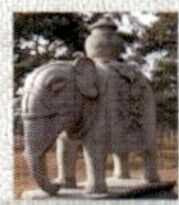

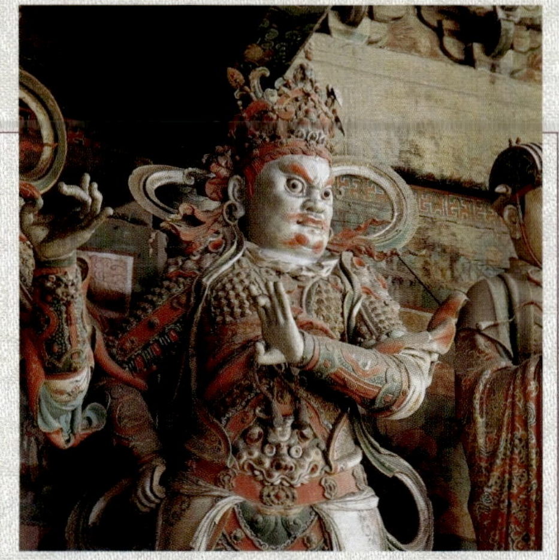

Some of the 28 Devas, Ming Dynasty. Dabei Hall, Dahui Temple, Beijing.
The statues in the Dabei Hall were executed in 1513, the eighth year of the Zhengde reign of the Ming Dynasty. They are tall, handsome and gorgeously dressed.

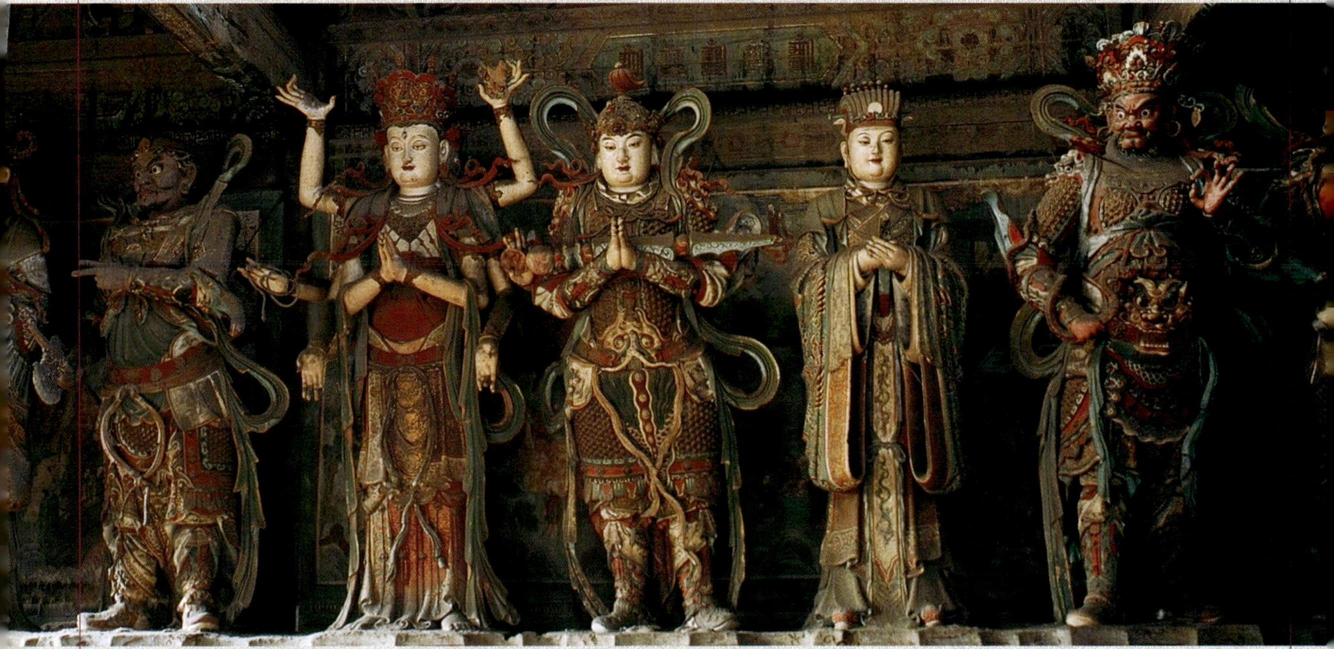

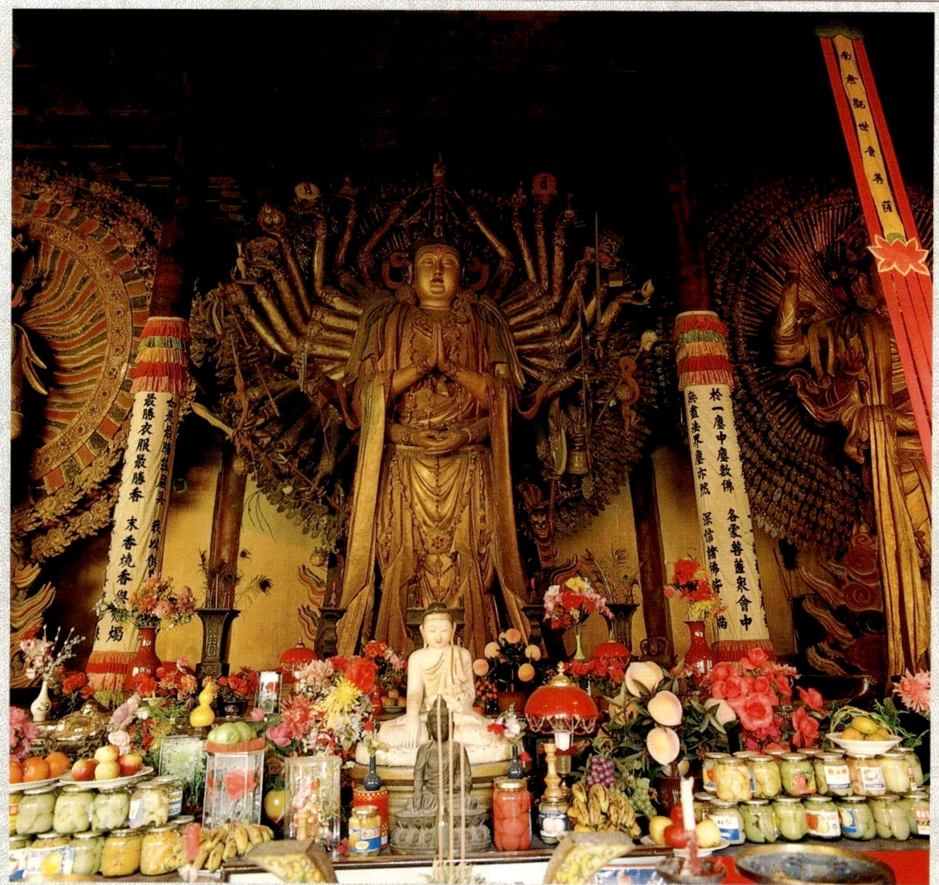

Goddess of Mercy with a Thousand Arms and a Thousand Eyes, Ming Dynasty. Chongshan Temple, Taiyuan, Shanxi Province. The sculptures in the Chongshan Temple were executed in 1395, including the 8.5-m-high Goddess of Mercy with a Thousand Arms and a Thousand Eyes, Bodhisattva of Wisdom and Bodhisattva of Universal Benevolence.

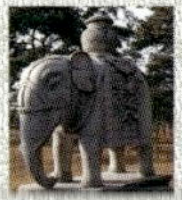

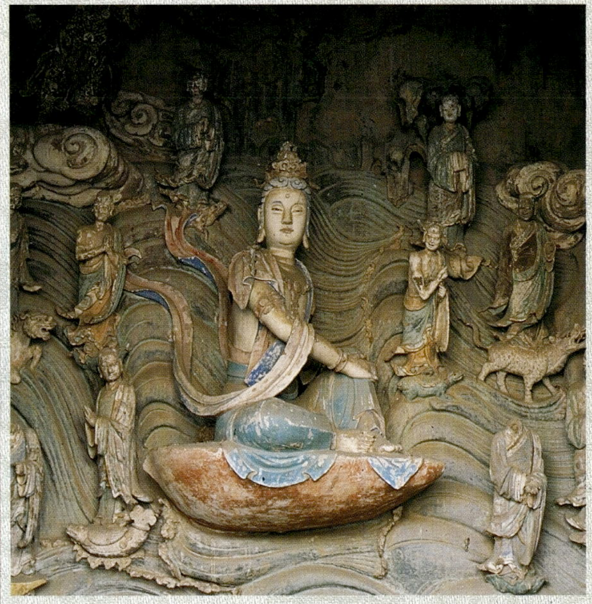

Goddess of Mercy Crossing the Sea, Ming Dynasty. Shuanglin Temple, Pingyao County, Shanxi Province. Shuanglin Temple was built sometime before 571, the second year of the Wuping reign period of the Northern Qi Dynasty, and was reconstructed in the period 1450-1456. In the 10 remaining halls, there are more than 2,000 painted sculptures of various sizes. Among them, the "Goddess of Mercy Crossing the Sea" is a particularly fine work.

Goddess of Mercy with 26 Arms, Ming Dynasty. Shuanglin Temple, Pingyao County, Shanxi Province.
The statue is symmetrical and gorgeously ornamented, and the arms are in different postures.

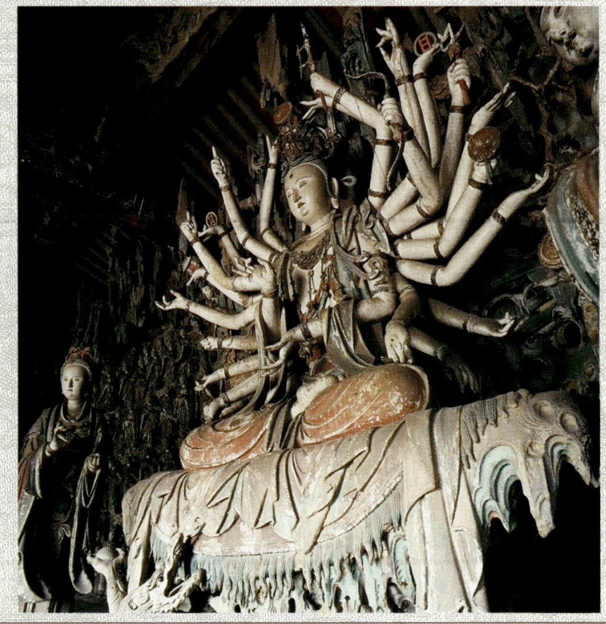

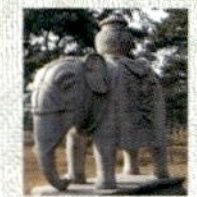

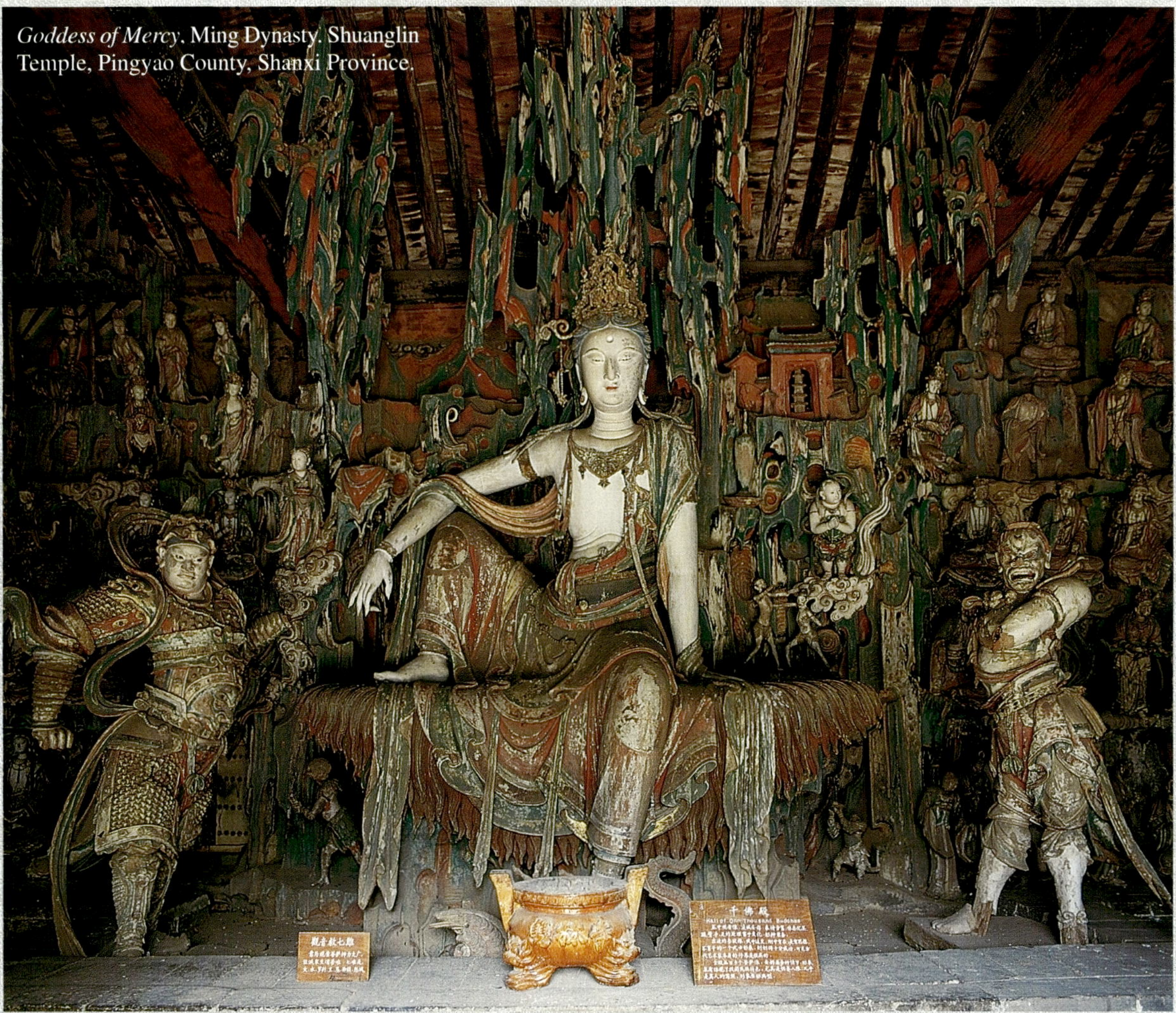

Goddess of Mercy, Ming Dynasty, Shuanglin Temple, Pingyao County, Shanxi Province.

Guardian Warrior (I), Ming Dynasty. Shuanglin Temple, Pingyao County, Shanxi Province. Standing majestically in front of the Heavenly King Hall of the Shuanglin Temple are sculptures of four guardian warriors, each three m high.

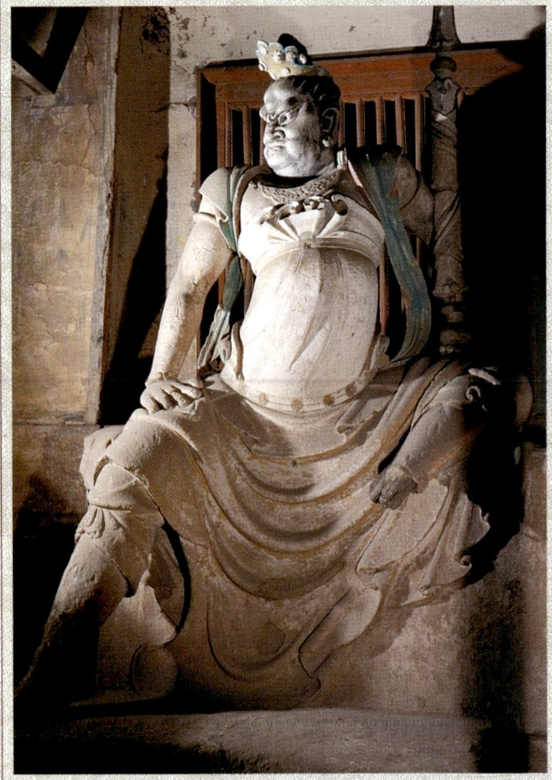

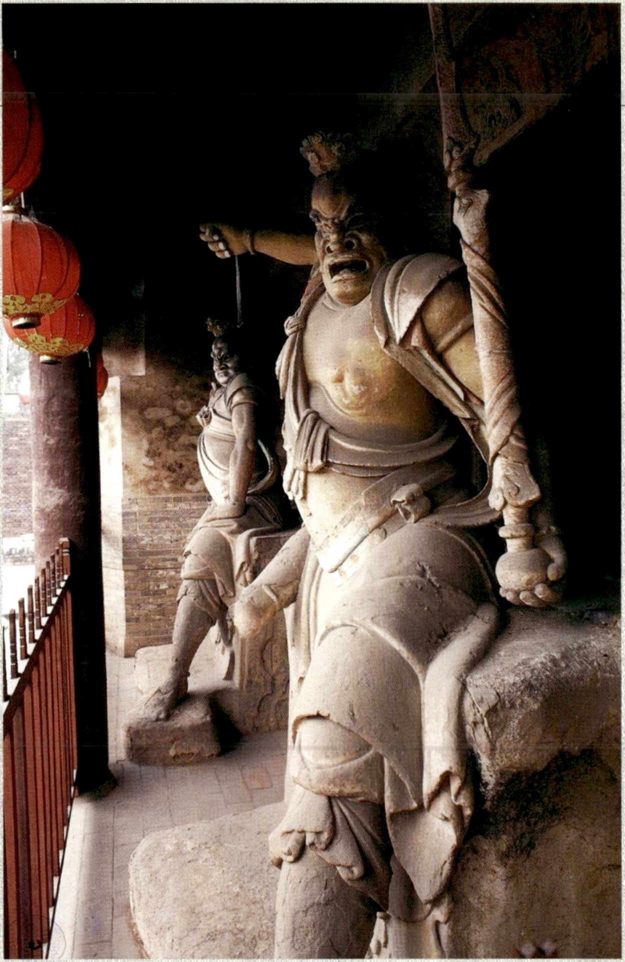

Guardian Warrior (II), Ming Dynasty. Shuanglin Temple, Pingyao County, Shanxi Province.

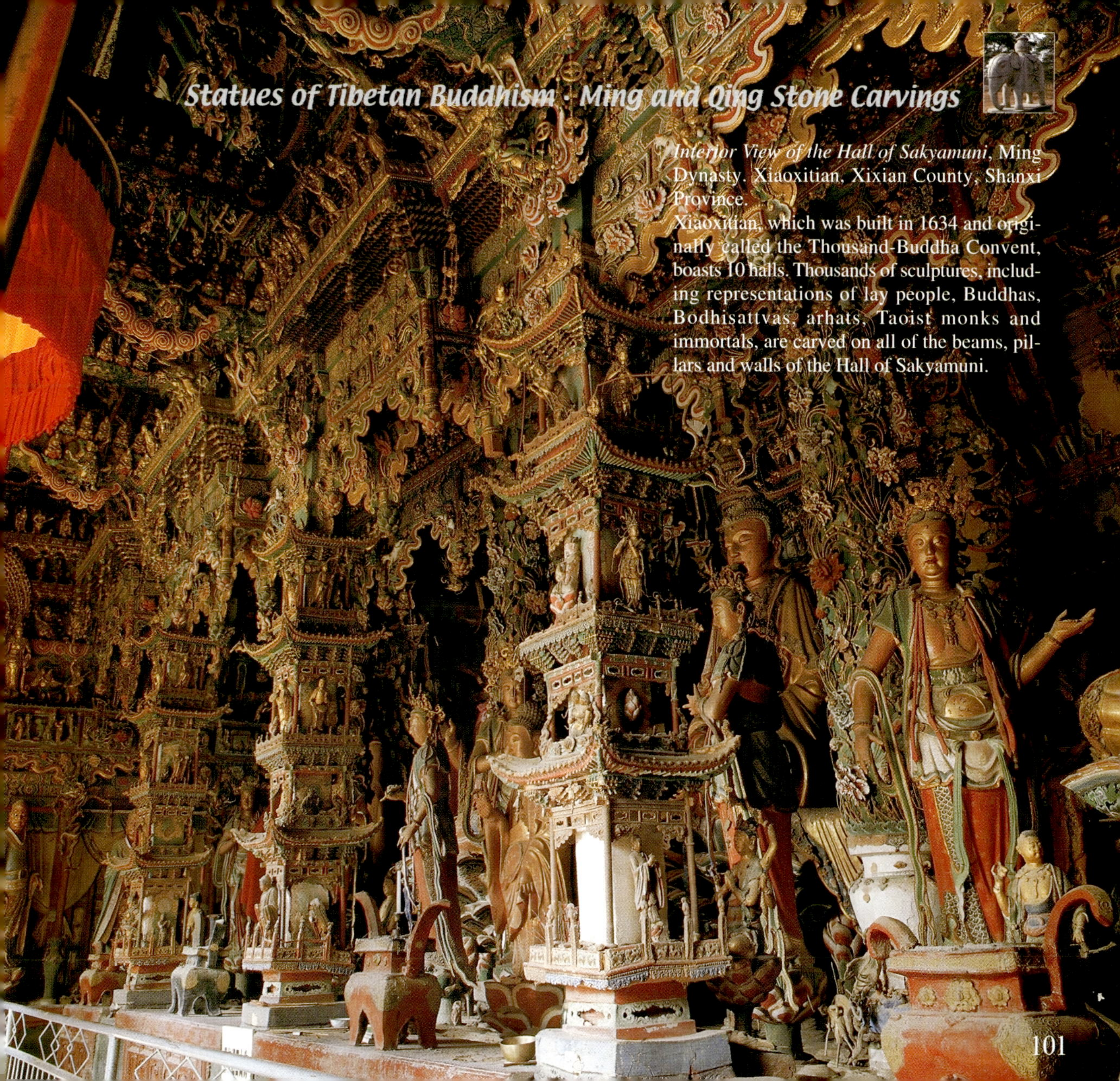

Interior View of the Hall of Sakyamuni, Ming Dynasty. Xiaoxitian, Xixian County, Shanxi Province.

Xiaoxitian, which was built in 1634 and originally called the Thousand-Buddha Convent, boasts 10 halls. Thousands of sculptures, including representations of lay people, Buddhas, Bodhisattvas, arhats, Taoist monks and immortals, are carved on all of the beams, pillars and walls of the Hall of Sakyamuni.

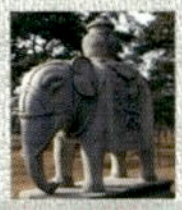

Ancient Sculpture

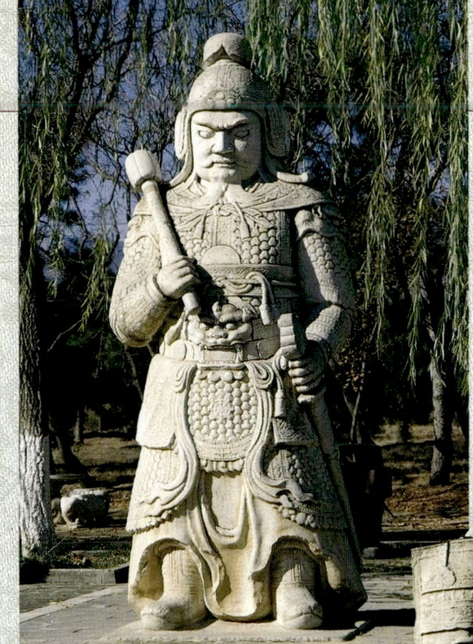

Military Officer, Ming Dynasty. Sacred Way to the Ming Tombs, Changping District, Beijing.

Stone Statues Guarding the Sacred Way to the Ming Tombs, Ming Dynasty. Sacred Way to the Ming Tombs, Changping District, Beijing. Situated at the foot of Mount Tianshou in Changping District, Beijing, the Ming Tombs are the last resting places of 13 emperors of the Ming Dynasty, therefore the tombs are also called the 13 Ming Tombs. Placed on both sides of the sacred path leading to the tombs area, the stone sculptures, including beast and human being figures, produce a solemn atmosphere.

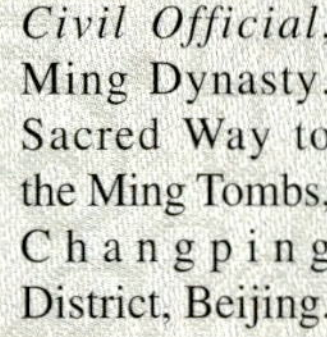

Civil Official, Ming Dynasty. Sacred Way to the Ming Tombs, Changping District, Beijing.

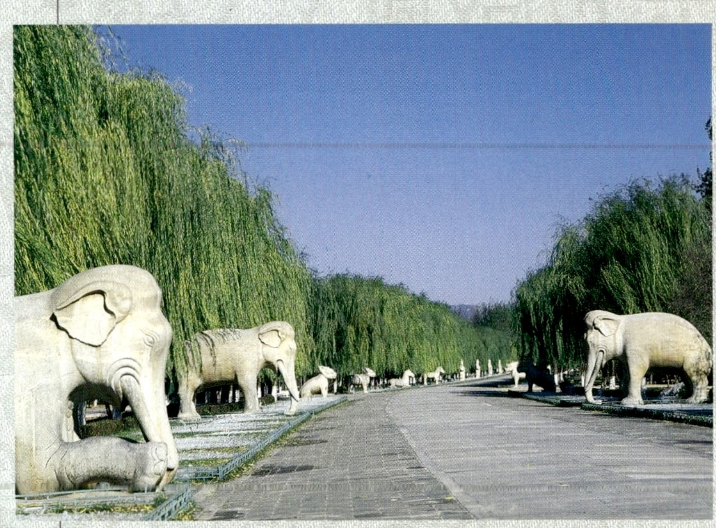

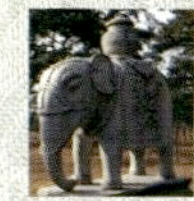

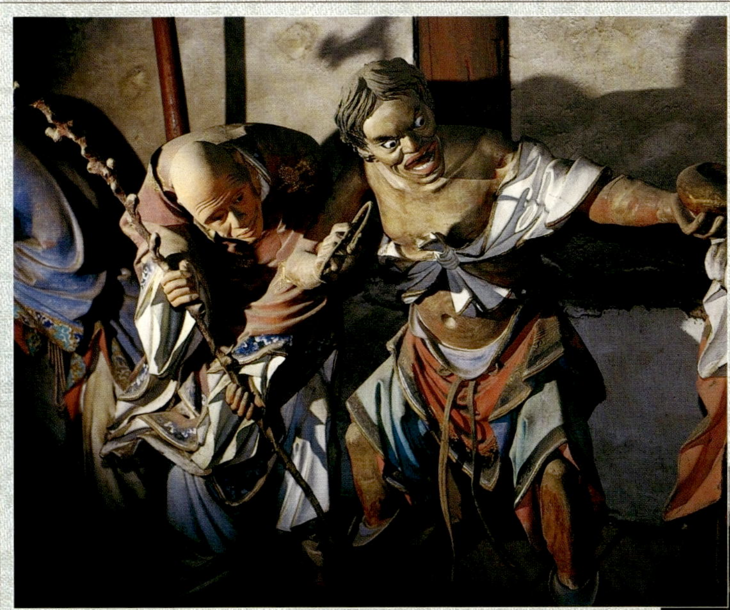

Arhat Statues (II), Qing Dynasty. Qiongzhu Temple, Kunming City, Yunnan Province

Arhat Statues (I), Qing Dynasty. Qiongzhu Temple, Kunming City, Yunnan Province. Situated on Mount Yu'an northwest of Kunming City, Qiongzhu Temple is renowned for its 500 arhat statues in full relief, with mountains and waters in relief as the background. The arhats, each about 1.2 to 1.5 m high and expressing the whole gamut of sentiments, represent various religious sects.

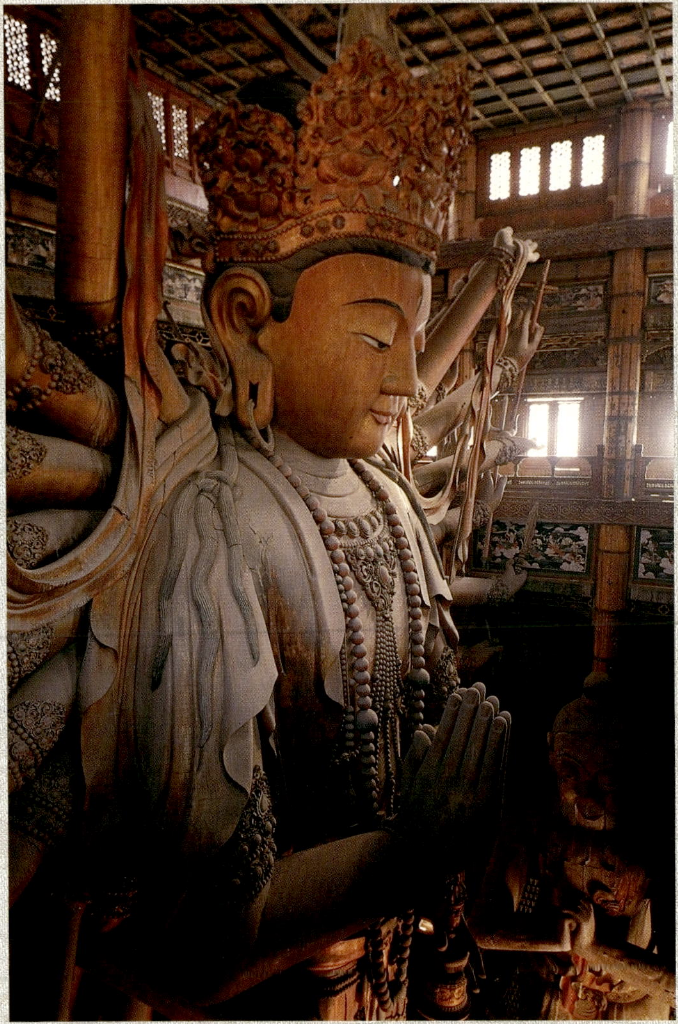

Close-up of the Goddess of Mercy with a Thousand Arms and a Thousand Eyes, Qing Dynasty. Puning Temple, Chengde County, Hebei Province.
Puning Temple is also called Big Buddha Temple, as it houses a 22.8-m-high wood carving of the Goddess of Mercy weighing 110 tons. The Goddess has 40 arms, with an eye in each palm.

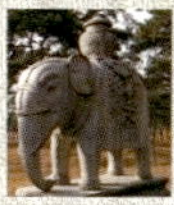

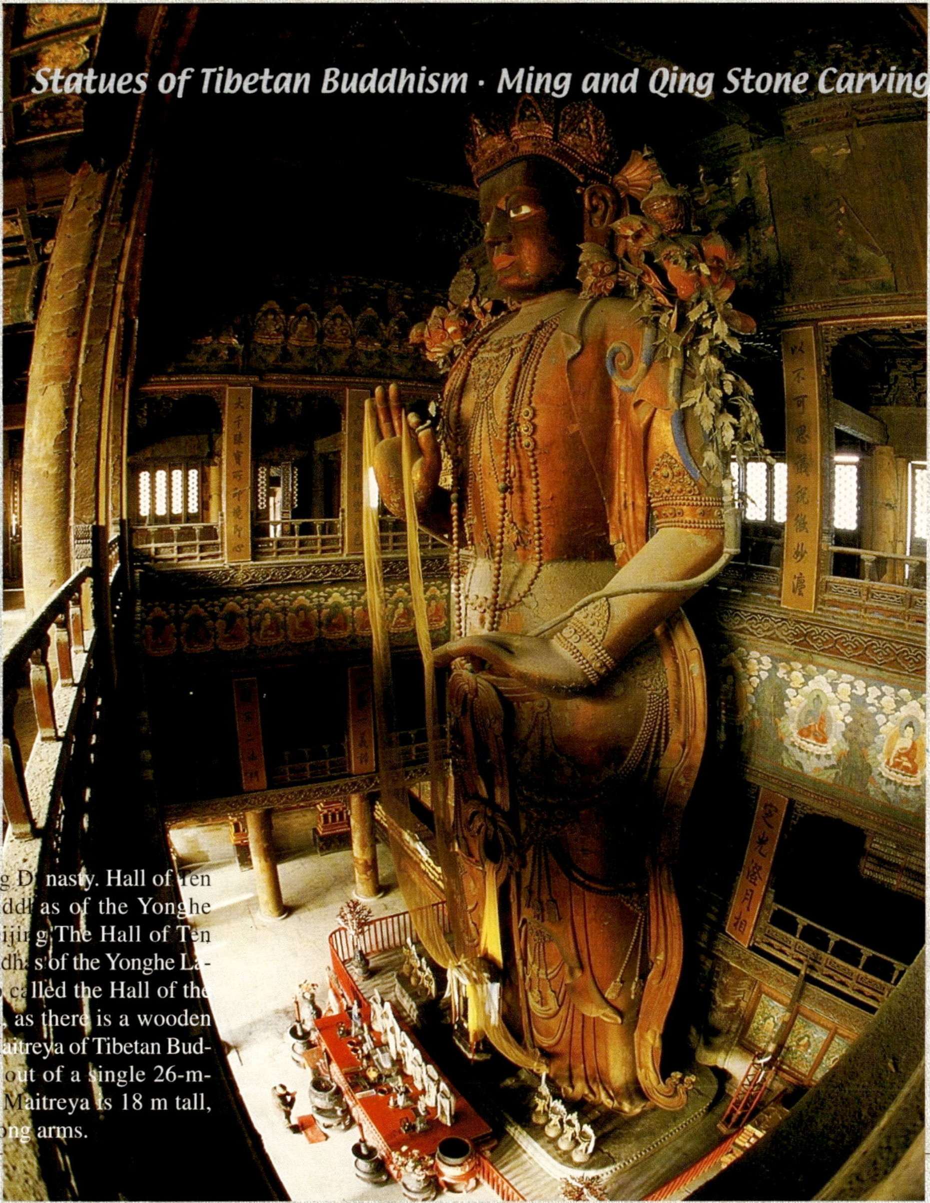

Maitreya, Qing Dynasty. Hall of Ten Thousand Buddhas of the Yonghe Lamasery, Beijing. The Hall of Ten Thousand Buddhas of the Yonghe Lamasery is also called the Hall of the Great Buddha, as there is a wooden statue of the Maitreya of Tibetan Buddhism carved out of a single 26-m-long log. The Maitreya is 18 m tall, and has 8-m-long arms.

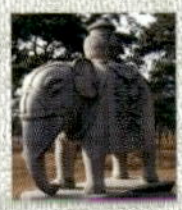

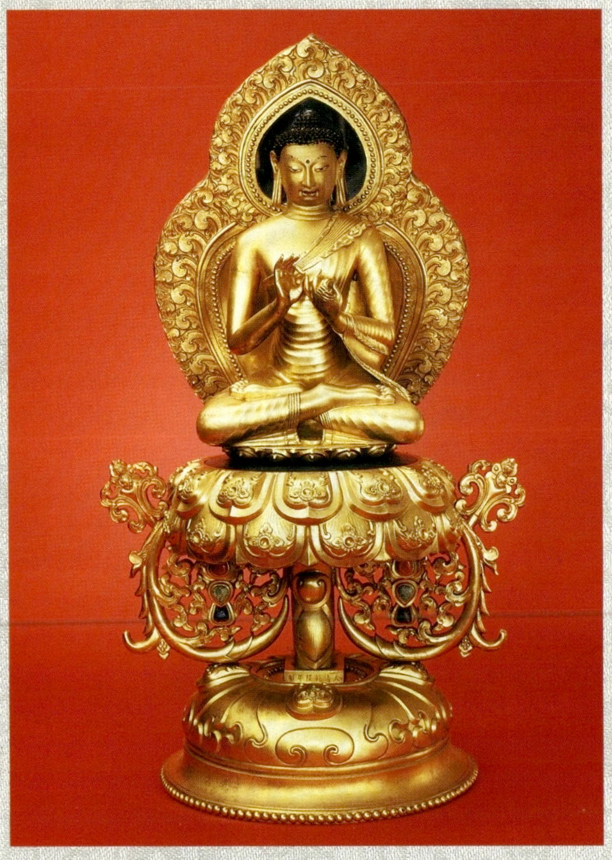

Seated Sculpture of Sakyamuni, Qing Dynasty. In the Palace Museum collection.

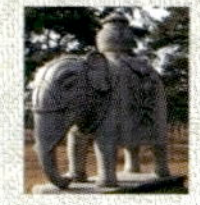

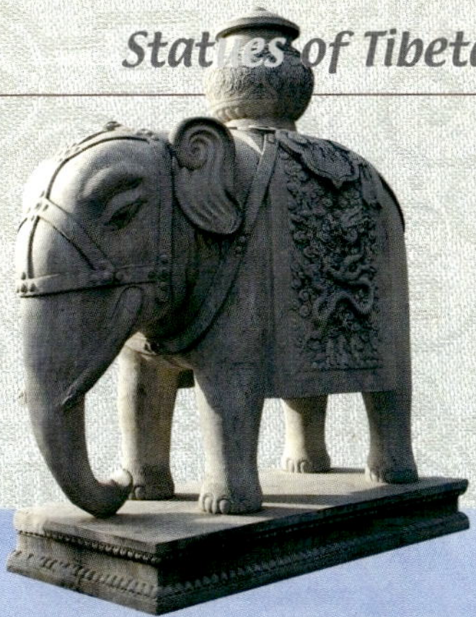

Stone Elephant, Qing Dynasty. The Tai Tomb, Yixian County, Hebei Province.

The stone sculptures of the imperial tombs of the Qing Dynasty continued the tradition of the preceding Ming Dynasty in contents and shapes—mainly representing civil officials, military officers, horses, mythical beasts, elephants, camels and lions. The only differences are in the costumes of the civil officials of the two dynasties.

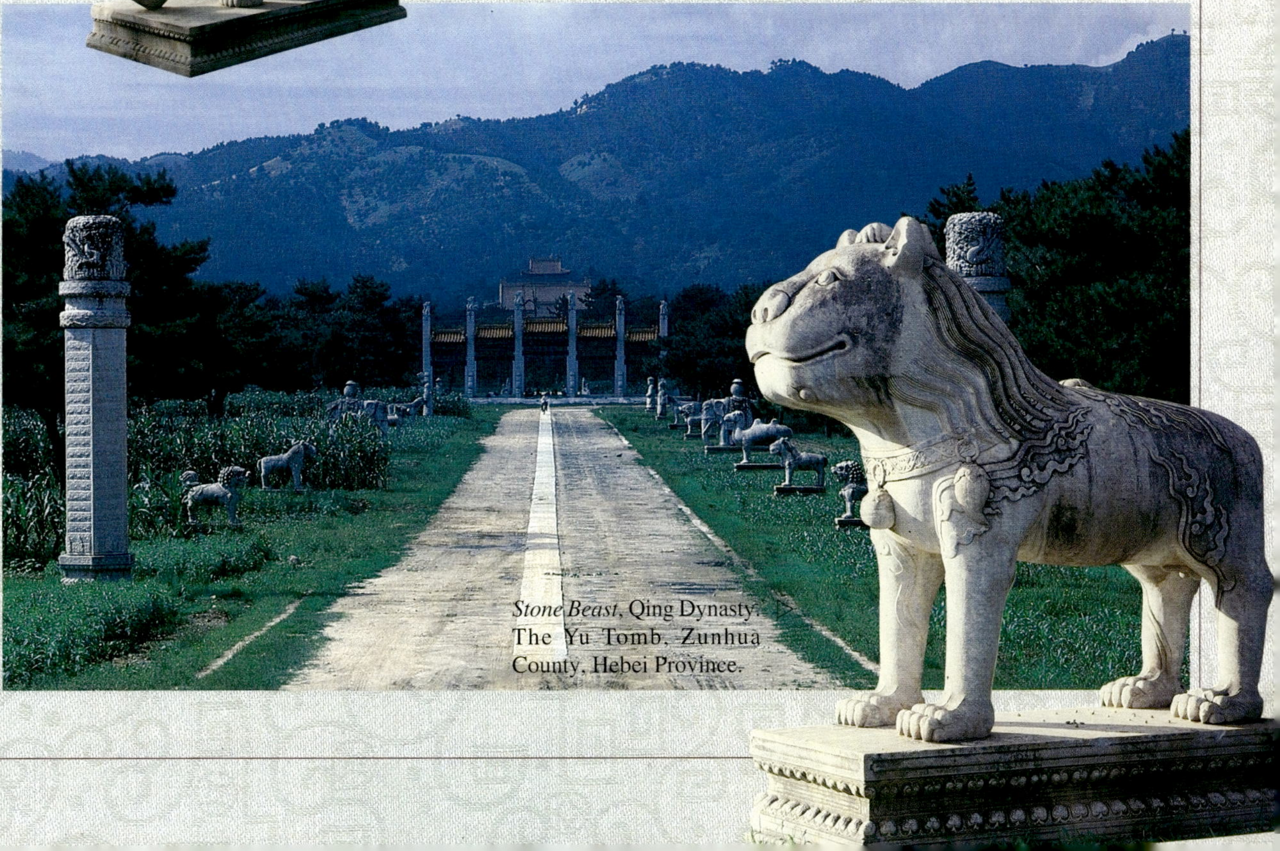

Stone Statue by the Sacred Way to the Yu Tomb, Qing Dynasty. The Eastern Tombs of the Qing Dynasty, Zunhua County, Hebei Province.

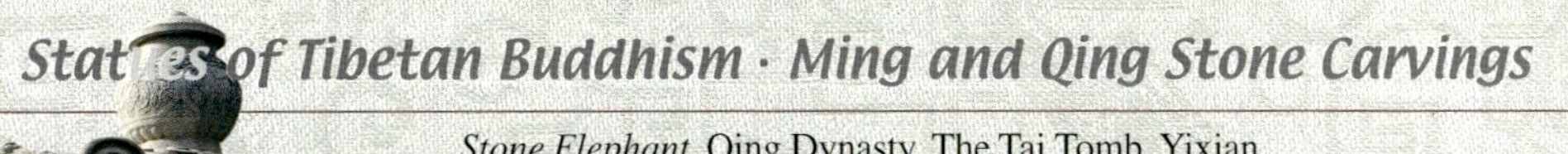

Stone Beast, Qing Dynasty. The Yu Tomb, Zunhua County, Hebei Province.

图书在版编目（CIP）数据

中国古代雕塑／《中国古代雕塑》编委会编．－北京：外文出版社，2002.5
（中华风物）

ISBN 7-119-03049-3

Ⅰ．中… Ⅱ．中… Ⅲ．雕塑－作品集－中国－古代 Ⅳ.J321
中国版本图书馆 CIP 数据核字(2002)第 023449 号

"中华风物"编辑委员会

顾　　问：蔡名照　赵常谦　黄友义　刘质彬
主　　编：肖晓明
编　　委：肖晓明　李振国　田　辉　房永明　呼宝珉
　　　　　孙树明　胡开敏　崔黎丽　兰佩瑾

执行编辑：孙树明
撰　　文：吴　文　孙树明
摄　　影：孙树明　李缙云　李振石　阎新法　江　聪
　　　　　罗忠民　王春树　白　亮　夏居宪　刘春根
　　　　　周沁军　陈志安　张宝玺　郭　群　兰佩瑾
　　　　　吴　健　王正保　顾　棣　朱熙中　孙立治
　　　　　高礼双　孙永学　谢　军　赵　岐　梁达才
　　　　　张克庆　曲维波　严忠义
翻　　译：许　荣　陈　平
设　　计：元　青
责任编辑：兰佩瑾

中国古代雕塑

ⓒ 外文出版社
外文出版社出版
（中国北京百万庄大街 24 号）
邮政编码：100037
外文出版社网页：http://www.flp.com.cn
外文出版社电子邮件地址：info@flp.com.cn
sales@flp.com.cn
天时印刷（深圳）有限公司印刷
中国国际图书贸易总公司发行
（中国北京车公庄西路 35 号）
北京邮政信箱第 399 号　邮政编码 100044
2002 年(24 开)第一版
2002 年第一版第一次印刷
（英文）
ISBN 7-119-03049-3/J·1584(外)
05800 （平）
85-E-527P

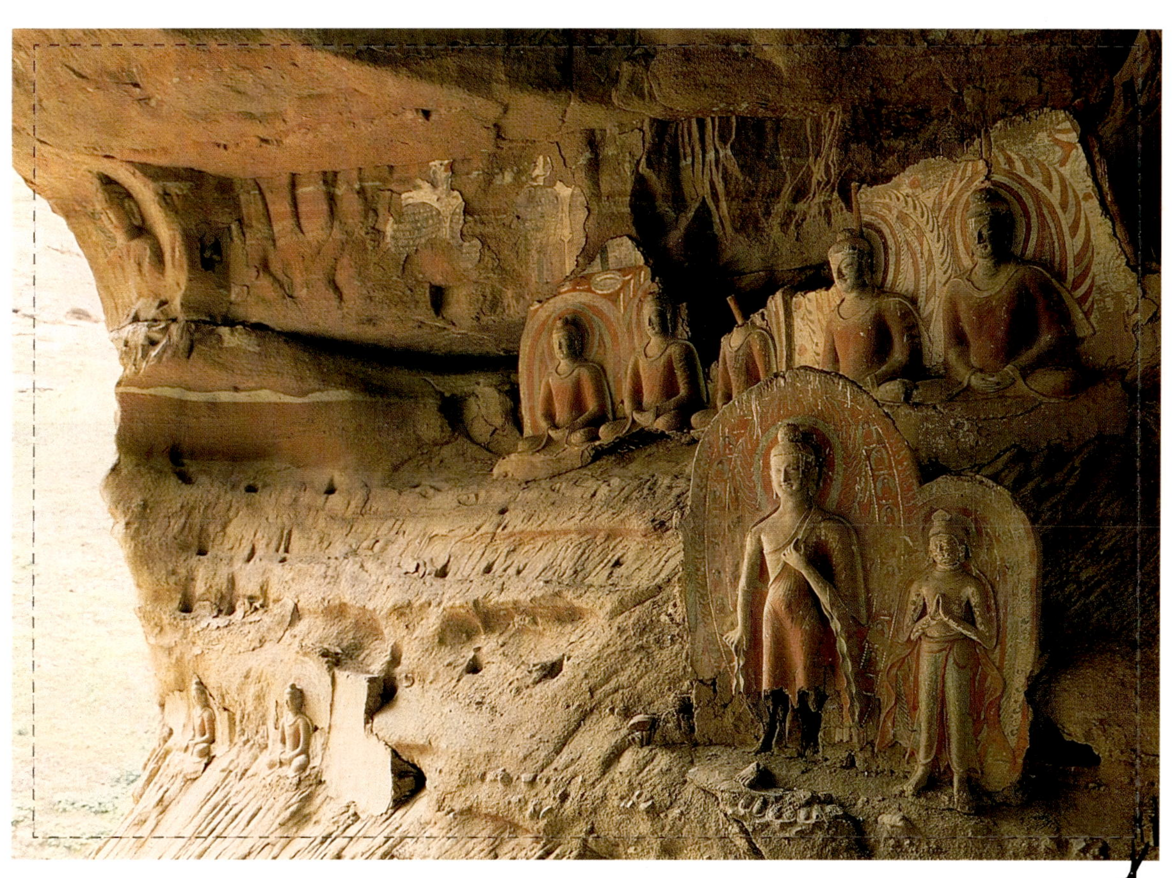

Post Card

FOREIGN LANGUAGES PRESS · 外 文 出 版 社

The interior of Grotto 169 of the Binglingsi Grottoes, Western Qin Dynasty. Yongjing County, Gansu Province.